RELATIONSHIP MARKETING: DIALOGUE AND NETWORKS IN THE E-COMMERCE ERA

Richard J. Varey

University of Salford School of Management

JOHN WILEY & SONS, LTD

Other Wiley Editorial Offices

John Wiley & Sons Inc., 111 River Street, Hoboken, NJ 07030, USA

Jossey-Bass, 989 Market Street, San Francisco, CA 94103-1741, USA

Wiley-VCH Verlag GmbH, Boschstr. 12, D-69469 Weinheim, Germany

John Wiley & Sons Australia Ltd, 33 Park Road, Milton, Queensland 4064, Australia

John Wiley & Sons (Asia) Pte Ltd, 2 Clementi Loop #02-01, Jin Xing Distripark, Singapore 129809

John Wiley & Sons Canada Ltd, 22 Worcester Road, Etobicoke, Ontario, Canada M9W 1L1

British Library Cataloguing in Publication Data
A catalogue record for this book is available from the British Library

ISBN 0-470-84341-1

Project management by Originator, Gt Yarmouth, Norfolk (typeset in 10/12pt Palatino)
Printed and bound in Great Britain by Biddles Ltd, Guildford and King's Lynn
This book is printed on acid-free paper responsibly manufactured from sustainable forestry
in which at least two trees are planted for each one used for paper production.

RELATIONSHIP MARKETING

Dialogue and Networks in the E-commerce Era

CONTENTS

PREFACE

This book on Relationship Marketing (RM) is unusual – it puts the concept of relationship, rather than marketing, at the centre of concern.

This book addresses the question of why managed communication is so central to business enterprise. The text is advanced and critical – to be complementary to the large and growing set of orthodox textbooks on marketing management, services marketing, customer service, and customer relationship management. The unique added value of this book is the specific emphasis on understanding relationship marketing as a business strategy within a framework that integrates marketing, e-commerce, corporate communication, and knowledge management. Therefore, the book has been written to theorize rigorously in order to provide a valuable examination of relationship marketing as a management approach.

The book develops a re-reading of relationship marketing in the light of the innovative thinking presented in Ian Gordon's practice-driven book on relationship marketing (1998), Professor Gummesson's (1999) text on marketing relationships, Professor Grönroos's recent text on service management and marketing (2000), and Professor Barnes's exposition of relationships as emotional bonds. The other side of the coin is presented – communication as the mode of interaction, and relationship as the shared context for meaning-making. This requires a critical communication theory drawn from Critical Social Science to avoid the damaging instrumentality of orthodox managerialistic accounts. Whereas as Christian Grönroos speaks of interactive communication, this book develops the management framework for responsive and responsible communicative interaction (part of the Corporate Communication system of managing that sees management, marketing, and public relations converging).

By continuing the debate beyond the prevailing rhetoric, we can re-present Relationship Marketing by re-viewing the quintessential logic, in order to discover possibilities for management practice that constructively transcend conventional wisdom.

Since relationship marketing principles have been (at least partially) relatively recently adopted in designing and deploying customer relationship management systems, the managerial framework developed in the book addresses the question of information and communication technology (ICT) as enabler and facilitator of the nexus of buyers and sellers.

The result of my writing is not a model of relationship marketing, but rather a model for the relational management of marketing.

I didn't write this book as a competing alternative to those of Ian Gordon, Evert Gummesson, Christian Grönroos, and Jim Barnes. Rather, I wish my work to be read as a complementary contribution from a communication perspective. In Professor Gummesson's terms, this text is the communication eyeglasses. Humbly, I propose my book as a scholarly reflection in response to Professor Gummesson's invitation in his recent book (1999). I asked myself, what is the idea behind RM, and what is the use of this thinking?

The aim of this book is not to add to an almost complete picture, but to offer an alternative view – to refresh the debate by re-viewing and re-presenting in order to discover. I am grateful to Professor Gummesson, once again, for his incisive and provocative thinking. My book thus looks at the buyer–seller relationship through an alternative (less managerialistic) facet of the inquirer's 'diamond' (Gummesson, 2001). This follows on from my previous book *Marketing Communication: Principles and Practice* (Routledge, 2001) in which I challenged the orthodox managerialistic view of marketing as a rational instrument, by bringing some work from social psychology and communication studies to help understand the trading situation (see Chapter 12, especially). There I began my critical review of the emerging relationship marketing tradition.

Lancashire, England
September 2002

References

Barnes, J. G. (2001) *Secrets of Customer Relationship Management: It's All About How You Make Them Feel*, New York: McGraw-Hill.

Gordon, I. (1998) *Relationship Marketing: New Strategies, Techniques and Technologies to Win Customers You Want and Keep Them Forever*, Toronto: John Wiley & Sons.

Grönroos, C. (2000) *Service Management and Marketing: A Customer Relationship Management Approach*, Chichester, UK: John Wiley & Sons.

Gummesson, E. (1999) *Total Relationship Marketing: Rethinking Marketing Management – From 4Ps to 30Rs*, Oxford: Butterworth-Heinemann.

Gummesson, E. (2001) 'Are current research approaches in marketing leading us astray?', *Marketing Theory*, Vol. 1, No. 1, 27–48.

ACKNOWLEDGEMENTS

This project came to fruition with the (often unwitting) effect of the following people. I thus wish to acknowledge:

- Professor Adrian Palmer for editorial direction, enthusiasm, and encouragement.
- Professor Bob Wood for inviting me into the Knowledge Management group at the University of Salford, and for his continuing and unwavering support of my scholarly aspirations.
- Professor Trevor Wood-Harper for enthusing about our critical inquiry in management and information systems.
- Members of the MSc Corporate Communication Management and MSc Managing IT classes who enthusiastically engaged in debate and theorizing about Customer Relationship Management (CRM) at the University of Salford.
- Heather Lloyd, doctoral candidate, for her diligent proof-reading, challenging suggestions, and queries on relevance to customers.
- Peter Murphy for his creative suggestions for the format of the book.
- Steve Hardman for believing in the possibility of building and floating something substantive to say about relationship marketing in a sea of fad and fashion.
- Sarah Booth for conveying my enthusiasm for the project to the Wiley editorial office.

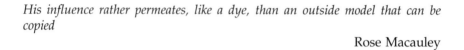

His influence rather permeates, like a dye, than an outside model that can be copied

Rose Macauley

This is another one for Pat and Joe

INTRODUCTION

I don't see Relationship Marketing (RM) as a replacement for Product Marketing, but more as a further option. The clever thing will be to figure out when to adopt this strategy, and when not to do so. Both may be operated harmoniously, as finding products for customers become more important than finding customers for products.

When Airtours plc announced their e-commerce strategy, they highlighted their intention to use 'leading edge technology in customer relationship management (CRM) to further identify customer needs' (www.airtours.com/emedia/body.htm). This heralded a 'revolution' in the selling of their products by enhancing their capability for 'listening and responding' (Airtours staff magazine, August 2000).

In 2001, we have a worldwide 'Customer Relationship Management' industry worth perhaps £20 billion. Around two of every three corporations have at least attempted a CRM project. A Google.com search of the World Wide Web identified 142,000 pages containing the term in July 2000. The same search term identified about 552,000 pages in July 2002 (63,600 pages for 'relationship marketing'). An international journal is published, and several online forums operate. Customer Relationship Management is currently a hot topic.

Perhaps direct marketing pioneer Lester Wunderman was the first to use the term *relationship marketing* in 1949 with a client. In the late 1960s, he gave a speech at MIT and described how ongoing dialogue and other forms of buyer–seller interaction could create long-term customer loyalty. This holistic view of what we now term CRM is comprised of customers, relationships, and management – not simply databases, software, customer service, sales, etc.

In the past 20 years, Relationship Marketing thinking has emerged from the services marketing management and industrial marketing management fields. For some, it is a 'big idea', even a paradigm shift providing a basis for a general theory of marketing. For others, this idea is no more than a passing fad. Curiously, the online www.CRMCommunity.com forum website mentions relationship marketing only twice!

In recent years, amid fears that our communications technologies may actually obscure the communication that we crave, *dialogue* has resurfaced. This is not a new idea, simply the re-emergence of the original oral tradition in reaction to the cacophony of modern electronically mediated communication and the blight of mechanization following the Industrial Revolution. This way of thinking about what is so human an activity centres interaction as fundamentally mutual since an initiative of one person is responded to by another – each participates in the social action of communicating that results in mutual emergent meaning through language use.

So, we should speak not of 'interactive communication', which is becoming fashionable in the specialized parlance of relationship marketing and service marketing, but, rather, of *communicative interaction*. This way of acting has been described as 'reasoning together' (Ballantyne, 1999, following Bohm, 1996) and is a third way of knowing (Shotter, 1993) that creates emergent knowledge. The tradition of the conduit metaphor, of sender and receiver, fails to capture and explain the richness of this social phenomenon.

In a hierarchy of ascending degree of reflection on meanings, dialogue is not possible in the growing crop of Customer Relationship Management systems when written as computer-automated (mediating) contact points and information resources. Presently, eCRM is capable of handling mere talk in an accumulation of transaction reports. This limiting purpose has been driven by the evidence that most public relations and advertising is merely monological talk. True, eCRM has developed out of customer contact and marketing information systems on the back of a burgeoning PC/Internet adoption. The problem remains one of how to encourage the recognition of the resurging need for dialogue, such that CRM and RM can be truly operated in the context of relating and not just objective informing. There is an as yet unmet opportunity to understand and facilitate the management of buyer–seller interaction fully in the context of a relationship process, with ICT support.

Integration through Synthesis

What follows is a critique of Customer Relationship Management enabled by new technology, that takes a re-reading of relationship marketing, marketing communication, and knowledge management in the light of Christian Grönroos's (2000) recent advance in service competition thinking. Grönroos has now taken the much needed step into relating and communicating, but, as yet, not far enough. What is required is a re-view (as suggested by Lee Thayer, 1997) of 'communication' away from the traditional emphasis on planned informing toward facilitated purposive conversation, leading to dialogue that is fundamentally productive (of identity, meaning, and knowledge – see Deetz, 1995, for explication of this argument).

Customer–supplier relating is not merely an issue within the context of managing. It is precisely the obverse. Managing is a 'problem' for solution within the context of people communicating (interacting in intercourse) for their own purposes. Christian Grönroos uses the term 'appreciation' in the final sentence of his latest book. I begin my inquiry with the concept of the corporate body as an appreciative (communicating) system. This has a profound impact on what must follow. The power of this approach is in the integration of ideas about knowledge management, e-commerce, marketing, and service management – around the concept of communicative interaction.

There is much evidence of the shift in attention in management knowledge from new product, to the development of the production process, to market research-based segmentation, and latterly to customers and relationships and the need for real learning about interaction behaviour. Today, much effort is applied to the strategic and tactical application of the notion of value-creating trading relationships, while less worth is given to plans and processes that only centre around exchange transactions.

What we need to know about Relationship Marketing is:

- What is a trading relationship?
- Why are they significant and important?
- How do they arise and operate?
- Who relates, and how?
- When and how do they initiate, grow, decline, and cease?
- What are the benefits?

Overall, this book locates Relationship Marketing as the central philosophy under-lying the Customer Relationship Management business strategy and information system. In order to be capable of delivering on the promise of a strong total customer trading experience, there must be a capability and resources for tracking and interacting. This enables the corporate sellers to serve by providing buyers and users with integrated seamless information and process resources for managing their relationships with them. Therefore, Relationship Marketing in the e-commerce era implies a managed network of policy, information, process, and technology architectures.

> *General advertising is Cyrano. He comes under your window and sings; people get used to it and ignore it. But if Roxane responds, there's a relationship. We move the brand relationship up a notch. Advertising becomes a dialogue that becomes an invitation to a relationship.*
>
> Lester Wunderman

> *Relationships – of all kinds – are like sand held in your hand. Held loosely, with an open hand, the sand remains where it is. The minute you close your hand and squeeze tightly to hold on, the sand trickles through your fingers. You may hold*

onto some of it, but most will be spilled. A relationship is like that. Held loosely, with respect and freedom for the other person, it is likely to remain intact. But hold too tightly, too possessively, and the relationship slips away and is lost.

Kaleel Jamison

References

Ballantyne, D. (1999) 'Dialogue and Knowledge Generation: Two Sides of the Same Coin in Relationship Marketing', *Proceedings of the 2nd WWW Conference on Relationship Marketing, Monash University,* Bradford, UK: MCB University Press, online @ www.mcb.co.uk/services/conferen/nov99/rm/paper3.html

Bohm, D. (1996) *On Dialogue,* London: Routledge.

Deetz, S. A. (1995) *Transforming Communication, Transforming Business: Building Responsive and Responsible Workplaces,* Creskill, NJ: Hampton Press.

Grönroos, C. (2000) *Service Management and Marketing: A Customer Relationship Management Approach,* Chichester, UK: John Wiley & Sons.

Shotter, J. (1993) *Cultural Politics of Everyday Life: Social Constructionism, Rhetoric, and Knowing of the Third Kind,* Buckingham: Open University Press.

Thayer, L. (1997) *Pieces: Towards a Revisioning of Communication/Life,* London: Ablex.

Chapter 1

THE NEW MARKETING

Building a better life, or fixing the leaking bucket?

A mass marketer is a hunter – a relationship marketer is a farmer
Don Peppers, speaking at the CRM Focus Conference, Boston 2001

The secret of success is sincerity. Once you can fake that, you've got it made
Groucho Marx (1895–1977)

Introduction

My starting point is this. A relationship is an antecedent to value-sharing buying–selling interaction. Satisfied customers get relevant, valued, fulfilled promises from their suppliers. Some (but not all) satisfied customers trade profitably with sellers they believe are 'my provider'. Read on to appreciate the basis of these claims.

The Relationship Marketing (RM) concept has become part of the 'plausible story' of the now burgeoning Customer (or Contact) Relationship Management (CRM) industry – eCRM (supposedly) marries a range of information and communication technologies with relationship marketing. But, is not the eCRM product a solution seeking a problem? What is the question for which CRM is the answer? In this book, I adopt a critical approach to show why so much relationship marketing practice fails.

This introductory chapter is, in part, an attempt to examine the co-optation of a well-accepted relational-oriented alternative variant of marketing that is in danger of becoming swamped and undermined (even lost) by an unreflective and narrow instrumental adoption. Many market system participants are subjected to no more than an expensive technology of alienative 'contact' – the system is capable of little more than data-driven reciprocal manipulation.

This depressing regime can be avoided with a more democratic and sophisticated trading 'unorthodoxy'. This requires the deployment of a critical communication theory within the principles of relationship marketing, then CRM, then eCRM.

Interaction is not merely a mechanism to enable exchange – interaction can be the mode of trading – value can be created, and not merely sold, through inter-action – by engaging in dialogical action.

Managing Relationships for Marketing

To the seller a market is a collection of buyers and potential buyers, some of whom can be attracted in to exchanges by tempting offers. To the buyer, a market is a set of supplier–product offerings from which to choose. A market is a source of rewards for exchanging, of expertise to do something, of information, and of referent power.

It seems worthwhile to ponder the apparent reinvention of relationship as a component of trading markets. How could it be that, until the final decade of the 20th century, marketing was seemingly not concerned with interaction, but merely with exchanges? Surely, a relationship was the context or environment within which such trading had meaning? By back-grounding relationship, a technicist marketing ideology placed communicating in the role of informing instrument or conduit – advertising flourished. Latterly, branding has surfaced in recognition of the active role played by people in constructing meaning. Now, it is difficult to pursue a logic that does not recognize the centrality of the concept of relating. But much of the burgeoning literature has simply married an unreflective instrumen-tal notion of information systems with a unreflective instrumental notion of marketing (Varey and Wood, 2001).

The problem lies in the politics and ethics of communicating (Varey, 2000). Gordon (1998) and Brown et al. (2000) are examples of well-written rhetoric on CRM. The resulting eCRM is unhealthy. Through our reflection, we see the present manifestations, in eCRM, of a convergence of relationship marketing and ICT as fundamentally flawed due to what we might term the 'intellectual BSE effect'. When a major new capability is heralded, yet constructed in the unreflective feeding of one distorted/flawed discourse upon another, a recipe for disappointment (at least) and the potential for a fall might reasonably be anticipated. Is the mutant that is being created from the damaged marketing and ICT (both spawned of a limiting managerialistic rationalism) really what we, society, want? Of course it is not. The challenge lies in widely recognizing the alternative ways of understanding the possibilities and their consequences, and in making good (ethically sound) choices.

Stephen Brown has been particularly vociferous in countering the erupting crowd frenzy that has raised relationship marketing (and therefore CRM, and especially eCRM) to the status of mantra and (yet another) strategic imperative. Brown and his colleagues, in considering the death of ('modern') marketing, saw relationship marketing as 'a false conceptual idol' (Brown et al., 1996, p. 14) and just one of a number of enthusiastic attempts to recycle 'long-dead' elements of the 'marketing' intellectual tool kit – part of 'the vast bulk of contemporary marketing scholarship [that] comprises (sic) little more than intellectual necrophilia' (op. cit., p. 11). Not too sensationally provocative then!

Brown is clearly concerned that relationship marketing, with the 'ostensibly communal, co-operative, egalitarian ethos of all-pervasive harmony' (Brown and Maclaran, 1996, p. 269), is no more than an enthusiastic pursuit (at least by some management gurus and their disciples) of a capitalist consumer society utopia.

The Narrow Conception of 'Marketing' – as a Management Technology

A typical recent definition of marketing is:

> *Marketing consists of individual and organisational activities that facilitate and expedite satisfying exchange relationships in a dynamic environment through the creation, distribution, promotion and pricing of goods, services and ideas.*
>
> (Dibb et al., 1994, p. 4)

This represents the popular conception of marketing as the application of economic theory to the efficient allocation of resources so that consumption can take place. This view is the foundation of almost all textbooks on marketing and implies a dominance and exclusivity of economic thinking and values and a limitation of marketing to transactions involving exchanges.

Despite the impression created by most textbooks that marketing sprang out of the early 1960s' US advertising industry, many activities associated with marketing, such as advertising and market research, pre-date the turn of the century. Bartels (1986) has pointed out that marketing emerged as part of an economic institution to meet the need of society for consumption. The emergence of a market economy was initially in a society comprising a range of institutions (or established social concerns): government, education, religion, recreation (leisure), arts, civic, international, and economic.

Marketing has, however, evolved as a technology for meeting the economic institutional (i.e. business) need for efficient distribution of manufactured goods and services. That is, marketing has become necessary for producers to dispose of their goods and services in an increasingly competitive world where supply now considerably exceeds demand.

Some of the more vocal members of our society might suggest that marketing has so far failed to fulfil an expected role in enhancing our lives. Recent evidence suggests confirmation of what many of us feel. While increasing consumption contributes to continued economic growth, our society may have already passed the peak of our quality of life and we are now seemingly experiencing a steady decline. Our notion of 'progress' perhaps has lost touch with human welfare and a sustainable environment in which to live.

Marketing as a technology has increasingly drawn heavily on quantitative tools (i.e. science-based analytical approaches to management). This has tended to narrow rather than broaden our view of marketing and its objectives (Cox, 1962, pp. 23–24). In doing so, marketing theory ignores or underplays the feelings of 'social man' while encouraging us to behave as rational managers and as 'economic man' (Eastburn in Lazer and Kelley, 1973).

There is a continuing presumption of the universality of marketing technology, even though it has evolved over the past 100 years as a function of specific, prevailing circumstances, subject to supplementation by progressive refinement. Most marketing theory has come from a progressive concentration on the technical aspects of the distribution of domestically produced goods in the capitalist-owned private sector of the USA. This has avoided responsibility for improving the quality and quantity of consumption (Bartels, 1986). A remaining and pervasive question is: Must marketing develop only as a business management technology or can it evolve as the social institution it was originally intended to be?

> *The marketing process has been seen as* business *meeting society's needs rather than as* society *meeting its needs through the institution of business.*
>
> (Bartels, 1986, p. 40)

> *The issue is whether marketing is an economic technology responsible to markets for distribution of goods and services, or an institution responsible to society for meeting those consumption needs in the context of society's ethical or spiritual expectations.*
>
> (Bartels, 1986, p. 41)

The Social Cost of Marketing

The narrow view of marketing has produced an overemphasis on 'managerial' marketing (*micromarketing* as discussed by Nason in Fisk, 1986) focused on the narrow interests of the individual producer in improving his or her efficiency in providing consumer satisfaction (Cox, 1964 quoted in Nason, 1986). Cox recognized the subservient role of business to the broader interests of society and the subordination of marketing to the goals of the firm.

> *We must at some point subsume our ideas as to the functions of marketing into our ideas of what our whole society is supposed to achieve for us.*
>
> (Cox, 1962, p. 23)

Cox has also questioned whether the cost, in monetary as well as non-economic terms, to society of achieving 'efficient' distribution (i.e. improved allocation) of goods and services is too high. Arising from these concerns the applied client-oriented discipline of *macromarketing* (reviewed by Nason in Fisk, 1986) was developed, in which client groups include both consumers and others not party to exchanges. This discipline is concerned with specific social impacts of marketing, such as:

- resource depletion;
- pollution;
- deception;
- obsolescence;

- discrimination;
- health and safety;
- financial losses;
- dissatisfaction.

Without explicit consideration of the total cost, to all parties, of decisions and actions (i.e. marketing transactions), marketers may not even be aware of their social impact through such actions as:

- built-in obsolescence;
- impact-creating packaging;
- product proliferation (see below);
- market share competition;
- product features that are convenient for the supplier and paid for by the consumer.

Do we really need 240 *sorts* of shampoo, 110 *types* of personal stereo, 75 *kinds* of toothpaste, 24 *models* of electric iron, and 347 *varieties* of Nike trainers? Clearly, Western society is geared up for variety – consider how many words we use to suggest variety and differentiation. Most of the current marketing textbooks urge marketers to compete through adding value by differentiation of products and services. Choice, we are led to believe, is a valuable part of our lives and worth giving up personal time for in order to browse, compare features, select, and decide!

Nason (in Fisk, 1986) has put forward the concept of **externalities** as spillover effects of economic transactions which may have social, environmental, or economic effects. These in turn may be foreseen or unforeseen, and may impact on those party to a transaction and those not party to the transaction. Negative social costs (i.e. *societal delivered value*: Kotler, 1994, p. 38 – the sum of all costs and benefits to all parties) can arise through the pursuit of self-interest, or unco-ordinated management decision-making with imperfect information, imperfect analysis, and/or imperfect knowledge. Anshen (in Lazer and Kelley, 1973) has argued that the failure of businesses to internalize the social costs of private operations has remained a problem, and that this may be resolved primarily by revising the nature of the *social contract*. This organizing concept describes the character and composition of relationships between business, government, non-economic organizations, and individuals.

As most marketing is taught around the micromarketing perspective of the single firm battling for supremacy with other firms and the trading 'elements', is it surprising that many marketers, even those who receive any formal marketing education, are unsure about their contribution to their society? Some writers are even beginning to question the validity of the 'competition paradigm' for business (see de Bono, 1993, for example) and society. It is clear from the recent upsurge in literature on value management that de Bono is not the first to argue that head-on competition will become less effective and that differentiation through value creation will be necessary in the future. Worryingly, this may be misinterpreted by some managers as a justification for even more waste, when what is needed is a move away from product and service proliferation driven by the narrow self-interests of single sellers, to a perspective which sees our society as a social system of which business is only a part. I have tried to develop my views on the social value of marketing elsewhere (Varey, 1994). It is uncomfortable to ponder the long-term consequences of the trend toward applying market-based efficiency arguments to all aspects of our lives. Do we really want all social interaction and relationships reduced (impoverished) to the level of economic exchanges between a 'customer' and a 'supplier'?

> As the language of 'the market' becomes the only valid vocabulary of moral and social calculation, 'civic culture' gradually becomes 'consumer culture', with citizens re-conceptualised as enterprising 'sovereign consumers'.
> (du Gay and Salaman, 1992, p. 622)

> Instead of reflecting people's diverse needs and wants, marketing produces (people as) consumers as it divides them into market segments, thus producing social stereotypical categories (such as gender and youth).
> (Alvesson and Willmott, 1992, p. 12)

An Application Gap

Most students take away a very narrow view of marketing as a set of activities and tools that are based on an implicit universality of economic values. Rarely is this view questioned as too narrow. But marketing is more than simply a system of communication whose objective is to transmit goods, people, and messages without regard to their nature (Cox, 1962, p. 18).

In considering an academic distinction between marketing as a business management technology and as a social institution, we can perhaps more clearly see that marketers in practice have almost exclusively pursued the lesser obligation, by focusing only on their own company, market, or industry interests.

Marketing is not merely a neutral technology, a bridge, for linking two worlds divided by a gulf (Cox, 1962), that is, the producer and the consumer. They (we), in any case, are all citizens of our society, subscribing to a set of ethics for behaviour. Of course, the question remains whether the code of ethics is a shared one.

People should not be viewed as markets (economic, physical, psychological, and social) but holistically as the 'whole person'. Consumption needs must be considered with respect to the individual's spiritual nature and endowed rights. If the marketer does not cater for the *whole person* then the danger is the intended or inadvertent violation of the spiritual and psychological nature of the human condition. Both the marketer and the consumer are whole people!

Is the prevailing view of marketing one of a process for imposing costs upon those who buy the goods and services, or as a process of adding value to goods and services? Is the view explicit in management decisions and actions and in marketing textbooks? In other words, does the manager seek productivity or efficiency? Buttle (1989), for example, argues that marketers can *create* needs as well as satisfy them. Value management requires a shift from seeing marketing as a set of undesirable but necessary activities to seeing marketing as an approach to integrating business activities around the production of (socially) worthwhile values. In this way marketing practice can be both socially acceptable and commercially attractive. We should take care to debate these issues with students of marketing.

> ... *confused terminology may be epidemic in marketing ... an impediment to others' efforts to think clearly about the discipline.*
>
> (Luck, 1974, p. 70)

I believe that marketing is capable of contributing more than it does as a technology, and this requires a 'both–and' conceptual approach which avoids unitary thinking in favour of pluralism (Bate, 1994, Chapter 3).

Marketing as a Social Process

Early scholars of the emerging discipline of marketing ignored society's spiritual and material expectations and pursued more the specific interests of producers and consumers. Producers' disposal problems became the focus of marketing interest. Management behaviour became the primary object of marketing scholars' interest. A generally held acceptance of the coincidence of social and economic interests was dropped. However, the discrepancy between the capability of an institutional technology and the satisfaction of social need has become evident:

> ... *social objectives are broader than technical objectives, the expectation of ethical and spiritual, as well as material, satisfactions in consumption exceeds the mere providing of goods and services.*
>
> (Bartels, 1986, p. 31)

A review of the application of the marketing concept is required because significant social changes are evident since the prevailing view of marketing emerged:

- the 'greed is good 1980s' has given way to the 'caring 1990s' and beyond;
- growth of 'non-consumption' markets in which self-fulfilment is displacing self-interest as the dominant motivator;
- the growing demand for respect of social and spiritual values in meeting consumption needs.

The responsibility of marketing management is shifting from that of producer–consumer relationships, to a recognition that each party is a person and no clear division exists. This requires a shift in thinking from profit objectives pursued through providing personal satisfaction derived from the consumption of material goods (an economic emphasis), to acknowledgement of responsibility to other institutions and the incorporation of sociological, psychological, as well as economic concepts, into management thinking.

Business has become 'big business' in modern life, and businesses have become major influencers of social stability and change. *Corporate social responsibility* is a voluntary commitment by managers to a wider range of responsibilities than to shareholders and to control by corporate and labour laws (Carroll, 1981). Corporate social responsibility focuses on ethical and discretionary responsibilities to conform or contribute to social values. Many managers, who are not trained to account for social responsibility in their decision-making, may not be unduly concerned or even fully aware that their decisions and actions inevitably impact on society. Some will argue that business is purely an economic instrument responsible to shareholders for profits and that concern for wider issues would put them at a competitive disadvantage. In any case, they would argue, altruism is for others to pursue.

Societal marketing is socially responsible marketing which takes account of and balances consumers' wants, company requirements, consumers' long-term interests, and society's long-term interests. Doyle (1994) has recently raised the need for a *balanced objectives* approach to differing stakeholder interests in marketing planning and business management. It is argued that socially responsible marketing can sensitively serve and satisfy consumer needs. This 'enlightened' marketing results in contributions to the firm's profits and to society. This is by no means a new perspective on marketing or business. Lazer, Lavidge, Kotler and Levy, Kotler and Zaltman, and Browne and Haas (all in Lazer and Kelley, 1973) discuss the responsibilities of the marketer to society and the pay-off for doing so. Social responsibility as 'good business' is also the theme of books by Solomon and Hanson (1985) and Embley (1993).

Of course, there is a clear distinction between social responsibility wielded as a tool of business (i.e. as a means to better profits) and the meeting of social obligations as an end in itself. The distinction must be made. On the one hand, social responsibility (which can be cynical in intent when a company conducts its business in a manner which is tolerable by society) is often constrained by a believed political need to 'control' industry and is intended to provide economic gain from meeting social needs (see Embley, 1993 and Solomon and Hanson, 1985). On the other hand, social responsibilities (when business is conducted as good 'corporate citizenship') results in a positive image and reputation, producing financial gain as a by-product. This will require a clear social contract and honest and thorough 'social accounting', which considers the total social cost–benefit of marketing and business actions. There is no societal gain to be had from cynical claims of social responsibility, which produce profits for individual private companies at the expense of others.

> *Business functions to satisfy the needs of the consumers. The first measure of the success of any business is how well it serves the consumers. If an operation is not in the interest of the consumers, it is not justified, no matter how profitable it may be to the owners . . .*
>
> (Converse and Huegy, 1946)

The social process perspective is a much broader view than that provided by economic considerations alone. Studying the discipline of macromarketing provides the broader view. This is the societal viewpoint required of management which was intended some 20 years ago, but largely still ignored in favour of seemingly outmoded, even irrelevant, economic emphasis in marketing thinking (see, for example, Ormerod, 1994) and especially teaching:

> *Social marketing is that branch of marketing concerned both with the uses of marketing knowledge, concepts, and techniques to enhance social ends as well as with the social consequences of marketing policies, decisions, and actions. The purview of social marketing is, therefore, broader than that of managerial marketing. It refers to the study of markets and marketing activities within a total social system.*
>
> (Lazer and Kelley, 1973, p. 4)

This contrasts sharply with the other apparently more popular (and narrower) view of social or societal marketing, as championed by Kotler and Zaltman (1971), which exhorts the use of marketing skills to further social programmes. Perhaps this popularity is due in part to the longevity of increasingly weakened economic concepts and the success of marketing gurus, such as Professor Kotler, in packaging and promoting easily understood concepts which have captured the 'rational' minds of 'economic man' as manager.

Marketing?

Marketing is understood as a knowledge enterprise, increasingly with an emphasis on the management of trading relationships. Our experience shows us that the thinking and talking of many practitioners and academics is largely unreflective, uncritical, and poorly theorized. Marketing, now almost ubiquitous in its application, remains largely a normative endeavour, with students almost universally concerned with how to 'market', rather than why?

In taking a critical reading of marketing (see, for example, Alvesson and Willmott, 1992, 1996), we find cause for concern in the discourse, the conception of knowledge, the model, and the way of seeing human relating. Fundamentally, we see a politically motivated explanation for the common conception of communication for marketing. We examine each of these features in turn.

Taking a Foucaultian view, the marketing idea can be seen as a professional ideology and a particular discourse, as well as a set of practices (Morgan, 1992). These are each taken for granted and have become a common sense ('truth') of market-based capitalism (i.e. a consuming society). Marketing management continues to colonize further domains of society as marketing knowledge is deployed for the management of markets. That there is a power effect of the knowledge created within the marketing system remains unrecognized or ignored (or hidden) by many advocates and practitioners. The language of marketing is spoken unreflectively.

> *Marketing discourse seeks to constitute the subjectivities of consumers and managers.*
>
> (Morgan, 1992, p. 13)

Almost the entire discipline of marketing (both practice and academy) is premised on a technical–rational view of the nature and purpose of knowledge. This positivistic and normative approach to knowledge drives a functionalist view of society and a scientistic pursuit of control through empiricist examination of phenomena defined in microeconomic fashion.

The whole marketing endeavour is thus cast by the prevailing 'technicists' as a neutral instrumental technology of exchange. The possibility of a social (political) process is unrecognized or ignored. A managerialistic[1] version of marketing is universally discussed, while a wide range of alternative schools of thought (see, for example, Sheth et al., 1988; Lazer and Kelley, 1973) lie undiscovered or discarded (even denounced) by 'true' 'marketers' (marketeers!). The challenging articles and books remain unread – the questions remain unasked or unanswered.

The unseen menace in this unreflective pursuit lies in the location of managerialistic marketing within the process of constituting a particular kind of society. Specifically, humans are treated as things (to be observed and manipulated), personal identity is reduced to ownership of commodities (brand), social relations are conceived in marketing terms (buyer–seller), and the question of the contribution of marketing effort to the social good is unasked by most.

The technology that we call marketing incorporates a particular way of seeing relationships and of seeing relating – people (agents), objects (products), and events (exchanges in 'consumption situations') (see Schmitt, 1999 for a showman-like elaboration of this terminology). Marketing has almost universally been taken to be 'the discipline of exchange behaviour' (Bagozzi, cited in Morgan, 1992), and the discourse has excluded concern for how 'exchanges' are mediated by asymmetrical power relations. So, markets are not understood as social systems, but as 'technologies of governance' (Morgan, 1992). This way of thinking favours those who manage (control) the markets by neglecting (veiling) structures of domination and exploitation. Social relations are then ignored or objectified as variables for managing. Giddens (1979, cited in Morgan, 1992) showed that exchange theory does not take account of power. So, we are left with marketing as a supposedly neutral technology for managing exchange – but the behaviour engendered is reciprocal manipulation – far from the supposed 'good' of 'free market forces'.

This should prompt us to ask, among other questions, what mental model prevails in marketing education, scholarship, research, and management practice? In a recent email discussion with David Ballantyne (a service management specialist at Monash University), he commented, 'I do see dialogue as a "creating value" term, whereas communication is a "circulating value" term.' Dialogue is proposed as 'reasoning together' (Ballantyne, 1999) – a special kind of communication, which is itself a special kind of interaction. Communication operated as a participatory social action is constructive of identity, meaning, and knowledge (Deetz, 1992, 1995), whereas the 'conduit metaphor' conception of communication, which

---

[1] Deetz (1992) defines managerialism as 'a kind of logic, a set of routine practices, and an ideology.' He specifies that it is 'a way of conceptualising, reasoning through, and discussing events' (a discursive genre) and it involves 'a set of routine practices, a real structure of rewards, and a code of representation,' and 'It is a way of doing and being in corporations that partially structures small groups and conflicts with, and at times suppresses, each group's other modes of thinking.'

is a foundation of managerialistic marketing, places it as no more than an informing technology. Then, there is no free exchange in a value-creating consumption situation. Rather, this possibility is precluded to result in reciprocal manipulation. Such manipulative communication circumnavigates value as it is dishonest, insincere, skirting around the truth. It is time that both the marketing discourse and the underlying ideology were more widely challenged.

The Problem of Scientific Knowledge vs. Moral Concern

Marketing theorists and science researchers continue to pursue 'scientific credentials' through a science of marketing as a source of objective reality. Marketing science is pursued as a way of achieving prediction and control over what is essentially a social world, in the same way that natural scientists seek mastery over the physical world of natural resources and machines. Marketing can be thought of as a part of a socially constructed and socially changed *social reality* (Silverman, 1970) which can be studied as part of social theory through holistic *human science* (Trusted, 1987) in which meaning is more important (Pylkkänen, 1989) than 'rational' competitive market ideology which encourages the application of tools and techniques for economic gain. This dogmatism perhaps only reinforces misguided values. Do marketers know their own values and assumptions? How many are aware of the non-economic values which impact and are impacted by their decisions and actions? How many marketers are aware of their own economic rationality, which uses everything as a means to achieve its end?

   If marketing knowledge is constructed as a science then the marketing scientist is in pursuit of knowledge of the material world based on (scientific) analytical and abstract thinking, which focuses attention on certain sets of relations while ignoring all others. This mechanistic and reductionist view has pervaded much of man's attempts to understand the world in order to control it, and has resulted in higher levels of complexity being interpreted in terms of simpler, and supposedly more basic, levels.

   The marketer seeks assumed cause–effect-type action–outcome situations in which marketing tools are wielded toward the achievement of rational *objectives* (this term is related to 'objective' in the 'scientific' sense). This rules-based thinking in which there is assumed a 'right way' to deal with a situation is *disintellectual* in the sense that real thinking is not required. This point is developed below. Sheldrake (in Pylkkänen, 1989, p. 97) sees the mechanistic world view as merely an abstraction from the way things are, and that this is an aberration in thinking rather than the basis of scientific rationality.

In Defence of the Beleaguered Marketing Concept

The marketing concept has been presented in many guises, and after 50 years' accumulated work marketing scholars have not yet managed to agree on a universal formulation or definition. Over 100 definitions have been published. This is probably not due to any difficulty in conceptualizing marketing as a business philosophy, a social process, and a management technology, but rather the obvious need of marketing 'experts' to differentiate their own definition for the next book!

Bell and Emory (1971) described the marketing concept as:

> ... the result of an attempt to operationalize a basic philosophy of marketing held by economists and marketing theorists.
>
> (p. 38)

The problem seems to be that the marketing concept is more often interpreted as operational than as philosophical, since managers believe that they hold the responsibility for pragmatic decisions motivated by generally short-term profits and competition. The long-run *total costs* to *all stakeholders* in marketing decisions and actions are generally not considered.

Contrast the view that marketing is:

> ... the management process responsible for identifying, anticipating and satisfying consumers' requirements profitably.
>
> (UK Chartered Institute of Marketing)

with Kotler's wider notion (1991) that:

> ... marketing is a social and managerial process by which individuals and groups obtain what they need and want through creating, offering, and exchanging products of value with others.
>
> (p. 4)

The scope and nature of marketing has been questioned by Bartels who has traced the history and evolution of marketing thinking and practice:

> ... the issue is whether marketing is an economic technology responsible to markets for distribution of goods and services, or an institution responsible to society for meeting those consumption needs in the context of society's ethical and spiritual expectations.
>
> (Bartels in Fisk, 1986, p. 41)

The marketing concept *is* appropriate for the future of mankind provided a long-term and balanced view is taken of the aims of its application and the resulting effects on the world we live in, including the physical and mental environments we inhabit. The problems now increasingly seen as consequences of activities associated with the notion of 'marketing' can be related to the apparent lack of awareness of a sense of the concept from outside the narrow economic value base. Kotler has defined the marketer as:

> ... someone seeking a resource from someone else and willing to offer something of value in exchange.
>
> (1994, p. 12)

This definition will guide the future marketing manager well if the long-run social costs of the resource use is considered and the notion of (economic) exchange is replaced with the idea of social transaction.

A very early definition of marketing shows a philosophy of customer satisfaction which has not been well operationalized in that customer orientation is often used as a means to achieve a company's profit objective, rather than as an end in itself:

> *Business functions to satisfy the needs of the consumers. The first measure of the success of any business is how well it serves the consumers.* If an operation is not in the interest of the consumers, **it is not justified**, *no matter how profitable it may be to its owners ... (emphasis added).*
>
> (Converse and Huegy, 1946)

Schumacher (1973) pointed out the essential non-economic values which many marketers may have given little thought to in their pursuit of short-term goals. These are part of the totality of human thinking which constructs our reality and experience, and these fit well with Weber's 'spheres of life' in religious, political, economic, legal, and aesthetic thinking (see Kuper, 1987, p. 264).

A New Marketing Manifesto for the New Economy?

We can examine CRM in a new light, revealing a re-view. Grant's (2000) new marketing manifesto explains the *brand as ideas to live by* (the new traditions). Kelly (1998) shows that the emerging new economy is a complex of networks of connectivity for communication that drive change (Table 1.1).

A new marketing is needed for a new kind of society that is becoming rooted in ubiquitous electronic networks that trade in ideas, information, and

TABLE 1.1 The new conditions (based on Kelly, 1998).

- Society is increasingly becoming networked to deal with messy complexity by decentralizing control
- Increasing returns are realizable in networks through self-reinforcing success
- Value derives from abundance. Only human attention is becoming scarce
- Networks reward generosity
- Members prosper as the network prospers
- Innovation pays off when the successful is abandoned to escape its eventual obsolescence
- Economic activity is migrating from 'places' to 'spaces' – multiple interactions with anything, anytime, anywhere
- Turbulence and instability are becoming the norm – selective disruption is called for (we can call this managed innovation) to sustain disequilibrium
- The most powerful technologies are those that generate and enhance relationships by connecting people
- Far greater production of wealth comes from inefficient discovery and the creation of new opportunities than comes from slavish, efficient problem-solving

TABLE 1.2 Possible futures for marketing (based on Grant, 2000).

New marketing as value extractor	New marketing as value creator
Subjection to 'new retailing' – ICT-based automated mass targeting and transaction	Participation in brand development through creative entrepreneurship
Passive customers	Independent, active customers
Production system as conformist, hierarchical bureaucracy	Business de-institutionalized around knowledge and ideas
Fragmenting society	Breakdown of cultural distinctions
Incremental change	Breakthrough innovation

relationships. So, communication is the foundation of society, culture, humanity, personal identity, and the economic systems. But not merely as an enabler – *as a transformer*. This new marketing is fundamentally different from what has gone before (Table 1.2), requiring us to explicate and reassess our mental models and assumptions in alternative orthodoxies.

Grant (2000) promotes the notion that brands are ideas to live by in post-traditional society. The shift to a new marketing is in the what and why (new purpose) of marketing, and not simply in the how (new digital multimedia) of marketing (Table 1.3).

These principles of relational marketing are explored further throughout this book.

Peter Drucker is credited with first defining the *marketing concept*:

Marketing ... is the whole business seen from the point of view of its final result, that is, from the customer's point of view.

(1954, p. 36)

Evert Gummesson advises that this is best implemented by operating not with marketing management, but with *marketing-oriented management*.

According to leading service marketing specialist Professor Christian Grönroos (2000), all businesses must now compete on service. The marketing process, then, comprises:

Understanding the market and individual customers by market research and segmentation analysis, and by using database information on individual customers so that market niches, segments and individual! customers can be chosen, for which marketing programmes and activities can be planned, implemented, and followed up; and to prepare the organisation so that marketing programmes and activities are successfully implemented (through internal marketing).

In *service competition* the core solution for a buyer is the prerequisite for the success of a trading relationship. This offering, together with the management of a

TABLE 1.3 A new Relational Marketing manifesto (inspired by Grant, 2000).

Grant's rule	Significance	Relational implication
Get up close and personal	The subjective basis of marketing as a social process, rather than the overemphasis of marketing as a rational/objective technology of demand management	Marketing is what people do together and not an inert technology
Tap basic human needs	Forget marketing positioning through distinctive brands – uniquely express fundamental human drives (sex, hunger, curiosity, order, social contact, and so on)	People are persons before they are customers
Author innovation	Redefine the brand as an author – a constant presence behind new ideas – rather than as a fixed identity	Interaction produces rather than reproduces identity, knowledge, and meaning
Mythologize the new	Marketing as constructive – the brand as a new tradition, rather than as the reflection of old traditions	Let buyers and users lead
Create tangible differences in the experience	Consumers have to believe that brand personalities *are* different	Work toward 'my brand'
Cultivate authenticity	Marketing must engage, not merely project ideals	Resist educating, controlling, and winning
Work through consensus	Put ideas into circulation, rather than direct selling messages	Preference through accommodation, rather than loyalty through persuasion
Open up to participation	Work with partners, rather than do things for supposedly impressionable passive consumers – customers as co-creators of the brand	Communicability – be receptive
Build communities of interest	Target audiences as active communities of interest, rather than as supposedly passive recipients identified by fixed habits and allegiances	Foster a 'we' way of doing things, in place of an 'us' and (against) 'them'
Use strategic creativity	Don't be limited by the capabilities of available mass media – use old and new media strategically to support a suitable gene	Foster ties through connections, not merely abstract 'messages'

continued

TABLE 1.3 (*continued*)

Grant's rule	Significance	Relational implication
Stake a claim for fame	Do interesting things that tell a memorable story – forget repetitive, hopefully engaging expressions of a brand identity	Show people by involving them and you in worthwhile action
Follow a vision and be true to your values	Recognize that a brand makes the corporation and can be a change agent – marketing must be true to the vision and values of the people doing it!	Take accountability, and not only responsibility, for your actions

number of additional associated services, forms a Total Service Offering and determines whether or not the firm will be a successful trader (Grönroos, 2000).

The central thesis of contemporary accounts of marketing is that effective competition in a global economy requires effective co-operation in a commercial network. Hunt (1997) points out that this idea requires us to abandon neoclassical economic theory, which views co-operation among firms as anti-competitive collusion. We will examine the notion of a portfolio of relationship assets further as we progress through this chapter.

At the philosophical level, Relationship Marketing differs little from generally defined marketing. Whatever else it is, Relationship Marketing is participatory. Buyers and sellers do it together, rather than marketers doing it to consumers. Today's society is very different to that in which the managerial version of marketing came to dominate. Now, a relationship emphasis is necessary. Buyers are more demanding, expecting a consistently good (in their terms) personal service.

Accordingly, Grönroos (2000) explains the role and scope of marketing as identifying and establishing, maintaining and enhancing customer relationships, which implies, respectively, that the process of marketing includes the following:

- market research to identify potentially interesting and profitable customers to contact;
- establishing the first contact with a customer so that a relationship emerges;
- maintaining an existing relationship so that the customer is satisfied with the quality and the value he or she judges to have received and is willing to continue to do business;
- enhancement of an ongoing relationship so that the customer decides to expand the content of the relationship by, for example, purchasing larger quantities or new types of good and service;
- sometimes terminating a relationship or coping when a customer decides to discontinue the relationship, in such a manner that the relationship can be re-established in the future under different circumstances.

Almost 30 years ago, Peter Drucker told us that a business exists to create and keep customers by innovating (see Drucker, 1973). Making and selling things is only part of the business story. Today, many, but still too few, businesses are organized to integrate manufacturing operations, finance, and work processes to assist marketing in product differentiation and customer servicing through personal contact.

> Marketing is a social process. 'Marketing is to establish, maintain, and enhance and when necessary also to terminate relationships with customers and other stake-holders, at a profit, so that the objectives of all parties involved are met. This is achieved by a mutual exchange and fulfilment of promises.'
>
> (Grönroos, 1994)

Another view from the Scandinavia Nordic school of thought is:

> *Total relationship marketing (TRM) is marketing based on relationships, networks and interaction, recognizing that marketing is embedded in the total management of the networks of the selling organization, the market and society. It is directed to long-term win–win relationships with individual customers, and value is jointly created between the parties involved. It transcends the boundaries between specialist functions and disciplines. It is made tangible through the thirty market, mega and nano relationships, the 30Rs.*
>
> (Gummesson, 1999, p. 24)

Relationship Marketing is an alternative approach to the traditional 4P (product, price, promotion, place) marketing mix management. What is managed is relationships that are the context for trading. All interactions in the trading relationship management (TRM) system are in preparation for, or the enactment of, trading exchanges. Table 1.4 summarizes two ways of explaining the role and function of marketing management.

Marketing mix management focuses attention on managing awareness and preference dispositions through the circulation of supplier and product information. Relationship marketing management seeks to establish individualized ties through strong personal appeal and continuing commitment.

Management, traditionally, has been thought of as dealing with things, including human resources. This reinforces an artificial separation into component disciplines (IS, marketing, accounting, etc.), yet there can be no ready separation in practice, since 'real' problems overlap any such divisions. Fulop and Linstead (1999) promote a view of management as inherently relational practice. This does not, however, emphasize the control of relationships. The job of the manager is to bring relationships into being and change them for mutual benefit. They note that relationships are with constituencies (or 'stakeholders'), are managed by action, through organization (NB, organization is *not* structure), among many wider sociocultural influences. So, relationships are managed through the performance of organized functions, tasks, roles, interpersonal interaction, and analysis.

Management co-ordinates action efficiently and flexibly to produce high-quality goods and services, and learning within the resources and constraints of

TABLE 1.4 Management of products or networks?

Marketing mix management	Trading relationship management
Recruit customers	Strengthen customer relationships
4Ps model	Economics and social psychology of trading relationships
Managerialistic use of the 4P toolbox of controllable variables	Marketing as a social system and Marketing Relationship as a process
Production orientation	Customer orientation
'Do to'	'Do for – do with'
Departmentalized function	Customer relationship life cycle model
Marketing as a technology	Co-production of valued service: interactive marketing function, perceived service quality
Active seller, passive buyer/consumer	Active participants
Promotional budget overhead	Relationship learning reduces interaction costs

the operating environment. This, in turn, produces improvement, creativity and innovation, and productivity in the production system. The system is then capable of profit-making by producing value for stakeholders. To understand the TRM system fully requires systemic consideration of 'total quality management', Management, Marketing, and Knowledge Management (ICT/IS).

The Origins of Relationship Marketing

Gummesson's (1999) Total Relationship Marketing approach recognizes the necessary shift away from manipulating the marketing mix, to managing the service system as part of a network of commercial relationships supported by a variety of technologies. This recognizes the central significance of customers' judgements of goods and service quality, and seeks to integrate all resources, including relationships, that can affect service system outcomes. Marketing management necessarily is recast as marketing-oriented management.

The shift from thinking of marketing as a machine for disciplining selling transactions, to thinking of marketing as a social process is a particular manifestation of a much wider 'shift of mind' to 'see the world anew' (Senge, 1990, p. 68). Systems thinking allows us to recognize the 'structure' that underlies complex situations by seeing wholes, rather than only parts. This is a way of seeing interrelationships rather than discrete entities, and patterns of change rather than static 'snapshots'. Therefore, people are seen as active participants in shaping their reality.

In a fragmenting, deregulating society it becomes more difficult to sustain a leading business on the basis of a short-term sales transaction orientation to policy/decision-making. Increasing competition turns managers' minds to keeping profitable customers trading, rather than making new customer connections. Enduring, learning relationships are now recognized as the necessary basis for sustainable productive business enterprise. As customers, we now demand quality in terms of what but also how we are helped to satisfy our needs and wants. We expect 'customer care' in terms of feeling involved in the process and outcome of product creation, purchase, and consumption.

> Nissan responded to their declining market share by changing their structure of organization and corporate philosophy to place customer satisfaction as their first priority. Development times and delivery lead-times were reduced, and a more sophisticated sense of what car buyers wanted was created. This helped to rebuild the company's fortunes and market position.

> I consider a comprehensive and sophisticated definition of marketing to be *human behaviour of engaging in exchange (a multilateral process in which each party expects to receive and to give value) or potential exchange within a market for the purpose of satisfying one's own needs by acquiring additional resources and their property rights and associated obligations* (see Houston, 1994, for elaborate engagement with the question of what constitutes marketing – and what does not). Roles of *buyer* and *seller* are enacted in a trading relationship.

In service businesses, there is no real separation of production, delivery, and consumption, so the buyer–seller interaction is part of the marketer's task, and this can only be fulfilled in a relationship with the customer. In industrial trading, the performance of repairs, servicing, maintenance, delivery, installation, and training requires not just close connections between seller and buyer, but also often other partners.

This requires more than simply expanding the after-sales service department. It requires the bringing of marketing, customer service, and quality into alignment – not as separate functions, but as a coherent value-creation chain (Christopher et al., 1991). Competitive strength comes from increasing the overall service element of the market offerings. In this way, total customer care, established on the principles of total quality management, becomes Relationship Marketing. This requires a holistic approach to co-create and exchange value with suppliers, manufacturing operators, and customers. One way to enable and facilitate real-time and near-real-time interaction is to use ICT at the interface of buying and selling action.

Recently, the relationship marketing process has been explained as the creation and development of 'value laden' relationships with stakeholders (Kotler et al., 1999). What is meant by this?

While sales specialists manage relationships with individual accounts to generate immediate revenues, and marketing specialists identify and attempt to

TABLE 1.5 Marketing issues of today and tomorrow (based on Gordon, 1998).

Customer expectations are rising	Increasing sophistication and knowledge of buyers
Market segmentation doesn't really work any more	Traditional approaches do not predict customer behaviour. Current and future trading value seems more appropriate
Best customers deserve best value	Customers are not equally important, yet few sellers reward those who are the kind of customers they want to trade with
Networks of relationships	Many people contribute to the value-creation performance of the end buyer–seller interaction, yet relationships throughout the value network are often not assessed
Data	Although volumes of data threaten to swamp many managers, often the right type of data needed to develop desirable trading relationships is scarce
Mass customization technology	Technology is needed to improve the trading relationship by integrating knowledge into production, human resources, and other business processes
Support	Managers need support from board directors and investors who understand that high costs are upfront and returns will not be immediate
Recognition and reward	Reward systems have to recognize the performance of the 'farmer' and not only the 'hunter', and recognize the role of teams in improving relationship quality
Relationships and capabilities	Otherwise, fragmented, unlinked initiatives that impact on customers have to be integrated and learned from – capabilities for building strong trading relationships have to be addressed
Organize by relationship and capability	Product management is not compatible with a Relationship Marketing way of trading – closer bonding with customers requires organization around relationship category

satisfy needs for market segments, neither, observes Gordon (1998), typically deals with the significant issues of contemporary trading. Indeed, market segmentation has produced corporate segmentation (divisionalized, isolated specialists) (see Table 1.5).

Quanxi revisited

There has been much talk in the West about Chinese-style business based on relationships in complex networks of assistance that extend familial support beyond the domestic family. Could this be the way to model marketing relationships, with advantages over the rules-based systems of governance? Professor Nigel Holden has observed that many Westerners have viewed quanxi as 'some kind of spiritual ectoplasm' (2002, p. 11).

The principle is that one should always do business first with close family, then neighbours, then former school and college classmates, and then, only reluctantly, with strangers – and only exceptionally with strangers who are foreigners.

Such trust-based trading is based on ties of interest and obligation (to not let the other person down). Such relationships are not merely about instrumental connections for resource allocation, but are built on dyadic, interpersonal social ties within webs of ongoing obligation and loyalty to the person.

As the cost of rules-based market economy falls (due to ICT), quanxi ought to become redundant. But will it? Why should we not adopt so human a way of trading in the West? Must scientific instrumental economic thinking prevail instead?

Relationship Marketing Values

Inappropriate basic marketing values and the associated practices mitigate against the positive effect of a relationship marketing strategy. So what values are needed? Gummesson (1999) provides the checklist:

- *long-term collaboration for mutual value creation* (win–win outcomes of a 'plus sum game' that emphasizes commitment for an extended duration, and care, over and above attraction);
- *all parties recognized as active* (either of the interacting parties can initiate innovation, etc. – the relationship is co-managed);
- *relational and service values* – bureaucratic–legal values are discarded in favour of treating customers as differing (within communities of affinity) exchangers of value (co-defined by them, in various forms).

Traditional marketing thinking is prejudiced in favour of the benefits of competition, while excluding collaboration as an inhibiting force.

Traditional marketing represented the consumer as a passive and receptive object to be acted upon through market interventions that would influence their attitudes and, consequently, their behaviour through 'targeted communications'. In this break from the tradition, the Relationship Marketing logic views the consumer as a highly active agent who acts productively on the basis of personal motivations (Figure 1.1). In this way, people can choose whether or not to engage in relationships, and this perspective brings partnership and negotiation to the fore in marketing thinking.

Transaction marketing	Relationship marketing
Focus on short-term performance and recruitment of customer for single sales	Long-term performance is the priority with attention to transaction history and potential, for customer retention
Management of a marketing mix	
Profit from goods	Marketing interaction (supported by marketing mix activities)
Attention to technical quality of product	
Quality is production concern	Customers less price-sensitive as value of benefits and solutions is realized
Customers are price-sensitive	
Market share is taken as customer satisfaction indicator	Quality of interactions is paramount
	Customer satisfaction assured by managing trading relationships
Customer information from *ad hoc* satisfaction surveys	Customer information from real-time ICT
Interface of marketing, operations and HR is given little or no importance	Functional interface is strategically important
Customer service not valued	Customer service is paramount
Little commitment to customers	Quality is the concern of all
Internal marketing is given little or no attention	Customer contact is frequent and co-operative
Contact with customer is largely promotional	Internal marketing is strategically important
Consumer packaged goods and durables	*Industrial goods and services*

FIGURE 1.1   The marketing strategy continuum (based on Grönroos, 1990).

The Driving Forces behind Relationship Marketing

Why has this way of thinking about the purpose and organization of marketing risen to prominence over the past 25 years? Palmer (2002) has conducted a simple PEST analysis to try to explain this shift in emphasis from discrete transactions to relational exchanges. This analysis is summarized in Table 1.6.

Palmer has no doubt that the development of Relationship Marketing has arisen from changes in the business environment that will have effects for some considerable time. The reduction in the power imbalance between buyers and sellers, of course, implies directly the significance of the trading relationship. Customer ties will have to become more sincere and authentic.

Ways of Explaining a Relational Basis for Marketing

As a so-called new paradigm of marketing, we should consider the theoretical origins of the principles and practice of Relationship Marketing. A range of bodies of theory is here briefly reviewed to provide some understanding of RM foundations.

TABLE 1.6 The environment for Relationship Marketing (based on Palmer, 2002).

Technological	Advent of information and communication technologies, enabling large-scale communication between seller and buyer, and the centring of knowledge as a resource. Manifest in card-based loyalty programmes
Social	The shift towards a more co-operative society, and the move away from traditional institutions (church, family, etc.) to the derivation of identity from commercial relationships. Increasing influence of female values of co-operation and reconciliation
Economic	Recognition of cost impact of customer retention and service interaction quality
Political	Regulation, leading to the abandonment of hierarchical control structures, through outsourcing to hybrid organization structures in 'free' markets

Neo-classical Microeconomic Theory

This theory emphasizes profit maximization in competitive markets in explaining relative prices, market equilibrium, and income distribution. Exchange parties are price takers seeking to maximize utility in price equilibrium markets. This assumes well-defined and stable preference structures where individuals independently worry about creating value. Firms are seen as engaged in market transactions to secure the resources they require for producing goods and services they sell in the competitive marketplace. Such market transactions incur the costs associated with the price paid, searching costs, negotiating and contracting costs, and costs of monitoring supplier performance.

The marketing management tradition based upon the idea of microeconomic maximization strongly distinguishes the trading environment and controllable decision variables in the marketing mix. It has thus been very useful in explaining value distribution among marketing actors.

However, it is doubtful that contemporary problems can be adequately dealt with by a microeconomic approach focusing on costs, functional differentiation, and market structures. It has limited applicability to transactional exchange situations, due to its inadequacy in providing insufficient tools for analysing exchange structures and processes within and between exchange parties. For example, contrary to the assumptions of microeconomic theory, consumers have a natural tendency to reduce choices. Also, the assumption of rational behaviour is often not realistic. Economists have generally viewed markets as social 'vacuums' in which buyers and sellers only know each other in their roles as dictated by the market (i.e. as no more than buyer and seller).

Transaction Cost Theory

Transaction cost theory (Williamson, 1975) uses arguments from microeconomics and institutional economics, contract law, and organization theory. In the original transaction cost theory, transactions were classified according to whether they occurred within a firm or between the firms in a market. Further developments examined the transaction cost advantages of different forms of internally and externally organized transactions within the constraints of bounded rationality and opportunistic behaviour. Axioms of this approach are that certain exchange characteristics give rise to transaction difficulties and that different governance mechanisms vary in their cost-minimizing properties.

Market transactions may become very costly due to human factors, such as bounded rationality and opportunism, and environmental factors, such as uncertainty and economically concentrated input or output markets. Transaction cost theory departs from the assumptions that individuals are limited in their cognitive capabilities and that they are inclined toward opportunistic and self-interest-seeking behaviour. Consequently, in situations when information is unequally spread among exchange parties, opportunistic behaviour is believed to prevail and exchange may be commercially hazardous. Opportunism is generally centred on deceit. In order to reduce the risks of being exploited by each other, exchange partners can safeguard their interests by making substantial transaction-specific investments that are uniquely related to the exchange relationship and that cannot be retrieved on termination. If both partners make such investments, they create incentives to maintain, or obstacles to leave, the relationship they are in by communicating their credibility of commitment to the relationship. Such investments in transaction-specific assets also create dependence relationships between exchange partners since they are difficult or costly to replace.

Every market transaction involves transaction costs that lead to inefficiencies for those engaged in these exchanges. Such transaction costs include costs of information search, of reaching a satisfactory agreement, of relationship monitoring, of adapting agreements to unanticipated contingencies, and of contract enforcement. Transaction costs can be subdivided into performance ambiguity and goal incongruence. Because of bounded rationality and the existence of transaction costs, a comprehensive contract related to controlling all aspects of a relationship is not a viable option for partners in a relationship. Instead, parties have to rely on 'incomplete contracting' involving the development of long-term relationships that permit sequential, adaptive decision-making.

Transaction costs are minimized by selecting a mode of relationship governance that is 'optimal', given transaction properties such as asset specificity, uncertainty, and infrequency, and that curbs bargaining and opportunism. Governance modes range from arm's length spot-market governance (external governance mechanism) and vertical integration (internal governance mechanism). In 'arm's length' exchange situations, buyers set sellers against each other in order to achieve lower costs. In vertically integrated exchange situations, buyers and sellers can reduce transaction costs by aligning their objectives and internal systems.

Under conditions of asset specificity, opportunism, and uncertainty, the transaction costs of arm's length market exchanges are far larger than those of more long-term relational exchanges. So, generally, a movement accompanies an increase in transaction costs from external to internal governance mechanisms.

This approach assumes that a firm will internalize those activities which they are able to perform at a lower cost, and that they will rely on market mechanisms for those activities in which other providers have an advantage (e.g. outsourcing). The framework helps to identify problems that can arise when idiosyncratic or transaction-specific investments are involved in an exchange relationship.

However, there are major limitations. The unilateral focus of transaction cost theory on the potential costs that are associated with idiosyncratic investments fails to recognize the potential value that is generated by these investments. Transaction cost theory focuses on the single criterion of cost-efficiency for shaping transactions. The role of other microeconomic criteria tends to be down-played in most transaction cost analyses. The term 'transaction costs' should also include positive returns that can result from exchanges. It does not take into account the interdependencies created between partners in a relationship, and generally only reluctantly acknowledges the potential contributions of power-dependence theory. Transaction cost theory is mainly preoccupied with the con-ditions that motivate exchange partners to structure relationships in a particular way, without specifying the mechanisms that provide the ability to implement these desired structures. It focuses on a relationship structure at one moment in time and neglects the possible dynamic evolution of a governance structure and transactions. The role and importance of people in the governance of exchanges is virtually ignored! The assumption of opportunistically inclined parties is overly simplistic and misleading. Empirical evidence demonstrates that human behaviour in relationships is not as Machiavellian as described in transaction cost theory. Sociologists stress that exchange is typically embedded in social structures in which opportunism is the exception rather than the rule. Transaction cost theory has failed to offer predictions about the implications of deviance from opportunism. Further, many exchanges are based on a gradual development of trust that helps exchange partners to lower transaction costs by safeguarding against opportunism. The implications of the effect of trusting behaviour on governance structures are generally ignored in transaction cost theory. The theory cannot adequately explain how it is that idiosyncratic investments occur in relationships that are not vertically integrated. Although transaction-specific investments play an important role in affecting relationships through creating dependence and 'locking-in' customers, they are not sufficient to explain long-term orientation in exchanges. Transaction cost analysis makes no allowance for safeguarding transaction-specific assets, other than by vertical integration, which is not always a feasible or relevant strategy.

Relational Contracting Theory

This is primarily rooted in contract law that applies to the legal rights of exchange parties and guides the planning and conduct of exchange. While classical contract law views exchange as composed of single, independent, and static transactions, modern contract law tries to deal with the dynamic nature of intermediate and long-term exchanges. Modern contract law explicitly refers to exchange planning and contract formation, to adjustments to established contract relationships, and to the resolution of contractual conflict.

Relational contracting theory has provided a rich conceptual framework that is able to capture the dimensions and dynamics that underlie the nature of exchange relationships as well as the belief structures and activities that are necessary for successful exchange relationships. MacNeil (1980) distinguished intermediate types of exchange between discrete transactions and complete internalization of exchanges. Such intermediate forms of exchange are termed 'contractual ways of exchange' or 'relational transactions', where exchange parties are still independent but at the same time coupled by weak or strong contractual agreements. Since a pure reliance on the mechanism of law can be costly in terms of both resources and time, and since unforeseen circumstances can affect the exchange relationship, extra-legal governance methods are needed. So, the concept of contract has been defined very broadly as a relationship between exchange parties who expect to sustain this relationship into the future. Therefore, contracts are about exchange because they capture the relations among parties and these relations project exchange into the future.

MacNeil's (1980) relational contracting framework describes types of contract in terms of the norms that are expectations about behaviour that are at least partially shared by a group of decision-makers. These differ in content and general orientation and may relate to particular kinds of behaviour. For example, while norms can be oriented toward a more discrete or a more relational nature (general orientation), relational norms may be translated into several different behaviours such as flexibility, mutuality, consistency, solidarity, creation and use of power, and information exchange. A general property of relational norms is their prescription of behaviours that are aimed at maintaining a relationship and their rejection of behaviours that promote individual goal-seeking. During an exchange act, buyers and sellers often establish norms that did not exist prior to this exchange.

Contracts can be based on the traditional promise of contract law (promissory norms) or more relationship-based promises (non-promissory norms). MacNeil (1980) argued that formal contracts guided by promissory norms do not play a substantial role in most relationships. Rather, it is the set of understandings among exchange partners or the 'implicit contract' guided by non-promissory norms that substantially affects relationships. Parties who engage in exchanges based upon implicit contracts are less in need of monitoring of their exchange partners or of building safeguards into the relationship.

Relational contracting theory deals with the criticisms that have been directed at transaction cost theory by including social dimensions of exchange, and by making clear that hierarchical relationship governance mechanisms are not the only mechanisms available. Consequently, the theory of relational contracting offers a valuable complement to Williamson's (1975) transaction cost approach. However, this theory has been criticized for failing to prescribe optimal types of governance to deal with specific characteristics of the exchange. Until now, relational exchange theory has mainly been used for descriptive and conceptual purposes.

Social Exchange Theory

People use cognitive schema to organize their perceptions of social interactions and relationships. The basis of social exchange theory is derived from marital theory, bargaining theory, and power theory. The qualities of interpersonal relationships have been extensively investigated in disciplines such as psychology and social psychology.

Social exchange theory compares the formation and continuity of a relationship with those of a marriage and places interactions between people at the core of relationships. This has inspired the development of the interaction approach of the Industrial Marketing and Purchasing (IMP) group. The IMP group examined the dynamics of interaction. Their interaction approach focuses on exchange episodes that are embedded in a framework of a relationship in which the parties adapt to one another in order to produce mutually beneficial outcomes. Marketing is seen as an interactive process occurring in a social context where relationship management is central (Grönroos, 1994). The IMP group considered the concept of interaction as a series of short-term social interactions that are affected by the long-term business process or 'atmosphere' that binds exchange parties together. They concluded that co-operation better explained this than did conflict and opposition. The interaction approach suggested six different types of bond: social, technological, knowledge, planning, legal, and economic.

While some scholars have used love or marriage as a metaphor for the type of relationship that should exist between a buyer and a seller, others have actually drawn on marriage theories to conceptualize buyer–seller exchange processes. When acting according to social norms, members usually expect reciprocal benefits in the form of personal affection, trust, gratitude, and, sometimes, economic returns. Social norms are generally defined as expectations regarding behaviour. Bagozzi (1995), for example, viewed reciprocity as an essential feature of self-regulation and mutual co-ordination in exchange relationships – the social mechanism by which actions of one party evoke compensating (responsive) actions by the other party.

Self-interest and the evaluation of relationship outcome are the basis of maintaining and exploiting relationships. The general aim of parties in interpersonal relationships is to derive benefits from their relationships that would not be accessible to them on their own. These benefits can include non-economic rewards and even altruistic rewards. The interpersonal attraction literature has directed attention to rewards flowing from perceived similarity or complementary resources such as money, information, or status.

Social exchange theory is not able to explain the processes related to relationship dissolution.

Equity Theory

Equity theory is related to social exchange theory, relative deprivation theory, and distributive justice theory, given their unifying basic premise that outcomes should be evaluated in a relative sense within some frame of reference. Equity theory focuses upon outcome evaluations that result from relationships characterized by economic productivity objectives. Equity theory postulates that parties in exchange relationships compare their ratios of exchange inputs to outcomes. Inequity is said to exist when the perceived inputs and/or outcomes in an exchange relationship are psychologically inconsistent with the perceived inputs and/or outcomes of the referent. Since parties sometimes need to evaluate each other before engaging in an exchange, role expectations play a crucial role in determining the equity level of a potential exchange relationship. Each party to the exchange has certain expectations about their own role as well as that of the other party. According to role theory, each exchange partner has learned a set of behaviours that is appropriate in an exchange context – this will increase the probability of goal attainment by each partner. Role stress can affect long-term relationships if role expectations are unclear (role ambiguity) or if actual behaviours deviate from expectations (role conflict).

Believed inequities lead exchange parties to feel under-rewarded or over-rewarded, angry, or resentful, and will affect behaviours in subsequent periods by encouraging these parties to change their inputs into the relationship, and thus result in suspicion and mistrust of the exchange partner. The closer the exchange relationship, the more likely it is that relationship participants will perceive inequity. If equity prevails, the ratio of one person's outcomes to inputs is assumed to be constant across exchange partners, which results in the satisfaction of exchange partners with their outcomes. Equitable outcomes stimulate confidence that parties do not take advantage of each other and that they are concerned about each other's welfare. Parties in a relationship can compare their own ratio to that of their exchange partner, to those of others who interact with their exchange partner at the same level, and to that of their best alternative exchange partner.

Though both equity and disconfirmation are comparison processes, these processes are viewed as conceptually distinct and complementary. While one person's outcomes and inputs are compared to those of the other party in equity processes, outcomes in general are compared to their expectations for those outcomes in expectancy disconfirmation processes. Equity theory is fundamentally different from cognitive dissonance theory. While cognitive dissonance research primarily focused on the relationship between a person and a product, equity theory research is concerned with a group process and an equitable distribution of benefits among people.

Equity theory explicitly recognizes the inherent inequality between exchange partners. In the case that roles are dissimilar, theories of distributive justice or 'expectation states theory' are useful in understanding exchange relationships. These theories require only that each party has expectations of the role of the other party, and interpret justice in terms of how well this other party performs on their role dimensions. Equity theory is more useful in commercial exchange situations than is social exchange theory (with its assumption of equal partners to the exchange).

Because contradictory findings have been generated on the effects of over-rewarding parties in a relationship, equity theory has declined in research popularity and application. A significant shortcoming of equity theory is the absence of a unifying framework that can explain both positive as well as negative effects of over-rewarding.

Political Economy Theory

The political economy paradigm integrates economic efficiency theories of organizations with behavioural power theories. It is an institutional analysis based on political science, sociology, and organization theory (Arndt, 1983). The political economy framework draws on social exchange theory, the behavioural theory of the firm, and transaction cost theory. Moreover, political economy theory is related to many of the subfields within marketing. For instance, the macromarketing school addresses the environment.

The political economy framework has most often been used in order to conceptualize structure and process in channels of distribution. It has also been claimed that it helps to better understand all types of relationship and alliance in marketing (Arndt, 1983).

Political economy theory views a social system as interacting sets of major economic and socio-political forces that affect collective behaviour and performance. Adopting analysts evaluate exchanges between parties on the basis of three dimensions: (1) polity–economy, (2) external–internal, and (3) substructure–superstructure (Arndt, 1983).

An essential characteristic of political economy theory is its simultaneous and interdependent analysis of political and economic systems of production and consumption. Economy refers to institutions that transform inputs into output and to the processes by which goods and services are allocated within and between institutions (ranging from market to vertical exchange processes). Polity refers to the power and control systems that legitimize, facilitate, monitor, and regulate exchange transactions. The economy and polity can be considered as allocation systems, allocating scarce economic resources and power or authority, respectively.

The main contribution of political economy theory results from its dyadic approach that integrates both economic and socio-political factors, and explicitly insists that economic and socio-political forces are not analysed in isolation. The value of the theory lies in its capacity of identifying socio-economic interactions between exchange partners in terms of their internal structure and external environment. It is considered to be a more appropriate paradigm than the microeconomic paradigm as it focuses on authority and control patterns, conflict and conflict management procedures, and external and internal determinants of institutional change. The value of political economy theory results from both its generality and its integrative potential. It is a fairly general theory that can support theory construction in a wide range of marketing areas. It is integrative in that it offers a unifying framework in which major economic and socio-political constructs can be used for comparing marketing relationships. The microeconomic and political economy paradigms are complementary rather than alternatives. The microeconomic framework, with its emphasis on controllable variables and problem solving, is appropriate in the normative marketing management tradition. However, for purposes of building positive theories in marketing, the political economy world view seems more relevant.

However, the theory is so comprehensive that it has proven difficult to apply empirically. Due to its complexity, political economy theory is often confronted with criticisms reflecting its methodological problems, vagueness, and incompleteness. It specifies many constructs and relationships that are difficult to capture through conventional research methods. At its present level, political economy is more vague and less precise than, for instance, the microeconomic paradigm. It may also be criticized for putting too little emphasis on performance or goal attainment of social units in terms of effectiveness and efficiency.

Resource Dependence Theory

The resource-based theory of the firm was developed from organization behaviour, economics, and strategic management, and has moved beyond the traditional emphasis on the microeconomic paradigm.

The ideas are based upon balance power theories, bilateral oligopoly and duopoly theories in economics, and relative deprivation theories of collective conflict. Many theorists regard dependence and power as central to explaining organizational and interpersonal behaviour. Yet, the traditional discussion of exchange in marketing generally does not focus on differences in negotiation power and the consequently unequal and unsatisfactory nature of exchange transactions. Resource dependence theory explicitly addresses these issues by examining sources of power and dependence in exchange relationships.

Resource-Advantage Theory

A resource is available to a firm to enable it to produce efficiently and/or effectively an offering to market that has value for one or more segments (groups whose members have relatively homogeneous tastes and preferences). Comparative advantage in resources allows the firm to occupy a position of competitive advantage in the marketplace. This results in a superior financial performance, with environmental limitations from societal resources, societal institutions that govern the operating rules, competitor actions, consumer behaviours, and public policy decisions. Innovation, in this view, is produced by learning in the process of competitive struggle.

Relationship Marketing is theoretically supported by the possibility that some kinds of co-operative relationships can enhance competition. Relationships are not part of the 'resources' in neoclassical theory. Yet, they are increasingly held nowadays to be valuable in the production–consumption process. The problem in neoclassical thinking is that relationships are not for sale (they are immobile) and have unique characteristics (they are heterogeneous), so they cannot be considered to be resources.

Hunt's Resource-Advantage Theory (Hunt and Morgan, 1995; Hunt, 1997) allows resources to be: financial, physical, human, organizational, informational, and relational. These resources need not be owned by the firm, but must be available for the purpose of producing value for some segment(s).

Relationships are thus conceived of as organizational capital. This element of the total value of a firm is growing in significance, and relationships are becoming the most important asset for many businesses. A relationship is thus viewed as a particular immobile pro-competitive resource.

Institutional Theory

This is an alternative, multi-constituent, and dynamic view that sees social actors in support of the corporation when institutional norms are upheld. The corporation is then seen as legitimate.

The Relationship Portfolio

Every potential and existing active or latent relationship should be scrutinized to ensure that it contributes to the firm's ability efficiently and/or effectively to produce a market offering that provides value to market segment(s). As pointed out by Grönroos's definition of RM, this should lead to efforts to initiate, maintain, develop, or terminate a relationship. The result is a contributing relationship portfolio – a set of advantageous relational resources. This relationship 'mix' should complement existing competencies and enable a position of competitive advantage – but it must be developed over time, since it cannot be selected at a single point in time. Requisite relationships must be strategically planned for and entered into only when promises can be fulfilled (as suggested by Grönroos's notion of what constitutes real Relationship Marketing).

From Customer Service to Customer Relationship Management

Customer service has been repackaged as CRM. Customer service is usually presented in managerialistic terms as beneficial for all – it ain't necessarily so!

From the provider's point of view, service delivery is fast becoming the only method of sustainable competitive differentiation as competing products become more homogeneous. From the consumer's point of view, service (attention, etc.) is what they have always wanted. Perhaps, then, we can now expect greater alignment of buyer and seller interests? However, how might this be brought about through management policies and practices?

The customer, apparently, has been placed at the heart of the management system (because they are an inescapable force?). Or has he or she? This is no longer seen as a marketing problem, but a problem of organization. Large-scale automation and (ICT) mediation have become the (obvious) co-solutions for the problem of organizing (disciplining) market exchange interactions. Relationship Marketing comes of age in an e-commerce society – electronic connections are then the means for direct interaction, negotiation, and partnership.

The claim is of the emancipation of the consumer – but power relationships between seller and buyer are asymmetric, thus CRM is simply technology-mediated hegemonic practices. For example, it is corporate agents who choose to describe market interactions as a relationship or collaborative, and when, and on what terms, to operate in 'relationships'. Many of us are still asking whether or not (all) customers really want a relationship with suppliers.

The rhetoric of RM/CRM is of a systematic/systemic apparatus for redressing power differentials (neither customer nor supplier is 'king'). In practice, argue Fitchett and McDonagh (2001), CRM is mostly effort to socialize and naturalize the imbalance of power.

Customer Service

The (flawed) logic of a sovereign consumer and free markets is justified by the notion of 'consumer choice' – that consumers know what they want, and are all-powerful (knowledgeable, mobile, active) in being able to choose and switch between suppliers, and this is readily understood by producers and sellers, but not necessarily acted on. Of course, producers are powerful in advertising and distribution, and thus retain a power advantage over buyers.

So, is the mantra 'the customer is always right', and the notion that s/he has a right to expect service of the highest quality a managerial manipulation, or a true *ethic of justice or care*?

The Nature of Service

An 'intangible' commodity is produced and consumed simultaneously in the interaction of employee and customer. However, there are also other 'invisible services' (e.g. cleaning) in which there is no direct contact between provider and buyer, and service transacted through the Internet where interpersonal interaction is indirect. So, then, what is the meaning of a 'trading relationship'? We will consider this question in depth in Chapter 2.

The Rhetoric of Serving, and Relating to, Customers

From the point of view of the business manager, concerns are costs, revenues, profit, and control of labour processes. At the same time advertising promises raise customer expectations – achieving 'good service' becomes problematic for the manager and the customer.

A service system has three constituencies. There may be instrumental exploitation of customers by managers in collusion with employees (attractive promises that cannot be met by the system), and of employees by managers in collusion with customers (attractive promises that cannot be met by the system). There is one further possibility – employees can collude with customers to resist managers' demands. Figure 1.2 is intended to suggest these reciprocal manipulations of collusion.

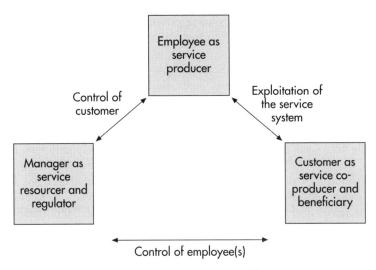

FIGURE 1.2   Service system collusions.

A False Logic?

Not everyone has been fooled by the 'co-operative rhetoric of relationship marketing' (e.g. Brown, 1994). Brown identifies Relationship Marketing as one of a number of what he terms philosophically unrobust 'catholicons'. I take this to mean that the logic of the belief in Relationship Marketing is found to be weak under careful scrutiny. This motivates a search for a more valuable and reflective interpretation of the idea and constitutive principles.

How is the customer sovereign? – either the seller is subservient in an authority relationship, or the contractual relationship is no longer biased toward the seller. The former is a pathological dependency that suggests unsustainable business, while the latter is a symmetrical partnership. How is this to be achieved? Does marketing operate as helping sellers to figure out how to meet consumers' expectations, or as helping consumers to become customers by clarifying unclear and unstated expectations?! Does common marketing practice allow the customer (as a choosing consumer) to participate as an (active) agent or merely as an object (to be manipulated)? Do we find arm's length technical contractual relations, and how are they transformed into relational contracts?

Who Are the Customers?

Rosenthal et al. (2001) identify customers in several guises:

- not producers, not citizens, but 'us' brought to life in our everyday talk;
- the final arbiter of product quality, thus to be understood and responded to;

- an accomplice of managers wielding power over employees;
- a conduit for employees' self-expression, with consequences for their identity and emotional well-being;
- a buyer, or beneficiary, or audience, or co-producer (resource).

Overall, customers are actors in relation to employees and managers.

It is becoming increasingly difficult meaningfully to categorize buyers on any basis other than actual buying behaviour. Therefore, the notion of market segments is no longer helpful. Each buyer is demonstrably different from all of the others, so aggregation of characteristics for prediction does not help. Until relatively recently, the requirements of individual customers were ignored in planning and promoting goods and services, because profiling, tracking, anticipating, managing, and serving uniquely were uneconomical. Dramatic falls in the costs of electronic systems have changed all of that. It is now possible to consider the personal (perhaps idiosyncratic) needs of all customers as individuals.

E-commerce

For some time, the principles of Relationship Marketing have been attractive, and yet could not easily be adopted because the ways of organizing and operating businesses (especially in terms of evaluating business success) provided few practical means of implementing the strategy.

Arguably, the advent of Internet-based electronic commerce (e-commerce) has significantly accelerated the transition from transactional to relational marketing 'philosophies' (Fitchett and McDonagh, 2001). E-commerce has introduced a practical medium for realizing the benefits of Relationship Marketing.

The argument for this is simple: consumers get greater and easier access to the market because information about competing offers is searchable, and marketers are provided with the information they need to do their job more effectively (e.g. market research, decision-making, and so on). It seems that the customer–supplier relationship is (capable of being) transformed in 'cyberspace'. According to Besser (1995), the technology we have called the Internet is one of several that, as part of a wider social change, are replacing public spaces and human interaction.

E-commerce is trade that occurs through the mediation of the Internet. Many predict that this new forum for trade will help to equalize the otherwise asymmetric power distribution (which the marketer dominates – they have more resources) in the customer–provider relationship.

The Challenge of New Conditions for Marketing

Dupuy (1999) speaks of the 'customer's victory' – that economic power has passed to buyers – in his examination of modes of functioning (i.e. forms of organization) of collective forms of production of the goods and services required for satisfying customers. He reveals a crisis of technical bureaucracies in business, at a time when customers want value providers to account for their behaviour, in the face of choice among alternative sources.

Dupuy's 'customer's victory' is a recovery of mutual confidence among buyer and seller. This arises through negotiation, rather than imposition, of who produces what. Providers have to be flexible/adaptable in the way they produce/deliver. This requires co-operative working of all actors in the production system (i.e. integration and co-ordination). The solution is value-sharing systems, not products.

Then, customers are known as individual people and groups, not as statistics. There is an inevitable chronic inability of 'knowledge by numbers' to comprehend consumer customs, expectations, way of life, and so on. We need the 'personal touch' in the well-oiled (risk-reducing) production machine. This is a social problem, not simply a corporate management problem.

The customer's victory (over the producers' processes) is a constraint on corporate (i.e. collective, privileged) business operations at a time in societal development when we experience not a product scarcity but a customer scarcity; hence, such moves as the ascendance of 'relationship marketing'.

It no longer makes much sense, at least from the customer's point of view, to organize production, marketing, and service as separate functions. The main challenges for marketing to face are (based on Gordon, 1998):

- *Conflicting timescales for business and marketing*. While investors and financial managers are demanding quicker revenue building and returns, customers want continuing associations that provide value at their own pace, thus avoiding those suppliers who 'take the money and run' or practice the 'hard sell'.
- *Changes in approaches to market segmentation*. Buyers and their behaviour are much more difficult to categorize than in days gone by. If actual buying behaviour is more meaningful than age, place of residence, race, gender, attitude, or lifestyle, then trying to manage market segments as categories of similarity does not make sense.
- *The design of personal preferences in to goods and services*. When the trading relationship lifetime volume and profit margin justify it, each customer's needs and wants should be considered in goods and services design.
- *Interpersonal communication*. Marketers need timely and relevant knowledge about what customers want to buy and when. Further, engagement through relevant and timely information provision, and participation in exchanges that are appropriate for both customer and supplier, can now be facilitated by advancing information and communication technologies.
- *Responsive customer service relationships*. Customer complaints should signal a broken value-creation process, since collaboration throughout the value chain casts the customer service function as the engagement of customers to ensure lifetime satisfaction.
- *Customer participation in pricing decisions*. Customers now expect to be able to choose options and to pay the associated price for what they value.

Experiential marketing

Recently, Schmitt (1999) has observed that 'the ultimate, humanistic, goal of marketing is providing customers with valuable experiences.' Managers must rethink their approach to the creation, design, management, and marketing of their 'products'. Holbrook and Hirschman (1982) first raised the idea of a fundamental shift in attention for those who try to manage the production–consumption relationship almost 20 years ago.

Experiential marketing is a move away from the traditional focus on managing products and communication artefacts and activity that emphasize the benefits of ownership and/or use. Products and services are thus produced to provide and enhance the sensory experiences of customers, or, in this case, visitors, enriching consumption and/or the trading relationship by making meaning. The US rail corporation, Amtrak, for example, define their brand as a combination of reputation, promise, and experience (Schmitt, 1999). In the service environment, where service is co-produced, people are the key experience providers. In live experiences, the live interpreter is the service deliverer, although other workers may support the production of the service.

Schmitt's framework identifies five modes of experience that might be managerially manipulated through product and communication, together with the pre-eminent providers of that aspect of the consumption experience:

- *sensing* – sensual appeal in sight, hearing, smell, taste, and touch (identity, signage, product presence);
- *feeling* – affective response to the corporation (or, in this case, attraction) and brand via experience providers (people, communication);
- *thinking* – engagement in elaborative and creative thinking to review assumptions and expectations (communication, co-branding, electronic media);
- *acting* – bodily behaviour pattern and lifestyle, and interpersonal (product presence, communication, electronic media);
- *relating* – expansion of private sensations, feelings, cognitions, and actions into a broader social and cultural context (people, Internet, spatial environment).

We can identify several components of the service consumption experience that place communicative interaction at the centre of the management problem. These are the participant and observer feelings of fun, excitement, sensory thrill, entertainment, engagement, and learning, and the associated imaginative, emotional, and evaluative judgements.

The service encounter may be thought of as playing out of a drama, for which the managerial task is the management of moments of truth. Indeed, Pine and Gilmore (1999) are clear that work *is* theatre, in that acting is the deliberate taking of steps to connect with an audience/customers/guests. A drama, then, is equivalent to 'strategy', the script is the work processes, and the performance is the offering.

We define the reality of our social setting by taking account of the physical environment, other people present, and their language used, gestures, and so on. Social reality, then, like a film or theatrical production, unfolds as actions occur and meanings are assigned – we come to appreciate our situation (Vickers, 1984). This drama is brought about in communicating (i.e. in interaction). Both 'audience' and 'actor' contribute inputs to the development and maintenance of a definition of their interaction.

Reverse Marketing

In some situations, the buyer takes the initiative in seeking suitable sellers. Take, for example, the 'auction' websites that place the onus for relationship management on the buyer. This situation has been termed *reverse marketing*, buyer initiative, or proactive procurement (Leenders and Blenkhorn, 1988). When this occurs, the provider has to respond through a *reactive marketing* process. However, this is a passive strategy that will not attract buyers to form trading relationships with the corporation.

Although this situation has been recognized, particularly in industrial and business-to-business marketing management, it has largely been taken to be the adoption of a marketing system by buyers in order to persuade an attractive supplier to supply.

What has largely been missed is that this concept of reverse marketing suggests that marketing communication systems must be able to cater for buyer-initiated interaction. Often, this responsibility for communicative interaction has been located with a customer service group and treated as an administrative task. So, the marketing communication system must be receptive as well as expressive – and providers need to expect that in some situations buyers will be hunting for suitable suppliers. Surely, this presents an (often unrecognized) opportunity for many supposedly customer-oriented corporations. Promise-making may have to be more receptive, accommodating, and responsive. These are all questions of communication system capability.

Reverse marketing – premised on the notion of attraction – assumes that the seller has control over market actions, yet either party may initiate marketing action – both are marketers – in seeking an exchange. We need to consider how the value provider manages the value chain to respond responsibly to the other's initiative in the two forms of reverse marketing – the seller attracts a suitable buyer, or the buyer attracts a suitable seller.

Implications for Marketing Managers

Marketers must identify those customers with whom a deepening relationship is profitable, uncover meaningful ways for customer and supplier to continue associating over the long run, and champion the changes in organization that will enable and foster this reorientation – they must enact a Relationship Management role. Rather than manage transactions, they will increasingly manage relationships.

Advertising and sales promotions can bring new first-time customers, and occasional repeat buyers. Relationship Marketing can build enduring trading relationships. Instead of pouring more water into a leaking bucket, Relationship Marketing aims to ensure that the bucket doesn't leak! I am indebted to Lisa O'Malley and Caroline Tynan, Nottingham University Business School, for this imagery.

The marketer has to identify the core value that will be delivered to a customer, and ensure that each customer can take charge of assembling the value they want.

Traditionally, marketers provided a product, at a price, accessible through a distribution system, and promoted through a media system. More and more, today, it is customers who choose what, when, how, where, and at what price.

Accordingly, Gordon (1998) explains Relationship Marketing as the 'process of identifying and creating new value with individual customers and then sharing the benefits of this over the lifetime of association' (p. 9).

This marketing strategy has some highly significant characteristics:

- New value is created and shared among producer and consumer.
- Value is created *with*, not for, customers.
- Business processes are designed around people, communication, and technology to support the value requirements.
- A real-time co-operative effort.
- Seeks to progressively bond more tightly over the lifetime of association.
- Builds a chain of relationships among stakeholders – suppliers, customers, producers, intermediaries, and shareholders.

Gordon (1998) highlights six focal issues for this 'new marketing':

- Information and communication technology – communicating with and serving each customer.
- Rethinking the scope of the business to serve selected customers as they wish to be served.
- Customers whose requirements are compatible with the strategy are selected for personal servicing, whereas others are rejected.
- The needs and behaviours of the selected customers will drive procurement, production, logistics, and human resource management. This requires the development of a chain of relationships among those who can contribute to providing for changing demands of customers: employees, suppliers, resellers and retailers, bankers, investors, and so on. Each will be able to benefit from the value created and shared by the corporation. Integration is needed across the organization interfaces (Wilson, 1994).
- The 4Ps marketing mix management approach has to be rethought and adapted into a relationship management way of working.
- Relationship managers manage relationships – they engage each customer in creating value by seeking meaningful benefits.

Gordon further identifies three enablers of Relationship Marketing that are central to our discussion of contemporary developments as marketing, customer service, quality, and e-technology collide:

- *Manufacturing technology*. The rapid development of technology capabilities and dramatic cost reductions have made possible the production and delivery of goods and services specific to the customer at prices affordable by buyer and seller. In this way, interactivity, enabled by ICT, etc. is able to deal with market fragmentation, allowing individuals to be addressed and served individually (consider just-in-time (JIT), total quality management (TQM), etc.).
- *Customer knowledge*. The ability to know customers and to serve them the way they wish to be served is crucial, and basic information profiles are generally inadequate. An ICT-based 'corporate memory' serves members of the relationship chain when it helps servers and their supporting managers to assess what they know and understand about a trading relationship.
- *Customer access*. Access limitations between marketers and customers are being overcome with the advent of more sophisticated and affordable ICT, including database, postal, Internet, specialized media, and addressable communication capabilities.

As a business strategy, Relationship Marketing is concerned with the employer's engagement with those who create value, and those who support this value creation, for which selected customers repeatedly pay. This is a particular form of psychological contract. This will be considered further in Chapter 2.

Summary

The 'old', currently pervasive marketing is characterized by scientistic analysis and a control-oriented reproductive conservatism. The emerging 'new' marketing thrives on insight, constant change, creativity, and humanistic values.

The market economy has produced a breathtaking array of goods for consumption and the concomitant feeling of choice (equals 'freedom'?). Quality and value for money, logically, can be improved through the mechanism of market competition. Indeed, marketing has become accepted as the 'most natural' of means of matching human desires with the means of satisfying them. In contemporary society, buying things, services, experiences, and sensations goes a long way toward giving meaning to our 'modern' lives. At what price?

Perhaps we have all suffered some of the 'brutal necessities' of the free market whose proponents seek to profit from basic human needs, such that citizenship is transformed in to 'consumership'. There are many noxious side-effects, and the most basic human needs remain unanswered (Seabrook, 1990). So, yes, I agree that marketing has produced much benefit and is a basic process of modern society. But, let's be careful that we reflect on what is actually done in the name of marketing. We can discern clearly and readily the triumph of (traditional) expressive, persuasive marketing in the management of demand for product. How, then, is Relationship Marketing an advancement or enhancement of now-pervasive principles and practice?

What is at issue is the extent of the interaction. This is far more significant in characterizing a relationship and a transaction. A house purchase or a building contract have a much greater degree of interaction, perhaps over a very extended period of time, and are much less frequent occurrences (i.e. less routine), than the purchase of a chocolate bar (which may or may not be repurchased). The degree, or intensity, of active personal contact determines the nature of the interaction. Therefore, the suggestion that a transaction is a one-shot sell–buy event, whereas relational trading is repeated, is too simple an explanation, and misses the point. Commitment (sometimes managerialistically termed 'loyalty'), or intensity (Lehtinen et al., 1994), or involvement, is the key feature. Transaction marketing may not be an alternative to Relationship Marketing at all. Each may be the poles of a continuum. This helps to answer the puzzle: Does a chocolate bar buyer have a relationship with the seller? Then, the answer can be yes, a low-commitment/involvement/intensity relationship. This idea is considered further in Chapter 2.

Pause for thought – how are sellers loyal to buyers?

To appreciate the significance of a Relationship Marketing strategy, we need to appreciate that marketing management is an integrating way of thinking about how to operate a business, and not merely some electronically mediated bundle of techniques.

Harley-Davidson are renowned for the degree of, and kind of, loyalty they inspire in their customers. This seems to be achieved by letting the customer manage the relationship. This has moved management beyond the orthodox ideas of selling, product marketing, brand management, and customer-driven marketing built on 'customer loyalty'. Today, customer-managed relationship marketing is practised by some corporations. We will return to the Harley-Davidson case in Chapter 6, and the notion of customer managed relationships in Chapter 7.

Peck et al. (1999) end their 500-page book on Relationship Marketing with a 9-page introduction to their 'relationship management chain'. In this book, I take up this model as a basis for defining a CRM system.

In Chapter 2 we will examine the central concept of marketing as an inter-active social phenomenon. We will see that a trading relationship can be treated by the seller as a means to produce data about the consumer or customer, and that this is premised on an adversarial notion of trading through the manipulation of a 'marketing mix', in which the product (benefits) provides the context. The alternative, we will see, is the relationship as the 'location' or context of linked co-operative exchanges of value in a network of interdependencies. A central question for both parties is this: is Groucho Marx in charge of the marketing management system?

References

Alvesson, M. and Willmott, H. (eds.) (1992) *Critical Management Studies*, London: Sage Publications.

Alvesson, M. and Willmott, H. (1996) *Making Sense of Management: A Critical Introduction*, London: Sage Publications.

Arndt, J. (1983) 'The political economy paradigm: Foundation for theory building in marketing', *Journal of Marketing*, Vol. 47, 44–54.

Association for the Advancement of Relationship Marketing, online @ www.aarm.org

Bagozzi, R. C. (1995) 'Reflections on relationship marketing in consumer markets', *Journal of the Academy of Marketing Science*, Vol. 23, No. 4, 272–277.

Ballantyne, D. (1999) 'Dialogue and knowledge generation: Two sides of the same coin in relationship marketing', *Proceedings of the 2nd WWW Conference on Relationship Marketing*, Monash University, Bradford, UK: MCB University Press, online @ www.mcb.co.uk/services/conferen/nov99/rm/paper3.html

Bartels, R. (1986) 'Marketing: Management technology or social process at the twenty-first century?', in G. Fisk (ed.) *Marketing Management Technology as a Social Process*, New York: Praeger.

Bate, P. (1994) *Strategies for Cultural Change*, Oxford: Butterworth-Heinemann.

Bell, M. L. and Emory, C. W. (1971) 'The faltering marketing concept', *Journal of Marketing*, Vol. 35, 37–42.

Brown, S. (1994) 'Marketing as multiplex: Screening postmodernism', *European Journal of Marketing*, Vol. 28, Nos 8/9, 27–51.

Brown, S., Bell, J., and Carson, D. (eds) (1996) *Marketing Apocalypse: Eschatology, Escapology and the Illusion of the End*, London: Routledge.

Brown, S. and Maclaran, P. (1996) 'The future is past: Marketing, apocalypse and the retreat from utopia', in S. Brown, J. Bell and D. Carson (eds) *Marketing Apocalypse: Eschatology, Escapology and the Illusion of the End*, London: Routledge, pp. 260–277.

Brown, S. A. (2000) *Customer Relationship Management: A Strategic Imperative in the World of e-Business*, Toronto: John Wiley & Sons.

Buttle, F. (1989) 'Needs: A social constructionist view', *Proceedings of the Annual Marketing Education Group Conference*, Glasgow Business School, pp. 1–30.

Carroll, A. B. (1981) *Business & Society: Managing Corporate Social Performance*, New York: Little, Brown & Co.

Christopher, M. G., Payne, A., and Ballantyne, D. (1991) *Relationship Marketing: Bringing Quality, Customer Service and Marketing Together*, Oxford: Butterworth-Heinemann.

Converse, P. D. and Huegy, H. W. (1946) *The Elements of Marketing*, Englewood Cliffs, NJ: Prentice Hall.

Cox, R. (1962) 'Changing social objectives in marketing', in W. S. Decker (ed.) *Proceedings of the Winter Conference of the American Marketing Association*, pp. 16–25.

de Bono, E. (1993) *Sur/petition: Going Beyond Competition*, New York: HarperCollins.

Deetz, S. A. (1992) *Democracy in an Age of Corporate Colonization: Developments in Communication and the Politics of Everyday Life*, Albany, NY: State University of New York Press.

Deetz, S. A. (1995) *Transforming Communication, Transforming Business: Building Responsive and Responsible Workplaces*, Creskill, NJ: Hampton Press.

Dibb, S., Simkin, L., Pride, W. M., and Ferrell, O. C. (1994) *Marketing: Concepts and Strategies*, 2nd European edn, London: Houghton Mifflin.

Doyle, P. (1994) *Marketing Management and Strategy*, London: Prentice Hall International.

Drucker, P. F. (1954/1955) *The Practice of Management*, New York/London: Harper & Row/William Heinemann.

Drucker, P. F. (1973) *Management: Tasks, Responsibilities, Practices*, London: Heinemann.

du Gay, P. and Salaman, G. (1992) 'The cult[ure] of the customer', *Journal of Management Studies*, Vol. 29, No 5, 615–633.

Dupuy, F. (1999) *The Customer's Victory: From Corporation to Co-operation*, London: Macmillan Business.

Embley, L. L. (1993) *Doing Well While Doing Good*, Englewood Cliffs, NJ: Prentice Hall.

Fisk, G. (ed.) (1986) *Marketing Management Technology as a Social Process*, New York: Praeger.

Fitchett, J. and McDonagh, P. (2001) 'Relationship marketing, e-commerce and the emancipation of the consumer', in A. Sturdy, I. Grugulis and H. Willmott (eds) *Customer Service: Empowerment and Entrapment*, Basingstoke, UK: Palgrave, pp. 191–199

Fulop, L. and Linstead, S. (eds) (1999) *Management: A Critical Text*, London: Macmillan Business.

Gordon, I. (1998) *Relationship Marketing: New Strategies, Techniques and Technologies to Win Customers You Want and Keep Them Forever*, Toronto: John Wiley & Sons.

Grant, J. (2000) *The New Marketing Manifesto*, London: Texere.

Grönroos, C. (1990) 'The marketing strategy continuum: Towards a marketing concept for the 1990s', *Management Decision*, Vol. 29, No. 1, 9.

Grönroos, C. (1994) 'Quo vadis, marketing? Toward a Relationship Marketing paradigm', *Journal of Marketing Management*, Vol. 10, 347–360.

Grönroos, C. (2000) *Service Management and Marketing: A Customer Relationship Management Approach*, Chichester, UK: John Wiley & Sons.

Gummesson, E. (1999) *Total Relationship Marketing: Rethinking Marketing Management – From 4Ps to 30Rs*, Oxford: Butterworth-Heinemann.

Holbrook, M. B. and Hirschman, E. C. (1982) 'The experiential aspects of consumption: Consumer fantasies, feelings, and fun', *Journal of Consumer Research*, September, 132–140.

Holden, N. (2002) *Cross-Cultural Management: A Knowledge Management Perspective*, London: Pearson Education.

Houston, F. S. (ed.) (1994) *Marketing Exchange Relationships, Transactions and Their Media*, Westport, CT: Quorum Books/Greenwood Publishing.

Hunt, S. D. (1995) 'The resource-advantage theory of competition: Toward explaining productivity and economic growth', *Journal of Management Inquiry*, Vol. 4, December, 317–332.

Hunt, S. D. (1997) 'Competing through relationships: Grounding relationship marketing in resource-advantage theory', *Journal of Marketing Management*, Vol. 13, 431–445.

Hunt, S. D. and Morgan, R. M. (1995) 'The commitment-trust theory of relationship marketing', *Journal of Marketing*, Vol. 58, 20–38.

Kelly, K. (1998) *New Rules for the New Economy*, London: Fourth Estate.

Kotler, P. (1991) *Marketing Management: Analysis, Planning, Implementation, and Control*, 7th edn, London: Prentice Hall International.

Kotler, P. (1994) *Marketing Management: Analysis, Planning, Implementation, and Control*, 8th edn, London: Prentice Hall International.

Kotler, P., Armstrong, A., Saunders, J., and Wong, V. (1999) *Principles of Marketing*, 2nd European edn, London: Prentice Hall Europe.

Kotler, P. and Zaltman, G. (1971) 'Social marketing: An approach to planned social change', *Journal of Marketing*, Vol. 35, 3–12.

Kuper, J. (ed.) (1987) *Key Thinkers, Past and Present*, London: Routledge & Kegan Paul.

Lazer, W. and Kelley, E. J. (1973) *Social Marketing: Perspectives and Viewpoints*, Homewood, IL: Richard D. Irwin.

Leenders, M. R. and Blenkhorn, D. L. (1988) *Reverse Marketing: The New Buyer–Supplier Relationship*, London: Collier Macmillan.

Lehtinen, U., Hankimaa, A., and Mittilä, T. (1994) 'On measuring the intensity in relationship marketing', in J. N. Sheth and A. Parvatiyar (eds) *Research Conference Proceedings: Relationship Marketing: Theory, Methods, and Applications*, Atlanta, GA: Center for Relationship Marketing, Emory University.

Lengnick-Hall, C. (1996) 'Customer contributions to quality: A different view of the customer-oriented firm', *Academy of Management Review*, Vol. 21, No. 3, 791–824.

Luck, D. J. (1974) 'Social marketing: Confusion compounded', *Journal of Marketing*, Vol. 38, 70–72.

MacNeil, I. R. (1980) *The New Social Contract: An Inquiry into Modern Contractual Relations*, New Haven, CT: Yale University Press.

Morgan, G. (1992) 'Marketing discourse and practice: Towards a critical analysis', in M. Alvesson and H. Willmott (eds) *Critical Management Studies*, London: Sage Publications, pp. 136–158.

Nason, R. W. (1986) 'Extremality focus of macromarketing theory', in G. Fisk (ed.) *Marketing Management Technology as a Social Process*, New York: Praeger.

Ormerod, P. (1994) *The Death of Economics*, London: Faber & Faber.

Palmer, A. (2002) 'The evolution of an idea: An environmental explanation of relationship marketing', *Journal of Relationship Marketing*, Vol. 1, No. 1, 79–94.

Peck, H., Payne, A, Christopher, M., and Clark, M. (1999) *Relationship Marketing: Strategy and Implementation*, Oxford: Butterworth-Heinemann/Chartered Institute of Marketing.

Pylkkänen, P. (1989) *The Search for Meaning: The New Spirit in Science and Philosophy*, Wellingborough: Crucible/Thorsons.

Rosenthal, P., Peccei, R., and Hill, S. (2001) 'Academic discourses of the customer: "sovereign beings", "management accomplices" or "people like us"?, in A. Sturdy, I. Grugulis, and H. Willmott (eds) *Customer Service: Empowerment and Entrapment*, London: Palgrave, pp. 18–37.

Seabrook, J. (1990) *The Myth of the Market: Promises & Illusions*, Bideford, UK: Green Books.

Schumacher, E. F. (1973) *Small is Beautiful: A Study of Economics as if People Really Mattered*, London: Abacus/Sphere.

Schmitt, B. H. (1999) *Experiential Marketing: How to Get Customers to Sense, Feel, Think, Act, and Relate to Your Company and Brands*, New York: Free Press.

Senge, P. M. (1990) *The Fifth Discipline: The Art & Practice of The Learning Organisation*, London: Century Business Books.

Sheth, J. N., Gardner, D. M., and Garrett, D. E. (1988) *Marketing Theory: Evolution and Evaluation*, Chichester, UK: John Wiley & Sons.

Silverman, D. (1970) *The Theory of Organisations: A Sociological Framework*, London: Heinemann.

Solomon, R. C. and Hanson, K. (1985) *It's Good Business*, New York: Harper & Row.

Trusted, J. (1987) *Inquiry and Understanding: An Introduction to Explanation in the Physical and Human Sciences*, Basingstoke, UK: Macmillan.

UK Chartered Institute of Marketing, Cookham, Berkshire.

Varey, R. J. (1994) 'Exploring the human face of marketing management', paper presented to the *Annual Conference of the British Academy of Management, University of Lancaster*.

Varey, R. J. (2000) 'A critical review of conceptions of communication evident in contemporary business and management literature', *Journal of Communication Management*, Vol. 4, No. 4, 328–340.

Varey, R. J. and Wood, J. R. G. (2001) 'When marketing met ICT: The mutant CRM child', paper presented to the *International Workshop on (Re-)defining Critical Research in Information Systems, Information Systems Institute, University of Salford, 9–10 July*.

Vickers, G. (1984) *Human Systems are Different*, London: Harper & Row.

Williamson, O. E. (1975) Markets and Hierarchies: *Analysis and Anti-Trust Implications, a Study in the Economics of Internal Organization*, New York: Free Press.

Wilson, I. (ed.) (1994) *Marketing Interfaces: Exploring the Marketing and Business Relationship*, London: Pitman.

Chapter 2

EXCHANGE RELATIONSHIPS

Partners exchanging valued resources in agreement –
'I win when you win'

Just what do you people mean by relationships?
psychologist, University of Maryland*

*What is a man if he is not a thief who openly charges as much
as he can for the goods he sells?*
Mahatma Gandhi (1869–1948)

*A relationship is defined not so much by what is said as by the
partner's expectations of behaviour*
Littlejohn (1992, p. 262)

Introduction

Exchange is widely taken to be the basis for 'marketing'. Trading relationships are
a special case of human relationships, such as we all have with family, friends,
colleagues, and members of the wider society. Here, I take a desirable trading
relationship to be a mutual experience (interaction) of a seller and buyer, in which
value is produced and shared profitably among participants. So, the aim of
Relationship Marketing is the accumulation of satisfactory trading and service
encounters, leading to active participation based on mutual disclosure and trust.
This helps to create an economic and personal bond manifested in affective loyalty
to the partner.

In this chapter, we ask:

- Are so-called marketing relationships any more than arrangements for interaction that are convenient for the seller?
- Relationship Marketing emerged from the special conditions of the business-
  to-business and service marketing fields. To what extent can this strategy be
  applied in consumer product businesses?
- Do trading relationships differ among consumer product, service, and
  business markets?

---

*Quoted from Grunig and Huang (2000, p. 26).

- How should a particular type of trading relationship be managed, and what portfolio of relationship types will yield the best competitive position?
- What benefits does a relationship provide for the customer?
- Is commercial exchange adaptive or generative (i.e. reproductive vs. productive)?
- Is an electronically mediated interaction really a relationship?
- When does a buyer discern something special that is more than a transient interaction event?
- What conditions would support an effective and efficient relational strategy?
- Is the concept 'relationship' only used metaphorically?
- How do we explain a trading relationship as a personal (social) asset?

When are relationships not relationships? Palmer (2001) points out that the term 'relationship' in discussions of relationship marketing is often used metaphorically for associations, between two parties, that are asymmetric in power, knowledge, and resources. These would probably not be described as a relationship in wider social terms.

Ledingham and Bruning (2000) suggest that the term 'relationship' is widely used as a primitive term (i.e. a word that has been accepted as having generally understood meanings and treated as a given). Yet, they argue, the term relationship stands for a complex phenomenon, for which there is no commonly shared, widely used definition.

In social anthropology, we find the question: How does core economic exchange occur within the greater 'sphere' of relational interaction? Economic exchange has functional purpose (action), while social exchange is symbolic in purpose (meaning).

The basic proposition is that *an exchange relationship is successful when there is*:

- mutual trust in each other's reliability and integrity;
- agreement on expectations of each other and the right to influence and decide goals;
- commitment to one another's goals and values and an accepted responsibility to maintain the relationship; and
- a feeling of satisfaction with equitable rewards that outweigh relational costs.

In this chapter, we examine the nature of the relationship that is initiated, maintained, and (at least in principle) terminated by relationship marketing management.

But, first, there is a problem of terminology to deal with. In the Public Relations field, there has been a growing adoption for some years now of a 'transactional' (in place of 'transmissive') explanation of human communication. To confuse matters somewhat, in parallel the marketing field has increasingly adopted 'relational' as an alternative to 'transactional'. Therefore, where one may speak of transactional interaction in public relations, a marketing colleague might use the term relational marketing – they might, in general terms have the same mode of interaction in mind. There has been a shift in emphasis in both fields from distant, impersonal to a more friendly personal touch in commercial relationships.

Most studies have taken the unit of analysis to be a party to a relationship. Focus on the relationship provides further valuable insights that raise managerial and social issues for scrutiny. So, communication is not some act of one or both individuals, but the process of their interaction.

We need to distinguish what helps to create a relationship, the relationship, and the consequences of the relationship. Commercial relationships are created for a trading purpose. Outcomes that are means to an end of continued, profitable trading can be applied as indicators of relationship quality. These include trust, mutuality of control, commitment to the relationship, and satisfaction with the relationship and resultant outcomes.

So, why manage marketing relationships? A logic of relationship marketing can be suggested:

> Communication adapts the *relationship* that is required for the committed *trading* that is necessary to produce mutual *enrichment*.

Note that this implies much more than attempts to secure a competitive advantage through the manipulable instrument of a relationship. Jacobs (1992) demonstrates that the two basic ways to live a life are *trading* and *taking*. She shows that much of the difficulty arises when a trading 'culture' is operated through a set of 'taking' values. Relational exchange is a form of governance (Mattsson, 1997).

When a trading situation does arise, it may not be a commercial buying–selling arrangement, since:

> *... many instances of relationship marketing do not have a 'customer' as one of the exchange participants. Strictly speaking, in strategic alliances between competitors ... there are neither 'buyers', 'sellers', 'customers' nor 'key accounts' – only partners exchanging resources.*
>
> (Morgan and Hunt, 1994, p. 22)

Grönroos (1990, 2000) convincingly provides the case for throwing away the 4Ps marketing mix management model of marketing, in favour of adopting a *relationship management strategy*.

One point that is seemingly missed in many so-called 'customer relationship management' systems is that people cannot have a relationship with a company, product, or technology interface, but they do have (mostly voluntary) relationships with other people.

In Relationship Marketing, buyers are not treated as targets to be reached, but as *partners* in the creation and sharing of value (in the widest sense). The relationship then becomes an important attribute of the offer, thus *differentiating* the seller from competitors.

There is a simple, yet powerful principle of Relationship Marketing as I understand it. Manage a personal relationship continuously with each customer, rather than with an aggregate market segment. This requires recruitment, joining, contributing, and benefiting. Buttle (1996) declares Relationship Marketing theory, as then explained, to be normative, using only an analogy of interpersonal relationships. I join Barnes (2001) in believing that to treat a trading relationship as inherently an interpersonal relationship is far more sensible.

The Relationship Concept

Much of what is termed 'relationship marketing' is no more than the use of one or a few techniques for creating repeat business for sellers. These include frequency marketing programmes (quantity discounts), contractual and structural barriers to exit, and customized messages targeted at a 'loyal' customer database. Few address the problem of genuine human relationships that are desirable. There is little understanding of what it takes to produce trading that we really want to do repeatedly and to encourage our friends, relatives, and colleagues to do (sometimes with us).

Professor Jim Barnes is one of the few marketing specialists to ask what is the nature of the relationships upon which our trading is/can be/should be managed? He points out (Barnes, 2001) that databases impede relationship formation when they are used to promote *at* customers, rather than to support the exchange of ideas and information *with* them. Such databases consist of transactional data only – often 'built' without the consent of the subjected buyer. That is, the data represents only the behavioural aspect of interactions. What, asks Professor Barnes, of emotions? Are the feelings toward a supplier (the people and the brand), their products, the relationship, and interactions taken into account? Barnes observes that feelings are not considered. Therefore, the database can facilitate contact, but much more is needed for a *genuine relationship*. Few writers, researchers, and managers approach the notion of a relationship from the customer's point of view. Indeed, observes Jim Barnes, relationship marketing techniques are the *antithesis* of a genuine relationship.

A relationship is the mutual recognition of some special status in the association or connection of exchange partners, that is, the result of a successful series of service encounters (adapted from Czepiel, 1990). Because service encounters are essentially social encounters, and service encounters require direct contact, there is a strong compelling logic for managing to build strong (parallel) economic and personal ties with customers. In other words, we should model all business outcomes as managed service encounters. This allows better serving, resulting in the desensitizing of customers to efforts to attract customers to competing suppliers.

Our relationships may be through kinship (family), tribe (social group), or with foreign strangers. There is increasing social distance (difference) and decreasing obligation to fairness and honesty. Trading transactions are with strangers, whereas the purpose of Relationship Marketing is to bring people into the tribe!

Wish et al. (1976) have set out dimensions of an interpersonal relationship that indicate some priorities for managing a marketing relationship (Table 2.1).

So, we should ask, how does a customer discern a trading relationship? In reading Broom et al. (2000) it is salutary to note that almost no reference to relationship(s) in the marketing literature properly defines the concept (this is true in other fields, too – except, perhaps, social psychology). The term 'relationship' is

TABLE 2.1 Dimensions of interpersonal relationships
(based on Wish et al., 1976).

Symmetry–asymmetry of roles	Equal–unequal
	Dominant–submissive
Valence	Co-operative–competitive
	Friendly–hostile
Intensity (degree of interdependence, frequency of interaction, felt commitment)	Distant–close
	Superficial–intimate
Setting	Social–work-related
	Informal–formal
	Socio-emotional–intellectual

accepted as having a generally understood meaning and is thus treated as a given (i.e. not requiring explication) in most descriptions and explanations of marketing (and thus, by implication, relationship marketing). There is (probably) no such precise definition of relationship in marketing and management textbooks and journals. The term stands for a complex social phenomenon that has not been widely conceptualized properly in the theory and practice of relationship marketing.

Relationships are continuous processes and every interaction has the potential for changing the relationship. 'Relationshipping', as Duck terms it, is actually '. . . a very complicated and prolonged process with many pitfalls and challenges. Relationships do not just happen; they have to be made – made to start, made to work, made to develop, kept in good working order and preserved from going sour' (Duck, 1991, p. 3). The expertise is that of the Relator (Spanish).

Emotions Matter

A relationship is a special situation when there is a genuine feeling and an emotional connection between two people that provides an emotional reward from the interpersonal interaction. Therefore, what is highly significant is the treatment of one person by the other in an interaction. Does this result in desirable feelings from the emotions invoked by what happens? Research by Barnes (2001) shows that people are much more disappointed by the treatment they experience than by products.

Relationships have to be defined in both behavioural and cognitive terms; that is, a relationship has both a subjective and an objective reality (Surra and Ridley, 1991). These provide the context within which each participant can interpret, understand, and predict the other's behaviour, and thus know how to behave toward the other. A relationship, then, is the product of interaction and the associated cognitive activity, and has distinctive emergent properties (Table 2.2).

As buyers we all, I would expect, wish to feel important and valued, rather than ignored and taken-for-granted or exploited. The manner in which others treat us is crucial.

TABLE 2.2 Emotions and feelings experienced in buying situations.

Positive (desirable) emotions	Negative (undesirable) emotions
Satisfaction	Anger
Pride	Regret
Surprise	Frustration
Happiness	Humiliation
Relief	Embarrassment
Contentment	Boredom
Delight	Disgust
Amusement	Scorn
Thrill	Disappointment
Gratification	Outrage
Trust	Indignation
Affinity	Annoyance
Assurance	Concern
Pleasure	Helplessness

Why Engage in a Trading Relationship?

The exchange process is simplified within a relationship, and non-economic needs can be met. An emphasis on resource exchange highlights the formation of a relationship when one has a resource that is required or desired by another – there is inherent dependency linkage. *Resource dependency theory* explains how an organization can survive, grow, and accomplish other goals by exchanging resources. Exchange theory defines relationships in terms of voluntary transactions for mutual interests and rewards. For example, six characteristics of interorganization linkages have been defined by Oliver (1990) (Table 2.3).

Systems theory is concerned not with entities, but with relationships, structure, and interdependencies among a set of interacting 'units'. Communication is the primary exchange in a social system, serving as the major determinant of relationships and the overall functioning of the system. Patterns of interaction

TABLE 2.3 Characteristics of business-to-business exchanges (Oliver, 1990).

Necessity	Stems from legal or regulatory requirements
Asymmetry	Potential exercise of power or control by one party over the other – desire for scarce resources may lead to surrendering of autonomy
Reciprocity	Co-operation, collaboration, and co-ordination in place of domination, power, and control
Efficiency	The arrangement reduces market transaction costs
Stability	Relative predictability under conditions of uncertainty
Legitimacy	Justification and the appearance of agreement with norms, rules, beliefs, or expectations

TABLE 2.4 Relationship, antecedents, and consequences distinguished (adapted from Broom et al., 2000, p. 16).

Antecedents	Social and cultural norms, collective understandings and expectations, resource needs, sensed uncertainty, other kinds of necessity
Relationship	Properties of transactions, exchanges, communication, and other interactions
Consequences (outcomes) (may become antecedents in subsequent episodes)	Goal accomplishment, dependency and loss of autonomy, routine behaviour, institutionalized behaviour

form the structure of the system. Importantly, structure and the process creating it are not the same.

Communication is the central means through which people pursue and service relationship functions that reflect joined, purposive behaviours of participating actors. Customers and suppliers interpret their exchange partner's actions in terms of both functional content and symbolic content. Motives, needs, behaviours, etc. are causes or contingencies in the formation of relationships. Relationships also have consequences that effect changes in the environment. So, relationships are the consequences of changes and the causes of other changes (Table 2.4). Antecedents explain why a relationship is entered into, while consequences explain what happens when parties actively relate.

Of course, people engage in buying behaviour with different motives in mind. Promiscuous buyers are attracted by 'bribes' and seduction. Special offers, discounts, and so on may be self-defeating in attracting those most likely to break off the relationship for a better offer. On the other hand, not defecting does not necessarily imply satisfaction and loyalty. The motivator may be no more than convenience and inertia. In some situations, customers are held 'hostage' by structural bonds and experience negative emotions.

Starting Conditions

Initiation of a relationship requires that one person makes an approach, presents an attractive proposition, establishes some rapport, and is liked by the other person (Bennett, 1996). Feelings of attraction and liking are very significant in relationship development. Attractiveness includes such feelings derived from judgements as ease of interaction, frequency of interaction, closeness, familiarity, nearness, similarity, mutuality, and interdependence. Likeability includes judgements of sincerity, dependability, truthfulness, thoughtfulness, and consideration. Of course, these are all dimensions of trust. There has to be some personal contact – exposure to another person alone can increase affect, but conscious actions have greater effect on affect.

> *Friendships, courtships and even casual relationships are begun only when the partners wish to enter them. By attending to the life-cycle position, social*

*circumstances and personality style of the individual one can more easily gauge
their likely interest in a relationship.*

(Duck, 1991, p. 48)

*The very creation of a relationship, its maintenance and development, are all
based on persuasion. No-one has to be in a relationship with anyone else and
all voluntary relationships are therefore rooted in our ability to attract (i.e.,
persuade) the other person to stay in the relationship.*

(Duck, 1991, p. 33)

The Interpersonal Theory of Carl Rogers, the humanist psychologist (Rogers, 1959), provides some understanding of what bonds people in relationships, helping us to see this from the buyer's point of view. Certain behaviours, attitudes, and communication foster trusting, bonded relationships. Therefore, an enhanced 'mix' of resources can be provided to relaters to foster mutually beneficial commitment in support of value creation in production and exchange. *Maintenance* of the status quo must be overcome to establish a new relationship. This requires trustworthiness, dependability, and consistency, by being open and sincere in expressive and unambiguous communicating. Accessibility, account-ability, commitment, and candour are all fundamental to lasting, healthy relation-ships. Most so-called trading 'relationships' lack one or more of these characteristics, especially accountability. *Enhancement* is concerned with the promotion of growth, learning, and change in healthy relationships. *Positive regard* is concerned with liking, approval, acceptance, and gratitude in personal dealings with others.

Managers need to be able to understand what is important to a particular customer, to be able to create a situation that is conducive to relating to each other (Table 2.5).

Buttle (1996) asks whether a corporate–consumer trading relationship can ever be truly reciprocal (see Figure 2.1). Can marketing operate beyond economic ties? Is the social basis for a relationship irrelevant in trading? Clearly

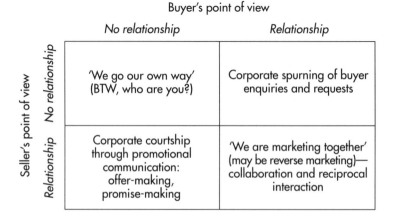

FIGURE 2.1   The relationship matrix.

not in many situations. So, what form of reciprocity exists in a marketing/trading relationship?

Is an exchange always sufficient? In what circumstances might a communal relationship be desirable? (Table 2.6).

Through interaction, might there be a shift from economic exchange transactions, to an exchange relationship, and then a communal relationship, at least for some?

The Internet is a small world

Are all humans connected by just six friends? In 1967 Sociologist Stanley Milgram proposed a theory that everybody in the world is connected through just six friends. He claimed that any one of us could find another person through a network of, on average, just six other people. This idea quickly became part of popular culture, but there has been little evidence to support the claim – until recently.

A digital version of Milgram's 1960s' experiment is under way in the *Small World Research Project* at Columbia University, New York. Using the postal service and email, randomly selected people are asked whether they know another person mentioned in the letter, and who else they know who might know this person. At each step, the identified person's name is given to the project co-ordinators. In Milgram's experiment, the average number of people the message went to before reaching its destination was just six (ranging from five to ten).

A second more ambitious project, the *Electronic Small World Project* is being conducted at Ohio State University. This aims to map social connections by asking 500,000 people about their email use. The information will be used to map the social patterns of the Internet to discover how small email social networks actually are. Follow-up investigations will examine how email relationships change over time, whether they differ from 'off-line' relationships, and whether the Internet transcends barriers of race, sex, and economics.

This research also tells us something about the nature of networks. These can be characterized as:

- scale-free – a few nodes have many links to other nodes, while many nodes have only a few links;
- clustering – relationships among nodes are not randomly distributed, but grouped;
- short path links – some groups are very closely connected.

More at http://smallworld.sociology.columbia.edu and Milgram (1967).

What is a Good, Strong Relationship?

Gutek (1995) distinguishes a service relationship from a service encounter. A *service relationship* arises through repeated contact between a customer and provider, so that they get to know each other as persons and as role occupants. They come to expect and anticipate future interaction and develop

TABLE 2.5 Characteristics of strong relationships (based on Barnes, 2001, ch. 5).

Trust	Confidence of desirable outcomes from interacting with another, based on predictability, dependability, and faith. The marketing task is to engender a feeling of reliance
Commitment	Motivates effort to preserve a relationship and to resist alternative offers, while viewing high-risk action as prudent in the absence of opportunistic behaviour – founded on satisfaction and investment. May be influenced by the actions of third parties (competing offers, etc.)
Investment	Expenditure of personal resources – time, emotional energy, sacrifice, shared memories, possessions, activities, and so on
Dependence	Each party relies on the other to satisfy certain functional and emotional needs – may be voluntary or involuntary (forced or imposed) dependence
Communicative interaction	Communicating people are relating people
Attachment	Feelings of liking, affection, shared values and goals
Reciprocity	A relationship is mostly defined by what each person provides for the other through exchange
Shared benefits	Those derived from ownership and/or use of a good or service, as well as the emotional benefits – risk reduction, reduced anxiety, recognition, preferential treatment, favours, etc.
Mutuality	Each interaction is affected by what has gone before and affects what may come about – the behaviour of one takes into account the behaviour of the other.

TABLE 2.6 Complementary forms of relationship.

Exchange relationship	Each person assumes that benefits are given with the expectation of receiving benefits in return – each keeps track of the other's needs in anticipation of an opportunity for reciprocal behaviour – each is concerned primarily with his or her own welfare.
Communal relationship	Each person is concerned with the welfare of the other – the receipt of benefit does not incur an obligation to return a comparable benefit

a history of, often lengthy, interactions that they can draw upon whenever interacting. A *service encounter*, on the other hand, occurs when a buyer engages in, typically, a single fleeting interaction with various providers, so that the provider and the buyer remain strangers to each other. Gutek points out that often a relationship is merely simulated in what is really no more than a series of (often isolated) encounters. These are the information-based pseudo-relationships so often found in direct mail and telesales programmes. The two modes of trading are distinguished by the time, effort, and care commitments of the parties. People engaged in encounters focus on how little commitment is needed, whereas those engaged in relationships attend to how much commitment is necessary.

Ledingham and Bruning (2000) have characterized the behaviour of participants in a high-quality relationship as follows:

- feeling of trust;
- sensed investment in the relationship;
- takes-into-account;
- demonstrated interest;
- understanding;
- honest and open about intentions;
- improves;
- serves;
- promotes welfare;
- socially responsible actions.

The character of a relationship depends on the longevity and strength of association, a well as the content of the interaction. Depending on the desirability of the relationship, the choice of partner, and efforts to develop the relationship, the relationship may be short and simple, with no future prospects. On the other hand, the relationship may be involved and complicated, and operate into the long term.

Attributes considered important in gauging long-term relationships (Grunig et al., 1992):

- reciprocity;
- trust – the basis of the 'license to operate';
- credibility;
- mutual legitimacy;
- openness;
- mutual satisfaction;
- mutual understanding.

Much of what Relationship Marketing is intended to accomplish can be realized by shifting our thinking from selling to customers, to doing business with buyers and users. The strength of a relationship derives from the underlying motivation and the intensity of interaction (Figure 2.2).

Individuals feel more committed when they believe that they have poor-quality alternatives to their relationships.

	Low commitment	High commitment
Low trust	Recurrent	Co-operative, bilateral
High trust	Discrete or opportunistic	Hierarchical (one party dominant)

FIGURE 2.2   Relationship strength (based on Donaldson and O'Toole, 1997).

What do we expect from the other person in a trading relationship?

Might we reasonably and justifiably expect that they are:

reliable, helpful, trustworthy, knowledgeable, credible, empathetic, competent, friendly but not familiar, unobtrusive, and a clear communicator?

The size of an individual's investment in a relationship also influences his or her commitment to it. Generally, investment resources include time, emotional energy, personal sacrifice, and other indirect investments, such as shared memories, mutual friends, and activities or possessions that are uniquely linked to a relationship.

Those individuals who are voluntarily dependent on their partners and who perceive poor alternatives to the relationship are both dependent and satisfied. On the other hand, those individuals who are dependent on relationship, yet see better alternatives to their present situation, are not voluntarily dependent and are therefore somewhat dissatisfied or entrapped.

Trust evolves out of past experience and prior action; dispositional character-istics are attributed to the partner, such as being reliable, dependable, etc.; trust involves a willingness to put oneself at risk; and trust involves feelings of con-fidence and security in the partner.

Weak ties differ from close personal relationships. Many weak ties develop within the electronic context of telephone services, computer bulletin boards, and a host of other emerging technologies currently being laid over more traditional restricted channels like the mail (Adelman et al., 1987, p. 133).

Exchange can occur between a firm and its customers without a relationship being in place. Occasional, short-term interactions do not normally deserve the sobriquet 'relationship' because of the unlikelihood of continuity and because of the absence of any form of subjective support to the participants.

Weak ties are significant in a developmental sense because all strong ties were once weak ties. Many of the day-to-day interactions that occur between an individual and the firms with which he or she does business would be a part of that individual's network of weak ties.

The implications of the link between weak ties and customer relationships in the services sector has been explored by Adelman et al. (1994). They suggest that reliance on weak ties as a means of social support will increase in the future, for several reasons:

- increased preference among people born after World War II for warm personal interactions in place of formal impersonal interactions;
- an increase in the number of singles;
- an increase in the number of elderly;
- an increase in the number of small businesses, which has resulted in a proliferation of firms that will be more suited to providing this type of support;
- the general economic prosperity and political stability that has been present for the last few decades, which has resulted in a sense of security that an individual's lower order needs will be taken care of, allowing a greater focus of energy on higher order needs.

Grunig and Huang (2000) took the 'relationship' concepts from Table 2.4 (above) and describe this category as 'maintenance strategies' (i.e. what is required to maintain relationships) by drawing on *conflict resolution theories*.

Knapp and Vangelisti (1992) provide descriptions of a range of incremental tendencies in the development and deterioration of a relationship (referred to as *interaction stages* in Table 2.7).

Qualities of the communication (exchange linkage) are independent of the communicators and include: symmetry, intensity, content, frequency, valence, and duration.

So, what is a 'good' relationship? In transactional marketing, outcome measures are obviously related directly to economic exchange (sales, profits, etc.). In Relationship Marketing, on the other hand, we must include relational process and outcome indicators. For example, disclosure in the form of suggestions, complaints, inquiries, intentions, decisions, and so on directly to each other (i.e. not via the media, regulators, etc.).

Trust (i.e. the confidence that a partner has in the other's reliability and integrity) and commitment (i.e. the enduring desire to maintain the relationship) lead to honesty and benevolence (concern for welfare) in sincere promise-making and promise-keeping. This can be expressed through excellent service, recognizing obligations. Each partner feels obliged to act responsively and responsibly.

Barnes (2001) has outlined four levels of genuine trading relationships (Table 2.8). These genuine relationships take into account the customer's point of view, especially considering what their expectations are of such a relationship. The relationship is mutually acknowledged and afforded special status by both parties as much more than occasional contact. There is an emotional basis for the relationship that is not simply discernible in repeat purchase, frequency of contact, duration of dealings, or similar behaviours.

Typically, the degree of personal involvement with each other is high for an intimate relationship, but low for a brand relationship (Figure 2.3). However, this

TABLE 2.7 Interaction stage behaviour in a human relationship (based on Knapp and Vangelisti, 1992).

Interaction stage	Example of typical marketing behaviour
Initiating – first contact and reactions	'Cold' sales call or mailshot
Experimenting – smalltalk to discover the other	Pre-presentation 'chit-chat' or a questionnaire
Intensifying – specific personal disclosure – 'we' and 'our'	Negotiation
Integrating – acting together, developing a shared history, and merging social circles	Buyer and/or seller boast of relationship (e.g. customer wears a sweatshirt bearing a brand logo)
Bonding – public ritual or formal contract – public commitment to gain social or institutional support for the relationship	Customer gives a testimonial in an advertisement
Differentiating – more separate endeavours	Customer seeks an alternative supplier
Circumscribing – less communication – of a more superficial nature	Conversation avoids mentioning a sale/purchase
Stagnating – little communication – increased tension	Neither party makes a follow-up call
Avoiding – effort to avoid any communication	Customer does not return sales calls
Terminating – open access ceases	Seller or buyer closes the account

TABLE 2.8 Levels of genuine trading relationship (based on Barnes, 2001).

Level	Characteristic features
Intimate	Friendly, highly involved, physical contact, disclosure of personal information (e.g. dentist, hairdresser)
Face-to-face	Meeting and conversation (e.g. retailer, hotelier, car mechanic)
Distant	Infrequent interaction, mediated by technology (e.g. utility services, ISP)
Brand	Rare or no contact (e.g. food products, clothes)

does not have to be so. It is possible to increase the strength and closeness at any level of relationship.

Customers indicate that they desire quite a different type of relationship, say, with a telephone company, than they do with a lawyer or a hairdresser. Different dimensions of the relationship take on different levels of importance in each case.

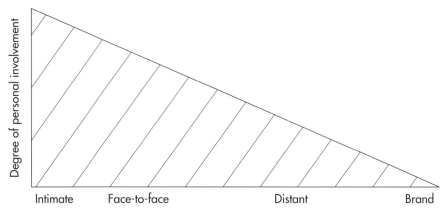

FIGURE 2.3 Relational involvement.

Growth Conditions for Genuine Relationships

Relationships flourish when we are effective in:

> ... *assessing the other person's needs accurately; adopting appropriate styles of communication; indicating liking and interest by means of minute bodily activities, like eye movements and postural shifts; finding out how to satisfy mutual personality needs; adjusting our behaviour to the relationship 'tango' with the other person; selecting and revealing the right sorts of information or opinion in an inviting, encouraging way in the appropriate style and circumstances; building up trust, making suitable demands, and building up commitment.*
>
> (Duck, 1991, p. 3)

Zabava Ford (1998) has explained three approaches to the customer–provider service interaction (Table 2.9).

Customer discretionary behaviour is the contribution that a customer may make co-operatively to the provider's business, for example, in displays of loyalty (faithful patronage) and promotion (recommendation to others). Zabava Ford points out that both manipulative service and personalized service tend to produce sales, whereas courteous service and personalized service generate customer satisfaction. Satisfied customers are more likely to comply with provider requirements and to remain loyal. It is loyalty that leads to co-operative customer discretionary behaviour. She also reminds us that interaction control may be exercised by seller or buyer. She also points out that deceptive, discriminative, and depersonalized service are all unethical.

The management problem is systematically and non-intrusively to ensure frequent face-to-face interaction, wherever possible, and to ensure familiarity and continuity. Multiple, integrated communication channels provide customers with choice in how they interact while capturing the total interaction picture. Customer involvement is essential, so solicitation of opinions, concerns, and suggestions is vital, as is the creation of additional value by improving service.

TABLE 2.9 Service approaches (based on Zabava Ford, 1998).

Courteous service	Manipulative service	Personalized service
All actions are instrumental, oriented to the creation of a bond of rapport through talking, to turn an encounter into an interaction	All actions are strategic, in pursuit of own interests.	All actions are discursive in pursuit of mutual interests, with a customer orientation.
	Rule-keeping, procedural, formal, distanced, emotionally detached, 'strictly business', treatment of all customers as the same, in order to control the interaction. This can also be accomplished through discrimination, scripts, directive questioning, and retention of initiative.	Typically, involvement in conversation (attention, appreciation, response), information sharing, and social support (caring, helping, and sensitivity) to rescue uncertainty and enhance self-esteem
	Alternatively, compliance-gaining by promising or threatening and the evocation or suppression of own emotions in order to appear to be positive are used to deceive the customer	

This is the basic rationale for eCRM (to be discussed at length in Chapters 5 and 6.

Relational Bonds

What, from the customer's point of view, constitutes a desirable relationship that, if continued, will be rewarding? 'Relationship' is inherently an interpersonal notion, manifest when there is much interaction with an associated emotional aspect.

McCall et al. (1970) describe five kinds of bond (Table 2.10). Each person as a customer will have a personal blend of these bonds. It is for the marketer to understand what is important to each person.

Managers attempt to bond customers through technologies, linked processes, co-branding, and personal friendships. A bonded trading relationship differs from a fleeting transaction. In the former, a purchase is the beginning of a process, whereas in the latter, a sale is the end of a process. In the bonded relationship, the participants ask, 'what have we done for each other lately?'

TABLE 2.10 Types of interpersonal bond (based on McCall et al., 1970).

Ascription	Inherent in relative social positions (e.g. father, banker)
Commitment	Semi-exclusive use of the other as a source of specified behaviours, role supports, or rewards
Attachment	Specific persons and their behaviours are build into role identities until a non-transferable relationship makes members vulnerable to the actions of each other
Investment	The resource cost of forming and maintaining the relationship – reciprocity is consideration for the other's investments
Reward dependability	A major reason for many relatinships to be formed and continued – in support of role(s)

Internet adventures with Kinder Surprise

Every Kinder Surprise chocolate egg contains a small toy and a unique magicode that can be input to the website as a personal password to take the child to an online adventure. This adds considerable value to the basic product, thus encouraging repeat purchase, by providing the adventure at very low additional cost to the manufacturer. Consumers can experience their very own adventure on the Internet by buying an egg.

Outcomes of Trading Relationships

Outcomes can be summarized (Table 2.11).

Morgan and Hunt (1994, p. 22) identify that '... commitment and trust are "key" because they encourage marketers to (1) work at preserving relationship investments by co-operating with exchange partners, (2) resist attractive short-term alternatives in favour of the expected long-term benefits of staying with existing partners, and (3) view potentially high-risk action as being prudent because of the belief that their partners will not act opportunistically.'

TABLE 2.11 Relationship outcomes.

Trust	Cognitive evaluation
Mutuality of control	Relative power
Commitment to the relationship	Degree of resource exchange
Satisfaction with the relationship	Affective evaluation

Commitment summarizes our experiences of dependence and directs reactions to new situations. Satisfaction has two components: (1) the degree to which a relationship provides valued outcomes by fulfilling important needs, and (2) the comparison level of alternatives, which is based on a qualitative expectation of what a relationship's outcomes ought to be in an ideal involvement, as well as comparison of one's own outcomes to the inputs and outcomes of a partner.

Variables useful in gauging short-term relationship effects in considering the extent of *co-orientation* (Grunig and Hunt, 1984):

- communication (extent of dialogue or mutual exposure);
- understanding (shared cognitions);
- agreement (shared attitudes);
- complementary behaviour.

Parasuraman et al. (1985) define a range of dimensions of customer appreciation of service quality:

- reliability;
- responsiveness;
- tangibles;
- assurance;
- empathy.

The latter two are essentially relational, concerned with the knowledge and courtesy of service providers and their ability to evoke trust and confidence, and with authentic caring and personal attention.

Relationship Marketing can be thought of as a win–win game in which value is created and shared, rather than simply redistributed by taking it from others. An RM-based management system produces value, rather than extracts it.

> Service quality > customer satisfaction > relationship strength > relationship longevity > relationship profitability (value acquired)

This has serious implications for CRM deployment. Managing a 'relationship' without realization of high levels of agreed service quality is a pursuit of satisfaction through cynical manipulation. Longevity of a relationship through 'lock-in' is coercive. This can degenerate into reciprocal manipulation – a lose–lose outcome.

The core values of sellers are displayed in their attitude to customers, the character of their relationships with customers, and the means applied to creating and sharing economic and social benefits in trading.

> **Trading value**
>
> - Experienced quality
> - Price/cost
> - Aesthetics
> - Performance
> - Reputation
> - Brand (a trust mark)
> - Peer pressure
> - Trendiness/fashion
> - Service
> - Association with a group (self-image)
> - Scarcity
> - Novelty
> - Nostalgia/sentiment

The Brand Relationship

A brand is an active relationship that customers know and value (McKenna, 1997). A significant brand provides meaning and is important to a person because it connects with their life, and they have behavioural, attitudinal, and emotional involvement. The managerial aim of branding is to establish a satisfying bond that sustains buying and recommendation. Based on Barnes's discussion of brand relationships, Figure 2.4 summarizes the branding progression from becoming aware of a name to bonding a relationship. Four stages of degree of involvement are discerned, each with an associated marketing (communication) objective.

A brand makes a promise by expressing what we are like, what we want to be, and an invitation to connect and bond (Simmons, 2000). Judgements of potential risk motivates the choice between buying a commodity product or a branded product (Figure 2.5).

Grant (2000) has redefined the notion of brand for contemporary society. He identifies the early brand as a guaranteeing trademark and sign of ownership. This evolved into a vehicle for the realization of aspiration to social ideals. Today, the

Naming: 'what is this?'	Awareness		Advertising
Associating: 'who is it like?'	Character	Progression in involvement	Positioning
Animating: 'do I like it?'	Personality		Selling
Relating: 'how important is it to me?'	Relationship		Bonding

FIGURE 2.4 Establishment of a brand relationship.

High risk of social loss or waste of resource(s)	Considerable assessment of repurchase option	Committed repurchase
Low risk of social loss or waste of resource(s)	Best value purchase	Routine repurchase
	Undifferentiated product (commodity)	Differentiated product (brand)

FIGURE 2.5   Consumer choice – commodity or brand?

brand encapsulates personal experience as a set of 'inward ideas' that people live their lives by, bringing meaning and order. This has replaced eroded and lost traditions. Advertising, packaging, etc. are representations of these ideas.

Christensen's (1993) Corporate Image Pyramid shows that the foundation of a corporation is the business idea. This is enacted through a set of values and norms (the corporate culture) and a conscious self-image (corporate identity). Corporate communication is the conscious expression of a desired profile for the corporation and business among stakeholders. It is they who form images of the enterprise. Perhaps it is helpful to consider the entire CI Pyramid as the building blocks of the corporate brand. The brand relationship in consumer markets is more distant than in business markets. In the former, emotions play a stronger part, while in the latter, rational thinking is more important. Therefore, consumers don't so readily detect mismatches of the profile consciously communicated by the seller and the foundation and culture observable in corporate actions.

Points of View

Marketing managers seem to view relationships primarily through the eyes of the company and their business, without sufficient regard for what the customer gets from the interaction (see Barnes, 2001, for elaboration). What is a rewarding relationship from the seller's point of view, will not be so for the buyer. How do the respective points of view differ? Marketers have to be able to answer this question. Experience, and research by Barnes, shows that mostly, from the seller's point of view, effort goes in to raising switching costs as a barrier to exit (service contracts, penalties, proprietary products, and processes, etc.), or a reliance on information from databases to promote *at* customers.

Sheaves and Barnes (1996) pose some stark issues for managers. It is critical that managers appreciate the fact that a relationship cannot be one-sided and that no relationship exists unless the customer believes it exists. Managers must also have a clear understanding of what a customer expects and demands from a relationship with a service provider; not all want the same things. Managers must also develop a better appreciation for the affective or emotional side of customer relationships. The concept of relationship marketing must mean more to customers than merely ensuring regular contact or rewarding them for continued patronage. Managers must realize that, in the minds of most customers, the concept of a relationship implies not only ongoing contact, but also a certain 'give and take', and the presence of a degree of warmth and intimacy.

The parties to a commercial exchange have differing points of view (interests, resources, assumptions, etc.) and, thus, different motivations. Two approaches to the resolution of such conflicts are problem solving and compliance gaining. The former is an integrative, symmetrical trust-based relationship of attempts to reconcile the interests of both parties, produce joint benefits, and accomplish win–win goal attainment. The latter is a control-based relationship of distributive, asymmetrical attempts by each party to maximize their own gains while minimizing their own losses (toward win–lose outcomes).

The 30Rs of Relationship Marketing

The extensive long-term study of relationship marketing undertaken by Gummesson (1999) identifies a large number of relationships that are not typically discussed when the focus is narrowly on 'the marketplace' (Table 2.12). Gummesson has comprehensively examined the situations in which interactions (active contact) arise for a variety of reasons. Gummesson identifies 30 relationships that are fundamental to the marketing activities of every business. Instead of managing the marketing mix, advises Gummesson, marketing-oriented managers have now to manage the Total Relationship Marketing system if they are to respond successfully to the very different, emerging marketing environment.

The advent of, first, exchange as the basis of market relationships (in the technical sense) and, later, relationship marketing both offer the consumer more and provide a managerial rhetoric of customer sovereignty. There is a clear emancipatory rhetoric (Fitchett and McDonagh, 2001).

TABLE 2.12 Location of 30 relationships (based on Gummesson, 1999).

Type of relationship	Nature of relationship
Mega	Non-market antecedent relationships at the level of society and the economy – the platform for market relationships
Market – Classic	Seller–buyer dyads, supplier–customer–competitor triads, and the distribution network (channels)
Market – Special	Service encounters and loyalty programmes
Nano	Intra-organizational (internal customer–supplier chains in internal markets)*

*See Varey and Lewis (2000) and Halal et al. (1993).

It is not necessary to study a dyad to identify whether or not marketing has occurred. Marketing exchange behaviour does not have to be described as dyadic behaviour. Yet, some non-exchange behaviour may be considered to be marketing behaviour, and some social exchange behaviour (if not all) is clearly marketing behaviour.

Is the 'exchange' concept still a viable basis for market relationships/ interactions?

The *relationship* is an important but much abused construct in contemporary marketing thought, and this requires an understanding of social exchange behaviour. *Social exchange theory* (see Chadwick-Jones, 1976; Gergen et al., 1980; and Cook, 1987, for example) explains social relationships as the means for exchanging physical and psychological (symbolic) resources. The relationship is maintained as long as the rewards of the exchanges exceed the costs, or until a more 'profitable' relationship becomes available. People enter into a relationship with a certain expectation for the partner's behaviour. Each has a desired level of satisfaction that is compared with that derivable from imagined benefits from other available relationships.

General Properties of Commercial Relationships

Who relates to whom? The unit of analysis here is the dyad of relaters:

- person to person;
- person to brand;
- firm to firm (really several connected person to person relationships).

What follows here is a conceptual map (Figure 2.6) that is intended to show that a dichotomy of person–firm is not very helpful since there are common features among the three classes of marketing relationship: services–consumer goods–producer goods. The commonality arises from the central concept of people relating together. The bold arrows suggest a managerial desire to move to closer relational relationships.

Relationship Marketing would be deemed successful for the traders if:

- person-to-person trading relationships were not asymmetric and hostile;
- person-to-brand relationships were long-term and intensive;
- firm-to-firm relationships were not distant, and relationship history was important to both parties.

There is potential to reposition/redefine the nature of a trading relationship by enhancing an asymmetric power-differentiating interaction to an apparently symmetric relationship.

Gummesson's (1999) extensive study of relationship marketing provides a valuable insight into the general properties of the relationships that concern the manager who manages through marketing-oriented management. These have been summarized in Table 2.13.

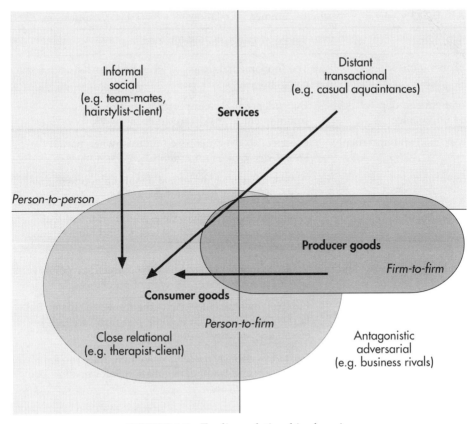

FIGURE 2.6   Trading relationship domains.

Iacobucci & Ostrom's (1996) study identifies fundamental properties of marketing relationships (Table 2.14), providing useful distinctions between services, consumer goods, and producer goods.

Some degree of collaboration is always at the core of a commercial relationship, while other properties feature according to the particular situation. Such properties can be identified in the evaluation of a relationship, allowing decisions about investment and termination.

Relationship Status

Trading relationships are more explicit at the start of the supply chain than at the final consumer end, where they may be unrecognized by the buyer. As Barnes (2001) has reminded us, a relationship only exists truly when the buyer believes that it does. At the same time, the level of possible intimacy increases as we move down the supply chain from raw materials extraction to consumption. The nature of the value production changes, becoming more directly relevant to the day-to-day lives of buyers.

TABLE 2.13 General properties of commercial relationships (based on Gummesson, 1999).

Property	Relevance to Relationship Marketing
Collaboration	The fundamental property – can be balanced with some competition
Commitment, dependency, and importance	Dependence makes importance, and requires commitment to make a relationship work
Trust, risk, and uncertainty	Close collaboration is based on trust when partial knowledge creates uncertainty
Power	Almost always asymmetrical, requiring goodwill and helpfulness for a successful relationship
Longevity	A relationship built over time is an investment that creates learning and understanding, and reduces risk and uncertainty
Frequency, regularity, and intensity	Points of interaction, only some of which are points of sale. Characteristics of the type of purchase–sale
Closeness and remoteness – proximity	Physical, mental, emotional – the former facilitates the latter – impersonal can become personal – feelings of credibility, security, understanding
Formality, informality, and openness	Forms of contract, consent, obligation, rules of interaction and trading, negotiation, information exchange, disclosure
√Routinization	Efficiency and effectiveness of procedures, rituals, level of attention
Content	Economic exchange – products and money – information and knowledge – value creation
Personal and social properties	Demographics, personality traits, patterns of relationships – direct and mediated

TABLE 2.14 Properties of marketing relationships (based on Iacobucci and Ostrom, 1996).

	Services	Consumer goods	Producer goods
Extent of interdependence	Few relationships are independent	Many asymmetric (dependence) buyer–seller relationships	All are symmetric, interdependent relationships
Close/Supportive	Few	Few	Contractual
Distance	Transactional	Impersonal	Relational
Power differential	Some	Much	None

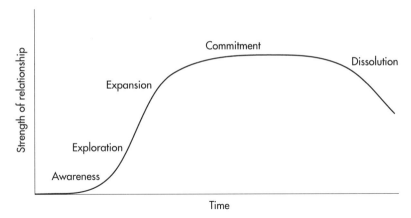

FIGURE 2.7 A buyer–seller relationship life cycle (Dwyer et al., 1987).

Consumers, buyers, and providers (sellers) seek to establish and maintain trading relationships when they believe that such an investment will enable them to accomplish the goals of their 'life projects'. The buyer–seller relationship has been likened to a marriage (Tynan, 1997). These ways of thinking about such relationships are drawn from the study of interpersonal relationships by social psychologists. Dwyer et al. (1987), on the other hand, used a life cycle approach to model the buyer–seller relationship (Figure 2.7).

In the exploration stage, parties try to attract the attention of the other to bargain and to understand the expectations, norms, and power of the other. Expansion occurs when the initial exploration succeeds in establishing the basis for a continuing relationship. Exchange outcomes provide clues about the suitability of this. Commitment reduces the need for searching for alternatives. The possibility of termination is always present, and the consequences are greatest once the parties have made significant investments in the relationship. The Relationship Marketing task is to sustain and maintain the trading relationship for as long as it provides benefits to the parties. If we refer back to the idea of a marketing mix, we can see that relationship development requires a fully integrated approach to managing the wide-ranging marketing communication situations (see Varey, 2001, for an elaboration of this idea).

The nature of the relationship and any gap between this and the desired relationship can be addressed by setting appropriate communication objectives. Several levels of commitment can be identified (Figure 2.8). A prospect has yet to establish a relationship, whereas a strong advocate is fully committed not only to product-purchase for himself but also to recommending to associates, friends, and family.

In marketing management, we are concerned with the interpersonal exchange of the buyer (consumer) and seller (marketer). Of course, other kinds of exchange occur in relationships between people and objects (products), themselves (intrapersonal), and other consumers (also interpersonal). In organizational exchanges, a person acts along with others, rather than alone.

Levinger and Snoek (1972) help us to understand the personal journey from isolated to mutual (Figure 2.9).

FIGURE 2.8 The ladder of consumer–buyer commitment.

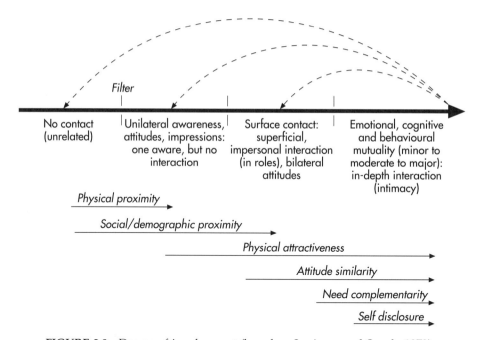

FIGURE 2.9 Degree of involvement (based on Levinger and Snoek, 1972).

Levinger and Snoek (1972) consider the difference between friendship, acquaintance, enmity, and formal interaction. They determined that degree of involvement distinguishes types of relationship. To involve someone means to implicate them or include them in some act. Therefore, in a trading relationship, there may be minimal personal involvement in product design and packaging, or a 'real' or 'genuine' relationship in a service situation where the process and outcome are negotiated. It seems sensible to explain the difference of transaction marketing compared to relationship marketing as an increase in the intensity of commitment and involvement. In this model, a relationship develops from awareness but no interaction, through impersonal interaction, to increasing degrees of mutuality, as the person mentally 'climbs the commitment–involvement ladder'.

Balanced reciprocity is dyadic, involving the exchange of items such that each party feels that they have received at least equal to that given up. When one party believes that they are not receiving at least equal value, they will attempt to bring the exchange back into balance or to terminate the exchange relationship. Sometimes alternative sources are not available, and there may then be no alternative but to continue with unbalanced exchange, with one party dependent upon the other and subject to their greed.

Commercial exchanges occur in a much wider environment in which exchanges of various kinds may occur at different levels (cultural, social, interpersonal, etc.).

When the outcome of an exchange exceeds the expected outcome, outcome satisfaction is likely. This may (other factors considered) encourage exchange re-engagement in the future. When this occurs, *relationship marketing* becomes possible. Then, exchange moves beyond a single act and becomes a process that does not always start nor end with a purchase.

Brand loyalty can be considered to be the consumer behaviour resulting from their determination of goal congruity (of themselves and the marketer with whom they exchange) and exchange satisfaction (see Gould, 1992).

There are two views on the significance of the relationship emphasis for managing through RM:

- relationship generalization – the relationship is a surrogate for quality in that buyers generalize positive feelings about a seller to core aspects of the good and associated service;
- rational evaluation – value is added to the good or service by meeting certain peripheral demands, but buyers are primarily concerned with core product quality.

When there is progression from low to high relational commitment – then the buyer uses commitment and trust as mediators for determining future activities with the particular seller. Does the seller seek commitment and trust from the buyer? Is this what is meant by loyalty?

Intelligent relationships

Companies do not only create value by making more intelligent product offers, but by developing more intelligent relationships with their customers and suppliers. To do this, the business must continuously re-evaluate and redefine their abilities and their relationships so as to maintain the flexibility of these value-creating systems, keeping them new and reactive. In this new value strategy the on-going dialogue between the company and its customers can explain the success and the survival of certain businesses, and the decline and failure of others.

(Normann and Ramirez, 1994)

Membership Relationships

We can distinguish differing types of service production (fleeting encounters and committed relationships) and differing forms of relationship of customers to providers (casual user and service system member).

Some products and services are provided and consumed without any real sense of a relationship. For example, a chocolate bar purchased from a street kiosk on the way to the rail station does not really bring seller and buyer together beyond a fleeting single transaction (a bar is picked up and some cash is handed to the vendor), although a relationship with the brand might be identified. There is no formal relationship (certainly the producer never meets the consumer). Payphone and bridge toll services are further examples.

On the other hand, some products and services require a degree of knowledge of the self and other to enable the transaction. For example, hotel and car hire require names, addresses, etc. Supermarkets scan customer 'loyalty' cards and credit cards at the checkout. Banking and magazine subscriptions are further examples of the operation of a subscription, account, or membership arrangement. Business-to-business trading is almost all conducted on an account basis.

The aim of RM is to convert buyer behaviour and status from fleeting casual encounter, through marketing interventions, to committed relationship.

Increasingly, this marketing work involves much more than promotion, and CRM or Relationship Marketing Management (RMM) is providing systems for customers to manage their own relationships with suppliers.

The crucial distinction is that membership is based on information, communication, and knowledge (see Chapter 3). There is a continuous relating of buyer and seller (seller and buyer), even when purchases are not being transacted.

The Tesco.com tribe

The online shopping service Tesco.com is attracting people who want shopping to be different from the traditional sojourn to the local supermarket every Saturday morning. Is this creating a community of alternative lifestylers? We will examine this phenomenon in Chapter 6.

A Relational Perspective on Relationships

It is hard to find any literature that does not treat a trading relationship as something to be established, owned, 'built', and managed by a supplier. This view that a relationship is nothing more than an object to be manipulated for profit is almost universal.

Hosking (1995) contrasts relational vs. entitative perspectives to show the folly of treating relationships as objects with existences independent of people and with intrinsic fixed and given meaning. In the discipline of 'managing relationships', thinking is almost universally stranded in very particular entitative taken-for-granteds. The personal characteristics of the individual person and context are treated as entities that exist separately and independently of each other. Relationships are understood as between entities, viewed as either subject or object. The subject is understood to act by gathering 'knowledge that' the other has certain characteristics and to achieve 'influence over' the other (as object) (Hosking, 1995).

A *relational approach* to organization, on the other hand, takes the unit of analysis to be relational processes as the vehicle by which person and culture are produced and reproduced. Subsequent talk of person and context then cannot treat them as independent entities but as outcomes of participation in conversations that construct identities, meanings, and knowledge (Deetz, 1992). So, a relational perspective assumes multiple, socially constructed (therefore personal) realities – constructed in the social processes of discourse. Meanings, local knowledge, and ongoing meaning-making processes are explained. This alternative explanation of human interaction is not generally found in the managerialistic (control-oriented) literature.

The technology that we call 'marketing' incorporates a particular way of seeing relationships and of seeing relating: people (agents), objects (products), and events (exchanges in 'consumption situations') (see Schmitt, 1999, for a showman-like elaboration of this terminology). Marketing has been taken to be 'the discipline of exchange behaviour' (Bagozzi, cited in Morgan, 1992), and the discourse has excluded consideration of how 'exchanges' are mediated by asymmetrical power relations. Accordingly, markets are not understood as social systems, but as 'technologies of governance' (Morgan, 1992). This way of thinking favours those who manage the markets by neglecting structures of domination and exploitation. Social relations are then ignored or objectified as variables for managing. Giddens (1979, cited in Morgan, 1992) showed that exchange theory does not take account of power. So, we are left with the notion that marketing is a neutral technology for managing exchange – but the behaviour engendered is reciprocal manipulation – far from the supposed 'good' of 'free market forces'.

Value in a Trading Relationship

Relationship Marketing is a management approach to enhancing trading relationships for 'profit'.

What might motivate a buyer to co-ordinate a trading relationship with a seller? Drummond and Ensor (2001) helpfully summarize benefits that may be received from continuing exchanges:

- mutually beneficial exchanges are sought – avoiding the limited returns from single transactions, providing greater value relative to alternative competing offers;
- needs and wants are fulfilled more satisfactorily than from a fleeting encounter;
- the seller provides more appropriate goods and services as solutions to buyer problems, derived from greater understanding and co-operative effort and a

focus on service quality in decision-making and performance evaluation – long-term commitments to product delivery and service provision;

- the seller organizes in a more coherent and buyer-focused manner;
- financial benefits such as quantity discounts, 'loyalty' and 'trust' discounts, or 'reward' points that can be traded for goods and services;
- social benefits of personal interaction, such as contact, belonging, support – trading 'friendship', symbolism (lifestyle and group identity);
- structural benefits accrue through automation (electronic data interchange (EDI), JIT, electronic point-of-sale (EPOS), etc.);
- the costs of switching between suppliers are eliminated;
- simplified decision-making.

On the other hand, benefits sought by the seller might include:

- Increased sales revenue and profitability from increased purchases, since less resource is expended in attracting consumers as first-time buyers to replace those who deselect the seller due to dissatisfaction with service quality (Reichheld and Sasser, 1990). Grönroos (2000) has shown how a balanced and co-ordinated traditional and interactive marketing system is required to cater for creation and development of profitable buyer–seller trading relationships. Relationship Marketing emphasizes continuance of a trading relationship rather than discrete transactional exchange satisfaction.
- Customer loyalty produces stability (revenues, etc.)
- Shorter sales cycles.
- Customers focus on promise-making and promise-keeping as only part of their assessment of relational quality.
- Avoidance of the limited returns available from single transactions.
- Reduced costs from scale economies and learning.
- Stability from customer retention and 'loyalty' – reduced service costs and increased employee retention.
- Free word-of-mouth advertising from satisfied partners.

With longevity in trading relationships, can come enhanced profit. There is no further recruitment cost (e.g. for persuasive advertising, special offers, and so on), premium prices are often paid for convenience and confidence, referrals are made, there is less need for supervision and experimentation, and, often, there are higher levels of spending.

Motivational interest in a relationship may be stronger in either party or to some extent balanced (Figure 2.10). This will determine the effort and the value. Assessment of rewards available is relative to what is thought to be available from elsewhere. Ability to choose whether to enter into or withhold participation, based on behavioural expectations, is also significant in evaluation.

In place of the tradition of 'need satisfaction', Relationship Marketing introduces the aim of 'promise fulfilment' – part of what is exchanged is promises. Of course, this begs the question: Why make promises and what if they are not kept? How prevalent is mendacity and outright lying by corporate agents in pursuit of business goals?

Supply–Demand buyer's market	**S–D** balanced market	Supply–**Demand** seller's market
Seller needs buyers – heavy competition Discrete transactions are best Seller-maintained relationship only when sellers act subserviently (dependency) Customer attraction strategy – promise-making	Bilateral relationship Interdependency A substantive symmetrical relationship Customer relationship maintenance through promise-keeping	Buyers need sellers – functional advantage Discrete transactions are best Buyer-maintained relationship only when buyers act subserviently (dependency) Reverse marketing

FIGURE 2.10   The effect of supply–demand balance.

Mini-case: selling (and buying) double glazing

After two hours of conversation about the merits of 'Brand X' double glazing, in which the emphatic and enthusiastic salesman makes a variety of attractive assertions and promises, an order is placed. In due course, the replacement windows are fitted, and the benefits of security and comfort are realized when the job is completed. Or are they?

Close inspection reveals two windows have not been fitted properly and a range of cosmetic damage. One window will not even open and close! It takes 25 telephone calls and 8 appointments, of which only 2 are kept by company staff, before the necessary rework is done satisfactorily. Then, it becomes known that the payment schedule offered cannot be met. Only the promised installation date was adhered to.

The problem? An underlying service incapacity (too much reworking needed?), shielded by staff who apparently routinely make promises that they know they cannot keep or naively believe are reasonable. Attempts to placate an irate customer simply turn into further aggravation. No professional managers with authority are accessible to customers. There are no obvious signs of a commitment to future trading! Finally, the letter of complaint to the MD remains unanswered.

How to Value a Trading Relationship?

The key to this major managerial priority (and puzzle) is to think in relational terms. Ask what value can be produced by managing a learning relationship instead of discrete, product exchange transactions. Table 2.15 summarizes some suggestions for performance indicators. Return on relationship and the value of a relationship are discussed further in Chapter 4. Helpful discussions can be found

TABLE 2.15 Criteria for evaluating relationship outcomes.

Personal value accruable	Corporate value accruable
Social contact	Revenues
Job satisfaction	Contribution of all sales
Stability and security	Cross-selling opportunities
Sense of purpose	New product ideas and applications
Co-operative working	Lifetime value
Recognition and reward	Profit premium
	Technology transfer opportunities
	Access to networks and alliances
	Word-of-mouth advertising and referral
	Asset appreciation (other resources depreciate)
	Improved service quality

in Johnson and Gustafsson (2000) and Anton (1996). Corporate measurement systems must be designed and employed with such logic as *only measure what you will strive to improve*. Ask your external customers and the internal customers they rely upon, *'what matters to you?'*

Summary

A seller is able to encourage the development of a relationship with a buyer through the way that the customer is treated by the organization, where the interaction takes place, the atmosphere in which it takes place, and the attempts undertaken to raise the interaction to a socio-emotional level.

A firm's ability to create a lasting relationship with a customer is determined not only by its own actions, but also by the actions of competitors.

The social psychology literature explains that relationships exist between individuals, not organizations. The literature stresses that both individuals must be willing to enter into the relationship in order for it to exist, and the individuals' perceptions of the relationship are crucial to the type of relationship that exists. At the very least, it is probably reasonable to conclude that it would be increasingly difficult for technology-based service providers to create strong, close relationships from the customer's perspective.

Exchange and communal relationships are not mutually exclusive. By ensuring that interpersonal contact is available if desired, and by training employees to recognize and cater to those customers who desire a more personal relationship with the firm, businesses may develop a more communal-type relationship with a customer.

The ability of a firm to establish close relationships with customers will be compromised in the future in those industries where the interaction between customer and firm is delegated to technology. Banks and other financial institutions, for example, are realizing that establishing and maintaining a close relationship is more difficult with those customers who have embraced the technology and deal almost exclusively with the bank through telephone banking and

TABLE 2.16 A meta-analysis of theories of relationship
(inspired by Donaldson and O'Toole, 2002).

From economics	Agency theory – exchange risk is reduced through co-operative working
	Transaction cost economics theory – cost-effective, bilateral trading structures arise under certain conditions
From behavioural sciences	Resource dependency theory – power imbalances create conflict when actors attempt to control access to scarce resources
	Social exchange theory – relationships are social constructions that operate under norms that govern the 'contractual' arrangements
	Interaction theory – interdependence in networks requires co-ordination and adaptation among participants

automated banking machines. In the future, banks and others will have to deal with such customers in a completely different way if there is to be a sense of relationship present. This requires improved 'personalization' of the technology and the establishment of other forms of personal contact to maintain communicative interaction with the customer.

As we saw in Chapter 1, a range of theories can be drawn upon to explain the nature of relationships for marketing managers. Donaldson and O'Toole (2002) very helpfully provide a summary of the perspectives, and the basic proposition of each is presented in Table 2.16.

In Chapter 3, we consider the almost synonymous concept of communicating and the way that this concept is treated in management studies. This reveals some considerable scope for developing the theory of Relationship Marketing.

Relationship Marketing is an asymmetrical, personalizing, long-term marketing process that results in bilateral benefits, and is based on an in-depth understanding of customer needs and circumstantial and behavioural characteristics. Initiative and dominance waxes and wanes as the respective party's interests and actions fluctuate. Can asymmetrical relationships prosper for both parties? Are asymmetrical power distributions necessarily inferior to symmetrical ones (see Grunig, 1992, for an extensive review of this point from both marketing and public relations perspectives).

Trading behaviour that is understood as discrete transactions is discouraged in favour of long-term repeat contact, but not all exchanges are part of an ongoing sequence of transactions. The two extremes are: single transaction (passing strangers) vs. committed trading (partners).

Supposedly, a relationship strategy works best (for both parties?) when a purchase requires a high level of involvement from the buyer because they believe there is the potential risk of loss.

A 'relationship' descriptor is metaphorical when we say that a manufacturer has a business relationship with a retailer, or that a consumer has a relationship with a retailer, but there is, nonetheless, a set of interpersonal linkages between representative agents of the corporations. Persons act on behalf of the abstract entities 'supplier', 'company', 'corporation'. Exchange partners provide emotional resources that support the maintenance of the relationship.

Managers (in particular, marketing managers) can usefully draw on a wider appreciation of studies from social psychology to gain a better understanding of the marketing relationship that provides the context for economic and 'human' exchange. Trading benefits are personally appreciated by buyers, owners, and users. They are not inherent in products. The nature of a trading relationship is often taken for granted and attention is given to the 'how' (i.e. process quality) rather than to the 'what' of the relationship.

Economists argue that exchange creates value since each party is better off after the exchange than they were before. A trading relationship may be valued in itself and not purely as an instrument of trade. The managerial problem is to realize a competitive strength from discerning those customers and trading situations where who interacts, and how, is valued in addition to what (good or service) is traded.

Interaction in a role (formal) relationship is determined by our knowledge of roles. Personal relationship interactions, on the other hand, derive from knowledge of the person. They inherently exhibit a greater degree of warmth, intimacy, and commitment.

With a few customers, face-to-face interaction is the natural way of trading. With many customers, impersonal contact is a necessary compromise – everyone loses something of the genuine relationship that Barnes (2001) so clearly describes. The limiting factor is the cost of communicating with customers. Automation and mediation is not the simple solution. We consider this further in Chapters 3 and 4 when we examine our thinking about communicating and managing relationships with CRM-ICT systems. Discrete transaction places people apart as objects to be manipulated. Interaction brings people together in co-operation. How do you want people to treat you?

In a business-to-business situation, there is formal formation and maintenance of a personal relationship, often underpinned by a written contract and official exchanges of information. In business-to-consumer situations, the relationship is (usually) impersonal – a state of mind – with a brand promise in mind.

Satisfaction does not necessarily lead to loyalty. Loyalty is founded on trust and liking, and brings stability to people's lives. Relaters may be forced together – co-operation is not necessarily a feature of a relationship. So-called 'loyalty' may be due to no more than convenience or lethargy. Dependency is not loyalty, but suppliers may crave the dependency of their customers (they keep buying and are not as price-sensitive as those who don't feel 'locked in'). Loyalty is fostered by repeated valuable consistent service quality and trust that the supplier and buyer have each other's best interests in mind. Of course, close ties also carry costs – lost independence, freedom of choice, and privacy.

Not all trading relationships are voluntary. What might be the benefit if more were? In Chapter 4, we ask is the Internet facilitating the balance of supply and demand by providing connections that make tie-building easier? Of course, that leaves us to ponder when (and whether) people want ties of what kind.

References

Adelman, M. B., Parks, M. R., and Albrecht, T. A. (1987) 'Supporting friends in need', in T. A. Albrecht and M. A. Adelman (eds), *Communicating Social Support*, Newbury Park, CA: Sage, pp. 105–147.

Adelman, M. B., Ahuvia, A., and Goodwin, C. (1994) 'Beyond smiling: Social support and service quality', in R. Rust and R. L. Oliver (eds) *Service Quality: New Directions in Theory and Practice*, Thousand Oaks, CA: Sage Publications, pp. 139–171.

Anton, J. (1996) *Customer Relationship Management: Making Hard Decisions with Soft Numbers*, Upper Saddle River, NJ: Prentice Hall.

Barnes, J. G. (2001) *Secrets of Customer Relationship Management: It's All About How You Make Them Feel*, New York: McGraw-Hill.

Bennett, R. (1996) 'Relationship formation and governance in consumer markets: Transactional analysis versus the behaviourist approach', *Journal of Marketing Management*, Vol. 12, No. 5, 417–436.

Broom, G. M., Casey, S., and Ritchey, J. (2000) 'Concept and theory of organization-public relationships', in J. A. Ledingham, and S. D. Bruning (eds) *Public Relations as Relationship Management: A Relational Approach to the Study and Practice of Public Relations*, Mahwah, NJ: Lawrence Erlbaum Associates, pp. 3–22.

Buttle, F. (ed.) (1996) *Relationship Marketing: Theory and Practice*, London: Paul Chapman Publishing.

Chadwick-Jones, J. K. (1976) *Social Exchange, Theory: Its Structure and Influence in Social Psychology*, New York: Academic Press.

Christensen, J. H. (1993) 'Public relations i et overkommunikeret samfund', *Mediekultur*, No. 20, 15–21 (in Danish).

Cook, K. (ed.) (1987) *Social Exchange Theory*, Newbury Park, CA: Sage.

Czepiel, J. A. (1990) 'Managing relationships with customers: A differentiating philosophy of marketing', in D. E. Bowen, R. B. Chase, and T. G. Cummings (eds) *Service Management Effectiveness: Balancing Strategy, Human Resources, Operations and Marketing*, San Francisco, CA: Jossey-Bass, pp. 299–323.

Deetz, S. A. (1992) *Democracy in an Age of Corporate Colonization: Developments in Communication and the Politics of Everyday Life*, Albany, NY: State University of New York Press.

Donaldson, B. and O'Toole, T. (1997) 'Relationship governance: The link between relationship structure and performance outcomes in industrial markets', *Proceedings of the AMA Conference on New and Evolving Paradigms: The Emerging Future of Marketing, Dublin*, Chicago, IL: American Marketing Association.

Donaldson, B. and O'Toole, T. (2002) *Strategic Market Relationships: From Strategy to Implementation*, Chichester, UK: John Wiley & Sons.

Drummond, G. and Ensor, J. (2001) *Strategic Marketing: Planning and Control*, Oxford: Butterworth-Heinemann.

Duck, S. (1991) *Understanding Relationships*, New York: Guilford Press.

Dwyer, F. R., Schurr, P. H., and Oh, S. (1987) 'Developing buyer–seller relationships', *Journal of Marketing*, Vol. 51, April, 11–27.

Fitchett, J. and McDonagh, P. (2001) 'Relationship marketing, e-commerce and the emancipation of the consumer', in A. Sturdy, I. Grugulis, and H. Willmott (eds) *Customer Service: Empowerment and Entrapment*, Basingstoke, UK: Palgrave, pp. 191–199.

Gergen, K. J., Greenberg, M. S., and Willis, R. H. (1980) *Social Exchange: Advances in Theory and Research*, New York: Plenum Press.

Giddens, A. (1979) *Central Problems in Social Theory*, Basingstoke, UK: Macmillan.

Gould, S. J. (1992) 'Marketing exchange as a product of perceived value and control', in J. N. Sheth. (ed.) *Research in Marketing*, Vol. 11, Greenwich, CN: JAI Press, pp. 115–146.

Grant, J. (2000) *The New Marketing Manifesto*, London: Orion Books.

Grönroos, C. (1990) *Service Management and Marketing: Managing the Moments of Truth in Service Competition*, Lexington, MA: Lexington Books.

Grönroos, C. (2000) *Service Management and Marketing: A Customer Relationship Management Approach*, 2nd edn, Chichester, UK: John Wiley & Sons.

Grunig, J. E. (ed.) (1992) *Excellence in Public Relations and Communication Management: Contributions to Effective Organizations*, Hillsdale, NJ: Lawrence Erlbaum Associates.

Grunig, L. A., Grunig, J. E., and Ehling, W. P. (1992) 'What is an effective organization?', in J. E. Grunig (ed.) *Excellence in Public Relations and Communication Management: Contributions to Effective Organizations*, Hillsdale, NJ: Lawrence Erlbaum Associates, pp. 65–89.

Grunig, J. E. and Hunt, T. (1984) *Managing Public Relations*, New York: Holt, Rinehart & Winston.

Grunig, J. E. and Huang, Y-H. (2000) 'From organizational effectiveness to relationship indicators: Antecedents of relationships, public relations strategies, and relationship outcomes', in J. A. Ledingham and S. D. Bruning (eds) *Public Relations as Relationship Management: A Relational Approach to the Study and Practice of Public Relations*, Mahwah, NJ: Lawrence Erlbaum Associates, pp. 23–53.

Gummesson, E. (1999) *Total Relationship Marketing: Rethinking Marketing Management – From 4Ps to 30Rs*, Oxford: Butterworth-Heinemann.

Gutek, B. A. (1995) *The Dynamics of Service: Reflections on the Changing Nature of Customer/Provider Interactions*, San Francisco: Jossey-Bass.

Halal, W. E., Geranmayeh, A., and Pourdehnad, J. (1993) *Internal Markets: Bringing the Power of Free Enterprise Inside Your Organization*, New York: John Wiley & Sons.

Hosking, D-M. (1995) 'Constructing power: Entitative and relational approaches', in D-M. Hosking, H. P. Dachler, and K. J. Gergen (eds) *Management and Organization: Relational Alternatives to Individualism*, Aldershot, UK: Avebury, pp. 51–70.

Iacobucci, D. and Ostrom, A. (1996) 'Commercial and interpersonal relationships: Using the structure of interpersonal relationships to understand individual-to-individual, individual-to-firm, and firm-to-firm relationships in commerce', *International Journal of Research in Marketing*, Vol. 13, 53–72.

Jacobs, J. (1992) *Systems of Survival: A Dialogue on the Moral Foundations of Commerce and Politics*, London: Hodder & Stoughton.

Johnson, M. D. and Gustafsson, A. (2000) *Improving Customer Satisfaction, Loyalty, and Profit*, San Francisco: Jossey-Bass.

Knapp, M. L. and Vangelisti, A. (1992) *Interpersonal Communication and Human Relationships*, Boston: Allyn & Bacon.

Ledingham, J. A. and Bruning, S. D. (eds) (2000) *Public Relations as Relationship Management: A Relational Approach to the Study and Practice of Public Relations*, Mahwah, NJ: Lawrence Erlbaum Associates.

Levinger, G. and Snoek, J. D. (1972) *Attraction in Relationships*, Morristown, NJ: General Learning Press.

Mattsson, L-G. (1997) '"Relationship Marketing" and the "Markets-as-Networks Approach" – a comparative analysis of two evolving streams of research', *Journal of Marketing Management*, Vol. 13, 447–461.

McCall, G. J., McCall, M. M., Denzin, N. K., Suttles, G. D., and Kurth, S. B. (eds) (1970) *Social Relationships*, Chicago: Aldine Publishing.

McKenna, R. (1997) *Real Time*, Cambridge, MA: Harvard Business School Press.

Milgram, S. (1967) 'The small world problem', *Psychology Today*, May, 60–67.

Morgan, G. (1992) 'Marketing discourse and practice: Towards a critical analysis', in

M. Alvesson and H. Willmott (eds) *Critical Management Studies*, London: Sage Publications.

Morgan, R. M. and Hunt, S. D. (1994) 'The commitment–trust theory of relationship marketing', *Journal of Marketing*, Vol. 58, 20–38.

Normann, R. and Ramirez, R. (1994) *Designing Interactive Strategy: From Value Chain to Value Constellation*, Chichester, UK: John Wiley & Sons.

Oliver, C. (1990) 'Determinants of interorganisational relationships: Integration and future directions', *Academy of Management Review*, Vol. 15, 241–265.

Palmer, A. (2001) 'The evolution of an idea: An environmental explanation of relationship marketing', *Journal of Relationship Marketing*, Vol. 1, No. 1, 79–94.

Parasuraman, A., Zeithaml, V. A., and Berry, L. L. (1985) 'A conceptual model of service quality and its implications for future research', *Journal of Marketing*, Vol. 49, No. 4, 41–50.

Reichheld, F. and Sasser, W. (1990) 'Zero defections: Quality comes to services', *Harvard Business Review*, September–October, 105–111.

Rogers, C. R. (1959) 'A theory of therapy, personality, and interpersonal relationships as developed in the client-centered framework', in S. Koch (ed.) *Psychology: A Study of Science*, Boston: Houghton Mifflin, pp. 184–246.

Schmitt, B. H. (1999) *Experiential Marketing: How to Get Customers to Sense, Feel, Think, Act, and Relate to Your Company and Brands*, New York: The Free Press.

Sheaves, D. E. and Barnes, J. G. (1996) 'The fundamentals of relationships: An exploration of the concept to guide marketing implementation', in T. A. Swartz, D. E. Bowen, and S. W. Brown (eds) *Advances in Services Marketing and Management: Research and Practice*, Vol. 5, Greenwich, CT: JAI Press.

Simmons, J. (2000) *We, Me, Them & It: The Power of Words in Business*, London: Texere Publishing.

Surra, C. A. and Ridley, C. A. (1991) 'Multiple perspectives on interaction: Participants, peers and observers', in B. M. Montgomery and S. Duck (eds) *Studying Interpersonal Interaction*, New York: Guilford Press, pp. 35–55.

Tynan, C. (1997) 'A review of the marriage analogy in relationship marketing', *Journal of Marketing Management*, Vol. 13, No. 7, 695–704.

Varey, R. J. (2001) *Marketing Communication: Principles and Practice*, London: Routledge.

Varey, R. J. and Lewis, B. R. (eds) (2000) *Internal Marketing: Directions for Management*, London: Routledge.

Wish, M., Deutsch, M. and Kaplan, S. J. (1976) 'Perceived dimensions of interpersonal relations', *Journal of Personality and Social Psychology*, Vol. 33, 409–420.

Zabava Ford, W. S. (1998) *Communicating with Customers: Service Approaches, Ethics, and Impact*, Cresskill, NJ: Hampton Press.

Chapter 3

INTERACTION, COMMUNICATION, AND DIALOGUE – OR INFORMATION?

Today, business is more like the dynamic relationship of dancing than it is like marriage or a one-night-stand*

Information is the oxygen of the modern age
Ronald Reagan

The centrality of language in human nature and existence means that relationships are dialogues
Professor Gwen Griffith-Dickson, Gresham College

Conversation – like hand-wrestling without the hands
William McIlvanney

Introduction

Most 'communication theory' in marketing explanation is Information Theory, borrowed from Shannon and Weaver's mathematical theory of communication, published in 1949. This 'information' explanation is concerned with accurately reproducing messages in the form of electrical signals. Yet, Relationship Marketing is a meaning-making social process of human interaction.

The relationship marketing literature generally discusses the products of communicating (trust, commitment, loyalty, and so on), but insufficiently attends to the management of the necessary social process (i.e. communicating). It is quite a different managerial mindset in play to say 'we must communicate to sell products', than to say 'we communicate, this fosters our relationship, and together we create the values we desire'.

In this chapter, we ask such questions as:

- Is relationship marketing simply a strategy for managing marketing communications?

---

* Inspired by Gummesson (1999, p. 5).

- Is a trading relationship no more than an instrument with which corporate marketers manipulate buying in their favour?
- Is 'customer loyalty' built on involvement and commitment? Does this require participation? Do buyers have to be willing to accept directives from sellers?
- Does the basic conception of 'exchange' limit the scope of relational marketing?
- Is exchange necessarily an emancipatory concept (in the sense of providing choice/freedom) to buyers?
- Is a 'relationship' a means or an end to 'communicating'? (do we communicate to establish and maintain a relationship, or do we relate in order to maintain communication?).

Increasingly, attention is being paid primarily not to 'organizations' (corporation is a more suitable term for the concept for organized collective action), not to products, not to customers, nor to communication processes, but to relationships. This is a fundamental shift in thinking from the idea of objects to be manipulated, to the notion of acting together.

The notion of relationship marketing merely as a technique is self-defeatingly instrumental, and the practices derived are largely incapable of accomplishing the espoused aims and objectives.

Information and Communication Technology (ICT) is viewed as an enabler and facilitator of the value exchange process – not the focus for analysis. In this book, the trading relationship is our primary concern.

My three selfs

Social psychology (see Stainton Rogers et al., 1995, for example) is a field that has not yet been explored adequately by marketing theorists. The work of social psychologists can help us to understand the significance of trading relationships, and has identified three interrelated self-representations:

- individual self – definable in terms of my personal traits;
- collective self – definable in terms of my group memberships;
- relational self – definable in terms of my close relationships of interdependence.

This has major significance for any social process, such as trading and marketing, since my participation in a social process produces this further version of 'me' in relation to 'we' and 'us'. Therefore, for example, a brand relationship is constructed in my attempts to recognize people like me who buy the product (or people I want to be like).

This theory also suggests that people differ in their orientation to relational concepts. Some people operate with this way of thinking while others do not. Yet, trading relationships are purposive meetings of strangers where our 'private' lives have to connect with the public realm of society. Who and what we are is tested, proved, undermined – made real – in our relationships. We largely know ourselves as we are known by others, and most of them know us only through our positions in relationships with them.

In part, our trading is motivated by the idea that things are valued for their predicted, hoped-for influence on what others will believe about us (Csikszentmihalyi and Rochberg-Halton, 1981). We pay attention to the expectations of *significant others*. How can buyers and sellers become significant others to each other? This seems to be a key question for RM practitioners.

Relating

We should reflect on the consequences of taking an entitative transaction as the basis for relationship market, when we can take an alternative relational interaction as the basis. In the field of 'managing relationships', thinking is almost universally stranded in very particular entitative taken-for-granteds. Personal characteristics of the individual person and context are treated as entities that exist separately and independently of each other. Relationships are understood as between entities, viewed as either subject or object. The subject is understood to act by gathering 'knowledge that' the other has certain characteristics and to achieve 'influence over' the other (as object) (Hosking, 1995). As we saw in Chapter 2, we can take the unit of analysis, instead, to be relational processes, thus opening up a recognition of multiple realities.

In being careful with our use of words to present concepts and theories, we can discern a very useful distinction between transaction and interaction. Our review of our conceptions of communication shows that the notion of information transmission can only make sense at the level of transaction. A participatory conception is required for making proper sense of interaction.

Following Brodie et al. (1997), it is necessary to distinguish the level at which relational marketing is operated. Therefore, relational marketing is distinct from transactional marketing, and may operate at the level of supplier firm *to* individual buyer (via database automation), at the level of individual seller *with* individual buyer, and at the level of seller firm(s) *with* buyer firm(s). In the classification discussed in Brodie et al., the former is termed Database Marketing, while the latter is termed Network Marketing. It is the other option that most interests me in this book. Interpersonal trading relationships are managed, in Brodie et al.'s terminology, in *Interaction Marketing*. The relationship and the behaviours of the parties are active and adaptive, reflecting the inherent interdependence and reciprocity. Interestingly, the study reported by Brodie et al. showed the diversification (enhancement?) of the practised approaches to marketing, with the adoption of more relational principles and practices in some situations, but not a wholesale rejection of transactional marketing (although this was most prevalent in consumer goods markets). Therefore, they rejected the notion of a paradigm shift to Relationship Marketing from Transaction Marketing, concluding that Relationship Marketing (in the three forms) is an expansion of the marketing management discipline, rather than a transformation (Figure 3.1).

Social identities connect us with other people and are the basis of our participation in social life, including trading. But are we citizen as consumer or consumer as citizen? Gabriel and Lang (1995) identify a range of roles (Table 3.1).

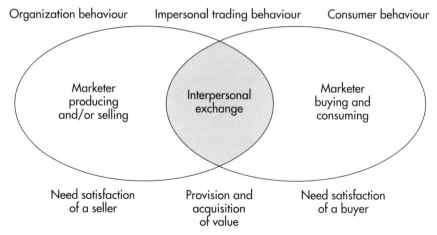

Organization behaviour   Impersonal trading behaviour   Consumer behaviour

Marketer producing and/or selling

Interpersonal exchange

Marketer buying and consuming

Need satisfaction of a seller

Provision and acquisition of value

Need satisfaction of a buyer

FIGURE 3.1   Marketers as value acquisition managers.

TABLE 3.1 How trading relationships identify people
(inspired by Gabriel and Lang, 1995).

Who/What is the consumer?	What is their stance in trading?
Sovereign	Choosing what and when to consume
Victim	Manipulated and outwitted by sellers
Explorer	In search of new experiences and meanings
Activist	Campaigning for collective rights
Communicator	Using objects in relating to others
Rebel	Using objects to express rejection and rage
Identity seeker	Seeking a real self in consuming objects
Hedonist	Experiencing personal pleasure

In examining Table 3.1, we should ask, 'what *can be* the nature of the trading relationship to provide the sought rewards?'

A Better Way of Explaining Communication for Relationship Marketing?

Communication processes penetrate all parts of the corporation, to some extent, thus modifying the position of (mostly the lower level) participants. We can usefully think of communication as a symbolic process by which orientations are reinforced or changed.

Theories of communication, stemming from different historical periods, differ in the emphasis given to issues of participation and effectiveness of presentation. Participation is concerned with: Who in a society or group has the right to con-

TABLE 3.2 Communication issues in marketing theory
(inspired by Duncan and Moriarty, 1998).

Marketing	Communication
Exchange	Relationship
Media channels	Feedback
Information	Signs and signals

tribute to the formation of meaning and the decisions of the group? Who has access to various systems of communication and can they articulate their own needs and desires within them (Deetz, 1992)? Effectiveness is concerned, on the other hand, with communicative acts as a means for the accomplishment of ends. The former is used to seek understanding and consensual decisions, while the latter is used as a tool to control.

A communication-based model of Relationship Marketing better addresses the needs of relationship building than does the traditional 4P functional marketing management model. Duncan and Moriarty's (1998) communication-based relationship marketing is a misnomer, since Relationship Marketing is inherently communicative. Indeed, relating and communicating are almost synonymous concepts.

We have to be careful about terminology here. Duncan and Moriarty, as do others, use the terms 'transactional' and 'relational'. They use the term 'transactional' in an explanation that is premised on the conduit metaphor of communicating. Therefore, their explanation of relational is entitative, not relational! The application of the conduit metaphor in explaining relationship marketing reduces the idea of a relationship to no more than a continuing series of informing transactions.

Traditionally, because marketing effect has been explained with a stimulus–response (sender–receiver) model, persuasion is taken to be synonymous with communication, but it is better seen as one of several particular subpurposes for communicating. All marketing actions are communicative – they need to be more interactive if they are to contribute to relational outcomes.

Table 3.2 summarizes the contribution of communication to marketing theory, revealing some significant alternative issues for attention in elaborating any explanation of trading relationships.

Why is this significant? In our alternative emphasis of marketing as a social process (rather than a neutral technology), compatible and/or agreeable meanings are co-produced for knowledge, and articulated in values, in desirable relationships through interaction. Relationships among customers, suppliers, and other stakeholders is a highlighted feature of 'the new marketing', as is interactivity (and concerns for balance, symmetry, and reciprocity). Feedback is more than expressed opinion on some act – it is a *reciprocal influence* – each party influences and is influenced. 'Messages' are expressions of intended meanings, but are subject to interpretation. Reception Theory (Eco, 1979) explains the receipt of information as always an interactive process of co-producing meaning.

Ford Motor Company: 'The Connection'

The objective for establishing 'The Connection' website was to link dealers in a network and to create for them customer 'feedback' that would permit dealers to respond locally, thus adding value to the customer's ownership experience. Ford owners can use an email network and are offered a range of benefits (for further details, see Grimm, 1999).

The Social System as Appreciative

Every observed act (interaction) of a person is interpreted by other people and so becomes communication only when meaning is attributed to it by the other(s) (i.e. when it is perceived *and* appreciated). Vickers (1984) could find no accepted term to describe the attaching of meaning to perceived signals to create communication. He thus referred to this mental activity and social process as 'appreciation', the code used as the 'appreciative system', and the state of the code as the 'appreciative setting'. This is how governing relations (or norms) are decided, executed, and changed. We will discuss this further as a valuable insight can be brought into our thinking about managing and learning.

Vickers (1984) clarified the nature of the problem. Culture and communication cannot be separated. For us to communicate and co-operate, we must share some common assumptions about the world we live in and some common standards by which to judge our own and each other's actions. These shared *epistemological assumptions* must correspond sufficiently with reality to make common action effective. The shared *ethical assumptions* must meet the minimal mutual needs that the members of our society require of each other. 'Culture' is the shared basis of appreciation and action which communication develops within any political system (a corporation and a market or consumption situation are subsystems of wider society).

We all have concerns, in response to each of which we construct an inner representation of the situation that is relevant to that concern. The *Appreciative System* is a pattern of concerns and their simulated relevant situations, constantly revised and confirmed by the need for it to correspond with reality sufficiently to guide action, to be sufficiently shared among people to mediate communication, and to be sufficiently acceptable for a 'good' life. The appreciative system is thus a mental construct, partly subjective, largely intersubjective (i.e. based on a shared subjective judgement), constantly challenged or confirmed by experience.

Only if the appreciative mind classifies the situation as changeable or in need of preservation, does the person devise possible responses and evaluates them with criteria determined by his or her other concerns. Therefore, 'problems' are discerned and 'solutions' sought. Action may or may not follow.

Vickers (1984) distinguished seven overlapping and coexisting ascending levels of trust and shared appreciation (Figure 3.2).

Note that dialogue – the ultimate level of appreciation – is a special kind of communication in which people 'reason together' (Bohm, 1996; Ballantyne, 1999).

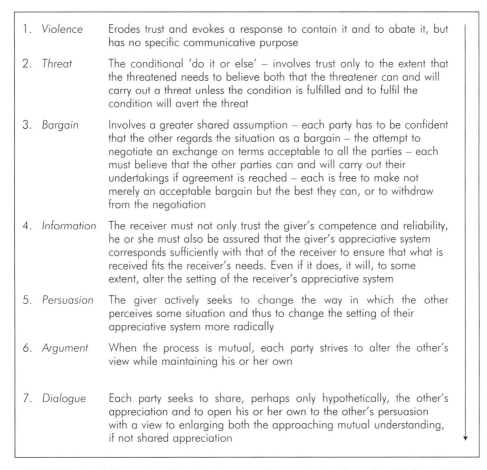

1.	*Violence*	Erodes trust and evokes a response to contain it and to abate it, but has no specific communicative purpose
2.	*Threat*	The conditional 'do it or else' – involves trust only to the extent that the threatened needs to believe both that the threatener can and will carry out a threat unless the condition is fulfilled and to fulfil the condition will avert the threat
3.	*Bargain*	Involves a greater shared assumption – each party has to be confident that the other regards the situation as a bargain – the attempt to negotiate an exchange on terms acceptable to all the parties – each must believe that the other parties can and will carry out their undertakings if agreement is reached – each is free to make not merely an acceptable bargain but the best they can, or to withdraw from the negotiation
4.	*Information*	The receiver must not only trust the giver's competence and reliability, he or she must also be assured that the giver's appreciative system corresponds sufficiently with that of the receiver to ensure that what is received fits the receiver's needs. Even if it does, it will, to some extent, alter the setting of the receiver's appreciative system
5.	*Persuasion*	The giver actively seeks to change the way in which the other perceives some situation and thus to change the setting of their appreciative system more radically
6.	*Argument*	When the process is mutual, each party strives to alter the other's view while maintaining his or her own
7.	*Dialogue*	Each party seeks to share, perhaps only hypothetically, the other's appreciation and to open his or her own to the other's persuasion with a view to enlarging both the approaching mutual understanding, if not shared appreciation

FIGURE 3.2 A hierarchy of levels of trust and appreciation (based on Vickers, 1984).

We must recognize the central role of human communication in the regulation of societies (Vickers, 1968). Nearly all that we know comes from communication, rather than from observation or direct experience. Our activities depend on communication: ways of clarifying experience, interests, standards, influence of others.

A social system (a market or service encounter sequence, for example) is a set of ongoing relationships between the person and 'organizations', governed by mutual expectations, which are usually embodied in roles. Each system has two sets of intimately linked relationships: functional – members to each other – and metabolic – the social unit to its surroundings. The regulator has three functions: noticing things about the situation (receiving information), evaluating the information (comparing it to a standard), and acting on the interpretation (selecting a response). Vickers termed this an *appreciative system*, pointing out that what is required is meaning, derived from information. Regulation is necessary to deal with problems of apportionment of scarce resources between conflicting claims and problems of conflicts between objectives (Table 3.3). Accordingly, policy-making deals with conflict as an important regulator of society, by constantly restructuring problems. Regulation is a process of mutual self-determination

TABLE 3.3 Conflict resolution strategies.

Contention	Try to convince the other to accept your position
Avoidance	Exit from the conflict (physically or emotionally)
Accommodation	Yield to some degree and lower your aspirations
Compromise	Meet part-way between preferred positions – neither is fully satisfied with the outcome
Co-operation	Work together to reconcile interests in a mutually rewarding relationship
Unconditional constructiveness	Do whatever is best for the relationship, even if the other does not reciprocate
Win–win, otherwise 'no deal'	If no solution that benefits both can be reached, then there is no deal (agree to disagree)

among conscious, communicating members (Vickers, 1984). Limits to regulation are due to the limitations of human communication in terms of our ability through collective processes mediated by communication: to generate an agreed view of a situation, to reach consensus on a course to pursue, and to arrive at common action to achieve it.

Acceptance arises from the apprehender's choices, not the initiator's intentions. Participants to a communicative event take part in a process of creating shared meaning. First, we interpret the situation, then act, influencing one another.

Communicating, then, is a joint social process in pursuit of appreciation. This inherently includes interpretation to derive meaning and judgement/evaluation. This, clearly, is much more complex than mere information 'sending' and 'receiving'.

Don't miss the Cluetrain

A powerful global conversation has begun. Through the Internet, people are discovering and inventing new ways to share relevant knowledge with blinding speed. As a direct result, markets are getting smarter – and getting smarter faster than most companies.

These markets are conversations. Their members communicate in language that is natural, open, honest, direct, funny, and often shocking. Whether explaining or complaining, joking or serious, the human voice is unmistakably genuine. It can't be faked. Most corporations, on the other hand, only know how to talk in the soothing, humorless monotone of the mission statement, marketing brochure, and your-call-is-important-to-us busy signal. Same old tone, same old lies. No wonder networked markets have no respect for companies unable or unwilling to speak as they do.

But learning to speak in a human voice is not some trick, nor will corporations convince us they are human with lip service about 'listening to customers'. They will only sound human when they empower real human beings to speak on their behalf. While many such people already work for companies today, most companies ignore their ability to deliver genuine knowledge, opting instead to crank out sterile happytalk that insults the intelligence of markets literally too smart to buy it. However, employees are getting hyperlinked even as markets are. Companies need to listen carefully to both. Mostly, they need to get out of the way so Intra-networked employees can converse directly with Internetworked markets.

Extract from the Cluetrain Manifesto [online @ www.cluetrain.com] (see also Locke et al., 2000).

Dialogue

Is unilateral 'loyalty' a sustainable condition? What of the supplier's commitment to the customer. When a buyer makes a complaint to a seller, what is his or her motivation? Customers, it has to be realized, evaluate outcomes of complaint handling.

Discussion and *dialogue* are two forms of conversation (i.e. ways of talking). Discussion is a purposive conversation that arises as people interact in presenting and defending their own respective view in search of the winning (best?) view that will support the decisions that must be made at the time. On the other hand, dialogue is a higher form of conversation that provides access to a common pool of meaning. People participate in a free and creative exploration of complex and subtle issues. There is 'deep listening' to one another and the suspension of one's own views.

Dialogue is *reasoning together in trust-based interactions* (Ballantyne, 1999). This theory is highly significant for marketing communication managers since dialogue and knowledge generation in relationship marketing create and contribute value for stakeholders – customers, suppliers, and other people.

Discussion and dialogue are alternative ways of talking – they are different modes of communication that are potentially complementary and can be valuably balanced as counterparts. Discussion is (reproductive) *competitive advocacy communication*, engaged in for reasons of conformity and stability. Dialogue is (productive) *collective inquiring communication* for learning and innovation. This terminology is drawn from Senge's (1990) very helpful discussion of Bohm's work on dialogue (see Bohm et al., 1991 and Bohm, 1996). Bohm also points out that, crucially, hierarchy is antithetical to dialogue.

Dialogue is a way of observing, collectively, how hidden values and intentions can control our behaviour, and how unnoticed cultural differences can clash without our realizing what is occurring. It can, therefore, be seen as an arena in which collective learning takes place and out of which a sense of increased harmony, fellowship, and creativity can arise.

It is worthwhile to revisit our earlier question on what we can imagine human communication to be like (see Matson and Montagu, 1967, for a range of perspectives) – and thus how we might try to manage communication for a purpose. Often we nowadays see the phrase 'interactive communication'. This is misleading. To be conceptually clear, *interaction* is any action that generates a response. In marketing systems, interaction is mutual and requires participation. *Communication* is a special kind of interaction that enables communicators to construct meaning by speaking and listening. These reflective conversations are entered into in order to get beyond the understanding of any one person (a 'third way of knowing' – Shotter, 1993) – so, dialogue moves from interaction to participation. This is where many writers on marketing have gone wrong – relationship marketing is much more about partnering (dialoguing) in co-operative relationships than it is about managing information. We need the term 'communicative interaction' to provide the necessary emphasis for the management task. Marketing managers manage communication systems.

Along for the ride

Buyers of a Harley Davidson motorcycle receive a one-year membership in The Harley Davidson Owners Group (HOG). They are mailed humorous reminder cards, club member magazines, and an easy-to-use renewal kit when they are due to renew their $40 annual membership. The campaign has produced a 75% renewal rate among the more than 400,000 members (generating $16M in revenue) (Newell, 2000).

All communication media are interactive, to a degree. Interactivity is not a feature unique to electronic/online information and communication technologies. Interactivity is not even a characteristic solely of a medium – it is the use of the media that determines the level of interactivity. The notion of interaction is often reduced to mere reaction – systems that set up the possibility of interaction do not ensure this feature in human communicating.

Market and customer information is typically responded to in predefined and self-confirmatory ways. So-called 'dialogues' are less open than is supposed. The notion of responsiveness implies some convergence of communicators. But managers pursue controlled adaptation to offset uncertainty and turbulence, therefore information exchange is controlled, adapting customers to the corporation in ways that are pre-specified by professional categories and routines (e.g. managing the marketing mix) (Christensen, 1997).

Making Understanding from Misunderstanding

A group of people who interact for the purpose of trading is a purposeful communication system. The Appreciative System is an interesting framework for understanding a communication system. Such a system is capable of overcoming the natural outcome of efforts to communicate – misunderstanding – that is inherent in the nature of language use (see Heyman, 1994). Counterproductive behaviour is exposed in such systems.

Much 'communication' and 'interaction' practice is ping-pong in nature, with individuals talking at/past/over each other – in a dyadic pair of monologues –

rather than with each other (reciprocal manipulation). Two temporally and spatially co-located, but independent, communication systems are operating in this situation. 'Feedback' is purported to complete the cycle, but often is little more than reaction (in the terms of the speaker). Heyman clarifies the manner in which each person contributes talk, but there is only limited communication. Note, however, that talking past each other in a monological dyad is not the same as dialogue. Communicating is better seen as interacting that co-constructs meaning by making context differences explicit, leading through common inter-pretation to a shared understanding. Why does this not naturally occur?

According to Heyman, language use (talk) inherently creates misunderstand-ing, because language is necessarily: *indexical* (context gives meaning to our talk) and *reflexive* (context depends on meaning). The context for understanding each other does not automatically arise (it is not pre-existent); we are responsible for creating our own context for understanding. The meaning of a situation comes from the combination of person, place, time, and so on. Talk is naturally ambiguous – we never know all that the other person knows. All language use is in a context, therefore meaning-making comes through interpretation. It is not the words of language that are the basis of communication, it is previous and current interaction that are at the heart of communicating, to provide understand-ing. Interaction does the communicating, language use clarifies. Experience may be past and present.

Misunderstanding arises when the communicators create differing contexts for understanding. In this context misunderstanding is differing understanding. Personal context is a taken-for-granted knowledge. The shared context necessary for shared understanding is created in interaction.

What are the implications of the inherent indexicality and reflexivity of language that is a barrier to shared understanding? First, interactors (communi-cators) each have a responsibility for creating shared context for understanding. Second, we need to understand misunderstanding to create shared understanding founded on shared context through strategic talk. Third, the service encounter (Grönroos, 2000, argues that all trading now centres on service) has to be a mutual context-creating interaction (we jointly create the world we experience).

Misunderstanding is natural but can be avoided through what Heyman calls Strategic Talk; that is, conscious effort to talk in order to create context and under-standing, using techniques of formulations, questions and answers, paraphrasing, examples, and stories. Strategic talk as a purposeful conversation is an interesting model for the conduct of a trading relationship.

The Participatory Conception of Communication

In adopting the conduit metaphor (of messages sent to receivers), management is taken to be a control mechanism located in a fixed structure. This is an instrumental model that treats communication as a means to a predetermined end, that of control by the sender or the receiver.

The traditional Communication Studies field has grown from the seed of Shannon and Weaver's transmissive model of communication, and should now be abandoned (this argument is developed further in Varey, 2000). No serious communication theorist would still accept this model, but it has been the most influential and reflects common sense, yet it is misleading. The endurance of the informational model of communication in popular discussion is a liability. In reflecting the naive realist notion of meanings as pre-existent and to be discovered so that we can transmit our thoughts to each other, this model fundamentally devalues the creativity of the act of appreciation. We should abandon unreflective (managerialistic) accounts of communication management and turn more to reflective (managerial) approaches.

The alternative participatory conception of communication promotes organization as structured human relationships (mutual, but not necessarily shared, expectations), but does not inherently and covertly support the deployment of power over others. Of course, this provides the threat of undermining the very conditions on which power and status are built – but do we want to create or reproduce?

In a turbulent social milieu, the manager role makes more sense as that of the steward of a responsive and responsible productive community. As router and filter in the shunting of information between isolates, the manager has no value-creating role.

Most of us are still operating in outmoded instrumental–technical (masculine agent) modes in pursuit of control – communication is seen as a conduit for the transmission or transportation of expressions of self-interest (i.e. informational for understanding) – these no longer suffice. Information conceptions of communication only work in situations in which consensus on meaning, identities, construction of knowledge, and basic values can be taken for granted – this is no longer a realistic view of our world. If we control through information systems, we are in danger of non-responsive self-referentiality – what Hayek (1990) called the 'fatal conceit' of human reason – we don't ask questions because we think we have the answers. Some crucial questions are never asked. Imaginary worlds are misrecognized as real. Management practice distorts, manufactures (artificial) consent, excludes, suppresses differences – asymmetrical power relations suppress natural conflicts. Social divisions are assumed to be fixed and in need of promotion. Consensus over problems, personal identities, knowledge claims, norms of interaction, and policies for directing joint action are assumed as the basis for interaction, when they need to be negotiated through interaction for creativity and to meet diverse stakeholder interests. When the 'corporation' is taken to be the senior management team, all other stakeholders are externalized as costs to be contained. Then, stakeholders are managed for the managers' benefit.

We must shift from our general belief in liberal quasi-'democracy' and its adversarial expression of self-interest, opinion advocacy, and persuasion, to a constitutive real participatory democracy of negotiated co-determination through interaction ('It's good to talk' is a moral stance). We need to move from controlling to stewardship – this requires a mindshift from self-interest to service, from patriarchy to partnership, from consent to co-ordination, from dependency to empowerment, from involvement to participation. Feminine inclinations toward communion are constructive.

'Communications' are best understood as interaction acts, not as objects and artefacts. We communicate when we interact. Communication is best understood as constitutive – interests should be understood as social products, often produced by decisions and opportunities. The moral question is are all positions granted an equal right of co-determination? Morally, psychology pursues reflective autonomy (of the person), sociology pursues legitimate social order (of the collective), and communication pursues equitable participation (in the social system). We need a communication theory of managing – this is largely a personal value decision – about why, rather than about how.

Relating, Involvement, and Participation

From the point of view of ensuring that systems are operating for requisite communicative interaction, involvement may be thought of as a mode of productive working, while participation is a means to produce involvement. Participation is a special case of 'organizational' or 'internal' communication.

From a communication perspective, participation is the discretionary interactions of persons and groups that result from co-operative links that cross the traditional worker–manager role and responsibility boundaries. A participation network is an alternative to a traditional hierarchical management system. Participatory networks are systems of exchange and integration, in that participation is an articulation of diverse interests and points of view. This is in contrast to the coercion and separation of the traditional structure. Thus:

> ... *worker participation comprises organizational structures and processes designed to empower and enable employees to identify with organizational goals and to collaborate as control agents in activities that exceed minimum co-ordination efforts normally expected at work.*
>
> (Stohl and Cheney, 2001, p. 357)

Participatory processes may be found as parallel structures such as quality circles and internal marketing, or as an integral part of corporate reorganization (work teams), or as a fundamental way of doing business (co-operatives). Workers engage in a range of activities with more knowledge of the business than otherwise, with an explicit effort to promote trust, support, and commitment to high-performance goals, and commensurate rights and responsibilities.

In everyday life outside the workplace, the mature person is considered normal if they initiate, plan, execute, and take responsibility for their own actions within the guiding framework of society's norms and laws. Strangely, still, in the workplace the situation is often very different. A person is then expected to be subordinate, passive, and dependent on the boss (more dependent at lower levels in the 'chain of command' and as the job controls the person).

Superiors are described by subordinates as considerate when they allow participation in decision-making and encourage communicative interaction. The subordinates then exhibit more positive attitudes and behaviours, and research has shown that this can result in greater job satisfaction and performance, and lower labour turnover and fewer grievances. Further research suggests that the effect of participation varies with personal need for independence and the nature of the work itself. Some other studies have suggested that it may even be the positive orientation of some employees that leads to positive descriptions of others' behaviour and even the invoking of participative behaviour.

Participation

As early as 1925, Follet argued that the most effective use of managerial authority is to establish personal face-to-face interaction, to seek feedback, and to elicit co-operation. Argyris (1957, 1964) identified incongruence between managers and workers, stemming from their very different goals. Alienation results from exclusion from decision-making, while dehumanization results from a cold, uncaring manner of management. Workers will act in the best interests of the corporation when they identify corporate goals as their own.

Likert (1961, 1967) stresses that the key element in initiating full worker participation in organizational processes is the development of supportive communication among workers and managers. The manager needs to act as a go-between by representing views from workers to executives and from executives to workers. The manager is thus a 'linchpin' for leaders and followers. Likert's studies resulted in four characterizations of alternative ways of managing (Figure 3.3).

Likert argues that System 4 is a generally beneficial alternative to the other ways of managing.

Participation is often sought through a programme of activities that promotes customer interests and reconfigures the corporation as a customer–supplier chain (du Gay and Salaman, 1992). Other purposes include the improvement of

System 1: Exploitative–authoritative	System 2: Benevolent–authoritative
Autocratic – tight control and authority	Softened autocracy
Motivation from fear of punishment	Complaints and opinions can be voiced
Little opportunity for participation	
Managers and workers are in conflict	Manipulative, since workers have no power or responsibility

System 3: Consultative	System 4: Participative–group
Communication and co-operation encouraged	Workers encouraged to participate in goal-setting and decision-making
Managers recognize value of hands-on information, but do not trust workers' judgement	Managers support workers, depending on their feedback and ideas
	Manager and workers identify with each other

FIGURE 3.3   Alternative management systems (derived from Likert, 1967).

productivity and performance, individual development, human rights, and 'riding the bandwagon for good public relations'.

What are the objectives of employee participation? Should participation be pursued in its own right, or as a means to improved productive efficiency, or to improve employee well-being? Greater autonomy and responsibility may benefit the person or the corporation, or both – but these outcomes do not necessarily result. The introduction of any system implies the need for extensive learning throughout an institution, in group problem-solving techniques and collective decision-making, for example. Benefits that might be realized through worker participation include increased support networks, the opening of level-spanning communication links, enhanced worker awareness of the 'big picture', and an enhanced knowledge-base in the operation of the business.

Orientation toward Directives

Deetz's (1995) analysis of political and decision practices provides a further insight into the significance of communication to the question of involvement and participation. Political practice deals with what is said (see Figure 3.4). So, language is taken to be used, at one extreme, to neutrally express in order to represent things that are taken to be fixed in the (internal) mind and in the (external) world. Therefore, interaction is taken to be a means for the reproduction of meanings, ideas, and so on that reside independently elsewhere. In the constitutive conception, however, things said (in speech and writing) are active in the production of meaning, judgements, and feelings. Discursive processes of making distinctions, attending to the world in particular ways, and of producing individual identity are active and fundamental.

Decision practices are those interactions in the collective efforts to resolve differences in groups and communities. These practices can be relatively open and participatory or closed and exclusive. Inclusionary practices are co-determinate through co-ordination, while dominatory practices are controlled. Informational explanations of interaction are premised in the desire for control, while dialogic communication extends co-determination.

Therefore, involvement is a negotiative expression in which information is widely distributed (although the processes of information formation are not explored) in the pursuit of determining the best of competing positions, by applying better argument and expertise. Participation, on the other hand, is a negotiative constitution based on giving voices to different positions, the negotiation of values and decisional premises, and the production of emergent integrative positions. Dominant positions can be contested in 'genuine conversation'.

These two approaches are contrasted with strategy and consent (Figure 3.4). Strategy is a dominant expression directly based on power, using rewards, propaganda, coercion, and manipulation to control motivation, attitudes, and action. Information is intentionally distributed in line with dominant group interests. Consent is a dominant constitution indirectly working through ideologies, common sense, routine and standard practices, and discipline. Choices for action are controlled hegemonically, casting contestations as irrational and ill

FIGURE 3.4 Orientations in social processes (derived from Deetz, 1995, p. 100).

informed. Information is widely distributed, but systematically distorted, while conflict is suppressed, and resistance is unfocused and actively discouraged.

In Deetz's analysis, strategy is clearly an information orientation (informing as a means), whereas participation is a communication orientation to managing (communicating as a mode).

Etzioni's (1961) comparative study provides a clear explanation of a range of types of complex organization in terms of compliance relationships. Compliance is a relation in which an actor behaves in accordance with a directive supported by another actor's power. Compliance is also the orientation of the subordinated actor to the power applied. Those who have power manipulate means over which they have command in such a manner that certain other actors find following the directive rewarding and not following it incurs deprivations. Therefore, compliance relations are always asymmetric, since the subordinates have less power. The means manipulated to support directives include physical, material, and symbolic rewards and deprivations.

The orientation (involvement) of the subordinated actor may be positive (commitment) or negative (alienation). This is determined partly by the degree to which the power applied is considered legitimate by the subordinated actor, and partly by its congruence with the action desired. So, in any compliance relationship, an actor exercises power, and another actor, subject to this power, responds to the subjection with either more or less alienation or more or less commitment.

Etzioni describes three kinds of power and three kinds of involvement, and indicates the range of possible associations that may be found in social units as they pursue goals. Power is an actor's ability to induce or influence another actor's behaviour in accordance with their own intentions. Incumbents of power positions have access to means of power over others who are subject to this power, and are thus subordinated. Those higher in rank are organizational representatives, while those lower in rank are participants.

Power differs in terms of the means employed to gain the compliance of subjects:

- *Coercive* power – the application of, or threat of application of, *physical* sanctions such as the infliction of pain, deformity, or death, or the generation of frustration through the restriction of movement, or control of the satisfaction of needs (food, comfort, security, etc.).
- *Remunerative* power – control over *material* resources and rewards through the allocation of payments, benefits, services, and commodities.
- *Normative/social* power – the allocation and manipulation of symbolic rewards and deprivations through leadership, manipulation of mass media, allocation of esteem and prestige symbols, administration of ritual, and influence over the allocation and manipulation of acceptance and positive response. The former is usually found in hierarchical relations, while the latter is more common in peer relations (hence the term social, suggesting informal).

All three kinds of power are exercised in most organizations, but to differing degrees. One kind is usually predominant. When two kinds of power are emphasized over a group at the same time, they tend to neutralize each other. Therefore, organizations tend to specialize in their application of power.

Etzioni also identified three types of involvement (Figure 3.5) – one means by which organizations realize their goals is the positive orientation of the participant to the organizational power. Involvement is the person's orientation to the (organized) corporation or institution as a power (or control) system. *Commitment* is a positive involvement, while *alienation* is a negative involvement.

The intensity of involvement can range from highly committed through mildly committed, to mildly alienated to highly alienated.

Etzioni applies the following definitions to all social units, not just business organizations.

Alienative involvement is an intense negative orientation, characteristic of hostile foreigners, and typical of isolated trading transactions in which each tries to maximize immediate profit for themselves. Each actor is treated by the other as a 'means' to their end. *Calculative* involvement is a low-intensity, positive or negative orientation that is predominant among those with continuing business contacts, and characterizes attitudes of, and toward, permanent customers. Actors

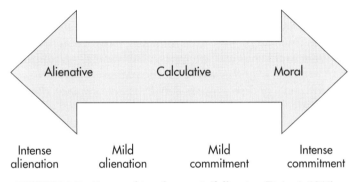

FIGURE 3.5   Zones of involvement (following Etzioni, 1961).

Relationship dyad	Form of compliance
Coercive–alienative	Coercive
Remunerative–calculative	Utilitarian
Normative–moral	Normative

FIGURE 3.6 Congruent compliance relationships.

are 'means' toward individual ends for each other. *Moral* involvement is an intense positive orientation of a devoted, loyal follower.

Pure involvement is based on internalized norms and identification with authority (in superordinate–subordinate) relationships, whereas social involvement exhibits a sensitivity to pressures of primary groups and members (in peer relationships).

Etzioni identified three congruent compliance relationships (Figure 3.6). The relationships are congruent when the kind of involvement due to other factors is the same as that produced by the predominant kind of power operating. Congruence provides effective organization.

Corporations require much more compliance than do other forms of collectivity. Involvement is positive when an action (directive) is conceived of as legitimate and gratifying.

Various types of participant may be discerned, defined by the nature of their involvement, their degree of subordination, and their level of performance obligations. Accordingly, customers and clients tend to have alienative involvement, while members (of a church, club, etc.) tend to have moral involvement. Employees, on the other hand, tend toward calculative involvement. Indeed, we could define involvement as the level of acceptance of a cultural system, and could thus expect to find various levels of acceptance. Elites (the dominant coalition, the executive group) more fully accept, and thus represent, the system (the corporation), while others (managers) may accept in part. Others may well be opposed to most of the system and some will attempt to maintain a subculture.

Arguably, teamwork and worker participation programmes are modern means of control and conflict suppression in the workplace (Deetz, 1992) that avoid authoritarian practices by fostering involvement. For example, some dignity is encouraged, producing high levels of self-worth, even in the face of deskilling. However, in the face of changes in expectations of participation, the very programmes that promote participatory democracy are usually implemented strategically for the 'management' of culture through teaching of value and loyalty (as a tool for control) rather than through any moral recognition of their social importance. Of course, these new systems do have democratic potential – yet they are almost always premised on, and dominated by, managerial precepts, assumptions, and practices. Teamworking produces reduced worker resistance, thereby enhancing managerial control. The context within which decisions are allowed is prescribed. The value of the team concept in enabling open discussions that would help meet the many potential corporate objectives is lost when goals are one-sided and participatory programmes are co-optive.

Such programmes are enacted by managers on employees, allowing only limited participation to a narrow set of issues by only one stakeholder. This extends managerial interests by reaffirming managers' controlling 'parental' positions (Deetz, 1995). The good things of loyalty and commitment (to the corporation) are sought, yet the participation allowed by an asymmetrical power distribution often results in control, subordination, and abuse. As a worker participation programme, the arrangement confirms (unchallenged) managers' prerogatives in issues and decisions, and workers participate only to the extent that they consent to the arrangement, and are deemed to be irrational or uncooperative if they resist. These programmes are often resisted by those who are supposed to be empowered, precisely because they function more to increase commitment and close down alternative perspectives than genuinely to represent stakeholders.

Explaining Communication in Participation Processes

Participation, of course, is not only the social condition for more people talking about more things more of the time. Much co-ordination is required, so frequent and complex interaction must occur. Communication networks will have greater range, diversity, interconnections, and information richness than those found in traditional, hierarchically organized corporations. Participatory communication (as distinct from 'objectively informing' communication) can increase commitment to acting on decisions and increase identification with work processes.

Human interaction can be explained, as we have seen, using either an informational approach or a communicational approach. Two metaphors for explaining human communication are discernible. The transmissive (conduit) metaphor is premised on the notion of distribution information and assumes fixed meanings and focuses on the codes and means of transmission. Therefore, 'communicators' engage in particular practices because:

> I already have the required meaning for this (desired) situation, and I talk to you because I want to change your choices of possible actions – I seek to persuade.

Social approaches to communication are in opposition to a psychological approach, and characterized as 'organic' rather than 'mechanistic', concerned with 'ritual' rather than 'transmission', and fundamentally 'interpretive' rather than 'scientific' or 'functional' (Leeds-Hurwitz, 1995, provides a comprehensive collection of essays around this 'new paradigm'; see also Gergen, 1999 and Putnam and Pacanowsky, 1983).

Social approaches to communication describe events occurring between people in the process of interacting. Interpretation focuses on the way individuals make sense of their work through their communicative behaviours. This is in contrast to the reporting of how events are perceived through a single individual's understanding. So, communication is thought of as inherently collaborative and co-operative visible behaviour, rather than as merely personal cognition. Social Communication Theory (Sigman, 1987) suggests that communication is not to be taken, in reductionist fashion, as a process through which individual cognitions are exchanged, or as a process of information transmission between isolated 'senders' and 'receivers'. Rather, interpersonal behaviour is a moment in social communication. A particular definition of what constitutes communication is adopted. This focuses on process as well as product or outcome. For example, Carey (1975) defines communication as 'a symbolic process whereby reality is produced, maintained, repaired, and transformed.'

Social reality is not seen as a fact or set of facts existing prior to human activity – it is created in human interaction (see Berger and Luckmann, 1966, for the classic exposition of this view, and Gergen, 1985). Berger and Luckmann analysed knowledge in society in the context of a theory of society as a dialectical process between objective and subjective reality. They concluded that people interact and produce meaningful behaviour patterns that construct a shared reality. We create our social world through our words and other symbols and through our behaviours. Such an approach requires that we question the validity of traditional 'scientific' experiments. The business of the interpretivist is not to reveal the world to us but to create some part of the world for us: 'Inquiry is the professional practice of the social creation of reality' (Anderson, 1990). Interaction is forwarded as a creative social accomplishment. Deetz feels very strongly that 'If the study of human communication is not ultimately the study of how we *make* the world in which we have our human existence, then it is as trivial as our dominant "model" of it would seem to say it is' (Deetz, 1995, p. 130). Further, 'Communication, then, is the process in which we create and maintain the "objective" world, and, in doing so, create and maintain the only human existences we can have' (Deetz, 1995, p. 203).

The central problem attended to is how social meanings are created. The focus is on people not as passive rule-followers operating within pre-existing regulations, but as active agents – rule-makers within social contexts. Identity is seen as a social construction, and the study of social role and cultural identity leads to the study of power and what happens when particular identities are chosen or ascribed by others. The concept of culture is central and is defined as the knowledge that people must learn to become appropriate members of a given society. Cultural contexts include the community in which particular communicative behaviours arise. Social approaches are mostly holistic – the study of interaction requires the whole picture to understand how the multiple components are related.

Reddy (1993) observed that our major metaphor for communication takes ideas as objects that can be put into words, language as their container, thought as the manipulation of these objects, and memory as storage. Accordingly, in this view we send ideas in words through a conduit – a channel of communication – to someone else who then extracts the ideas from the words. A consequence of this metaphor is that we believe that ideas can be extracted and can exist independently of people. We also expect that when communication occurs someone extracts the same idea from the language that was put in by someone else. Meaning is taken to be a thing. But the conduit metaphor hides all the effort that is involved in communication, and many people take it as a definition of communication.

Mantovani (1996) heralds the obsolescence of the *old model of communication* as the transfer of information from one person to another. No longer should we be satisfied with an outmoded model which conceives of communication as the transportation of an inert material – the information that actors exchange with each other – from one point to another along a 'pipeline'. There is in this view no account of the co-operation that stimulates reciprocal responsibility for interaction and the series of subtle adaptations, which occur among 'interlocutors'. Nor does the old model consider that communication is possible only to the extent that participants have some common ground for shared beliefs, they recognize reciprocal expectations, and accept rules for interaction which anchor the developing conversation. The old theory of communication treats knowledge as an object (i.e. as a body of information as independent facts to be processed) existing independently of the participants that can be carried through channels and possessed by a receiver when communication is successful. The new, *alternative conception of communication* is of a common construction of meanings. Information is not moved from one place to another – it is always a means to an end, produced and used by social actors to attain their goals in daily life. Knowledge arises out of action – what we know is bound up with what we do (Weick, 1979, 1995). Knowledge is a social phenomenon:

> We collectively know not just something more but something different from what any of us individually knows.
>
> (Taylor, 1999)

Therefore, the participatory (dialogic) conception or ritual metaphor implies characteristically different practices from those of the adopter of the transmissive metaphor of communication. They seek personal interaction or interpersonal action – communicative interaction:

> Meaning is always incomplete and partial, and the reason that I talk to you is to better understand what I and you mean, in the hope that we can find more satisfying ways of acting together – I seek to create and learn.

Communication is about transformation, not information (Deetz, 1995). Of course, the connection between the explanation of interaction as informational (neutral and self-evident) and managerial control is both obvious and self-conscious. Even as contemporary notions of management emphasize culture, empowerment, diversity, and participation, they are grounded in an informational (self-defeating) conception of communication. Informing and communicating are *alternative* ways of interacting, with different objectives (control vs. co-determination).

A conception of communication is needed that is capable of providing fundamentally a negotiative, participatory democracy to replace the commonplace, control-centred corporate structures, and participation and empowerment programmes that are based on adversarial free expression, the pursuit of self-interests, and information-based rational decision-making. This would allow the necessary reintegration of the management of work with the doing of work (Deetz, 1995).

Summary

A genuine relationship can begin when two people carry out reciprocally successful acts of attribution, thus defining and putting the other in a particular position. As consumers (buyers) and sellers, we think, feel, decide, and act in relation to ourselves and others. The Appreciative System explanation helps us to a more comprehensive understanding than does the widely used decision-making model of consumer behaviour and marketing theory.

In developing a relationship, both parties talk and listen. Marketing that only talks to supposedly listening customers is unrealistically one-sided, and thus misguided and incomplete. If we explain communication as a participatory social process of making knowledge, meaning, and identity, we can avoid the counterproductive behaviour of reciprocal manipulation. Communicating can be taken to be a cycle of act, interact, and react.

The 'interactive' school of marketing, as distinct from the managerial school that prevails in the textbooks, examines the balance of power between buyers and sellers in interdependent exchange relationships (see Sheth et al., 1988, for a thorough review of 12 schools of marketing theory). Either party may conduct marketing activities – neither party can act in isolation. Social exchange is seen as the fundamental foundation of marketing. This requires a participatory conception of communication.

Communication is a much more inclusive, more encompassing concept than persuasion (includes inquiring as well as advocating). Marketers are then listeners, requestors, suggestors, promisers, and so on, and not only advertisers. In the jargon of eCRM, 'contact' then has a much richer meaning. Contact points are moments in time at which meaning is co-constructed – they are points of appreciation. These may be natural – part of the product in use. Or, they may be contrived – one party makes an effort to communicate with the other.

The communication objective of 'shared understanding' is better termed *compatible understanding*, since 'shared' implies an apportioned, singular way of thinking. Therefore, marketing is taken to be value-making rather than value-taking, in a network of relationships constituted by interacting communities of particular world views.

Communication objectives can contribute to the accomplishment of interaction objectives, that contribute to relationship objectives, that contribute to business objectives. Corporate memory is the totality of what we know and understand about the trading relationship – suggesting that an eCRM system should support marketers' appreciations.

Integrated Marketing Communication (IMC) is an essential contributing way of organizing for Relationship Marketing. This integrates traditional media advertising, direct marketing, public relations, and other marketing communication acts, with buyer-driven and seller-driven communicative encounters in the production and consumption of goods and services and customer service.

Relational bonds are not limited to customers. Stakeholders can have more than one type of bond with a seller. Employees can also be shareholders and competitors can be customers, for example.

The Relationship Marketing way of trading set out here recognizes the significance and consequences of the power balance in seller–buyer relationships. The customer is not assumed to be subordinate. Each party has an equal right to participate in a process of dialogue (a marketing conversation). Both are motivated to participate in communicating with the other. Either may initiate interaction, for the other to respond (each is a correspondent).

Questions of power cannot be sensibly ignored in a relationship. Parties are entitled to ask 'how is value produced?' and 'who is entitled to some of it?'.

Trading is a mode of relating. Who loses when trading relationships are treated as commodities?

Communication is not a component of Relationship Marketing, but rather the mode of interaction. Traditional marketing communication is inefficient and costly, as well as being received as manipulative. Outcomes are limited because customers are not involved.

The language of Relationship Marketing differs from the tradition of marketing as persuasion:

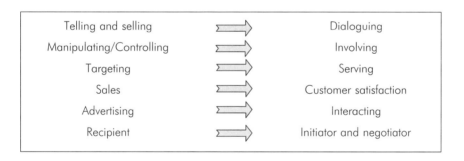

Telling and selling	⟹	Dialoguing
Manipulating/Controlling	⟹	Involving
Targeting	⟹	Serving
Sales	⟹	Customer satisfaction
Advertising	⟹	Interacting
Recipient	⟹	Initiator and negotiator

The unit of analysis for managing trading is shifting from predominantly products and producers, to people, social processes, and social systems – markets are networks of bonded relationships, with actors, activities, and resources. Interpersonal communication is a processual element of relational networks.

Adaptation of resources and/or ways of operating brings about co-ordination of exchanges for mutual benefit (performance, bonds, atmosphere). Each interactor creates his or her own interpretations and can reinterpret from differing points of view. The managerial need is to recognize marketing as socially constructed from processes of negotiation, in particular contexts, between people. It is to consider Relationship Marketing as relationship management that we turn to Chapter 4.

References

Anderson, J. A. (1990) *Communication Yearbook*, Vol. 13, Newbury Park, CA: Sage Publications, p. 14.

Argyris, C. (1957) *Personality and Organization*, New York: Harper & Row.

Argyris, C. (1964) *Integrating the Individual and the Organization*, New York: John Wiley & Sons.

Ballantyne, D. (1999) 'Dialogue and knowledge generation: Two sides of the same coin in relationship marketing', *Proceedings of the 2nd WWW Conference on Relationship Marketing, November–February, Monash University*, Bradford, UK: MCB University Press, @ www. mcb.co.uk/services/conferen/nov99/rm/paper3.html

Berger, P. L. and Luckmann, T. (1966/1971) *The Social Construction of Reality: A Treatise in the Sociology of Knowledge*, New York: Doubleday.

Bohm, D., Factor, D., and Garrett, P. (1991) 'Dialogue: A proposal', speech transcript, @ www.davidbohmbooks.com.

Bohm, D. (1996) *On Dialogue*, London: Routledge.

Brodie, R. J., Coviello, N. E., Brookes, W., and Little, V. (1997) 'Towards a paradigm shift in marketing? An examination of current marketing practices', *Journal of Marketing Management*, Vol. 13, 383–406.

Carey, J. W. (1975) 'A cultural approach to communication', *Communication*, Vol. 2, 17.

Christensen, L. T. (1997) 'Marketing as auto-communication', *Consumption, Markets & Culture*, Vol. 1, No. 3, 197–227.

Csikszentmihalyi, M. and Rochberg-Halton, E. (1981) *The Meaning of Things: Symbols in the Development of the Self*, Cambridge: Cambridge University Press.

Deetz, S. A. (1992) *Democracy in an Age of Corporate Colonization: Developments in Communication and the Politics of Everyday Life*, Albany, NY: State University of New York Press.

Deetz, S. A. (1995) *Transforming Communication, Transforming Business: Building Responsive and Responsible Workplaces*, Creskill, NJ: Hampton Press.

du Gay, P. and Salaman, G. (1992) 'The cult[ure] of the customer', *Journal of Management Studies*, Vol. 29, No. 5, 615–633.

Duncan, T. and Moriarty, S. E. (1998) 'A communication-based marketing model for managing relationships', *Journal of Marketing*, Vol. 62, No. 2, 1–13.

Eco, U. (1979) *The Role of the Reader*, Bloomington, IN: Indiana University Press.

Etzioni, A. (1961) *A Comparative Analysis of Complex Organizations: On Power, Involvement, and Their Correlates*, New York: Free Press.

Follett, M. P. (1925) 'Giving of orders', lecture transcript republished in D. S. Pugh (ed.) *Organization Theory: Selected Readings*, London: Penguin Books.

Gabriel, Y. and Lang, T. (1995) *The Unmanageable Consumer: Contemporary Consumption and its Fragmentation*, London: Sage Publications.

Gergen, K. J. (1985) 'Social constructionist inquiry: Context and implications', in K. J. Gergen and K. E. Davis (eds) *The Social Construction of the Person*, New York: Springer-Verlag.

Gergen, K. J. (1999) *An Invitation to Social Construction*, London: Sage Publications.

Grimm, M. (1999) 'Ford connects: Hatches massive relationship program via Web', *Brandweek*, Vol. 40, No. 1, January, 19–20.

Grönroos, C. (2000) *Service Management and Marketing: A Customer Relationship Management Approach*, 2nd edn, Chichester, UK: John Wiley & Sons.

Gummesson, E. (1999) *Total Relationship Marketing: Rethinking Marketing Management – From 4Ps to 30Rs*, Oxford: Butterworth-Heinemann.

Hayek, F. A. (1990) *The Fatal Conceit: The Errors of Socialism*, Chicago, IL: University of Chicago Press.

Heyman, R. (1994) *Why Didn't You Say That in the First Place?: How to Be Understood at Work*, San Francisco: Jossey-Bass.

Hosking, D-M. (1995) 'Constructing power: Entitative and relational approaches', in D-M. Hosking, H. P. Dachler, and K. J. Gergen (eds) *Management and Organization: Relational Alternatives to Individualism*, Aldershot, UK: Avebury, pp. 51–70.

Leeds-Hurwitz, W. (ed.) (1995) *Social Approaches to Communication*, New York: Guilford Press.

Likert, R. (1961) *New Patterns of Management*, New York: McGraw-Hill.

Likert, R. (1967) *The Human Organization: Its Management and Value*, New York: McGraw-Hill.

Locke, C., Levine, R., Searls, D., and Weinberg, D. (2000) *The Cluetrain Manifesto: The End of Business as Usual*, Cambridge, MA: Perseus Books.

Mantovani, G. (1996) *New Communication Environments: From Everyday to Virtual*, London: Taylor & Francis.

Matson, F. W. and Montagu, A. (eds) (1967) *The Human Dialogue: Perspectives on Communication*, New York: The Free Press.

Newell, F. (2000) *Loyalty.com*, London: McGraw-Hill.

Putnam, L. L. and Pacanowsky, M. E. (eds.) (1983) *Communication and Organizations: An Interpretive Approach*, Newbury Park, CA: Sage Publications.

Reddy, M. J. (1993) 'The conduit metaphor: A case of frame conflict in our language about our language', in A. Ortony (ed.) *Metaphor and Thought*, 2nd edn, Cambridge, MA: MIT Press.

Senge, P. M. (1990) *The Fifth Discipline: The Art & Practice of The Learning Organisation*, London: Century Business Books.

Shannon, C. E. and Weaver, W. (1949) *The Mathematical Theory of Communication*, Urbana, IL: University of Illinois Press.

Sheth, J. N., Gardner, D. M., and Garrett, D. E. (1988) *Marketing Theory: Evolution and Evaluation*, Chichester, UK: John Wiley & Sons.

Shotter, J. (1993) *Cultural Politics of Everyday Life: Social Constructionism, Rhetoric, and Knowing of the Third Kind*, Buckingham, UK: Open University Press.

Sigman, S. (1987) *A Perspective on Social Communication*, New York: Lexington Books.

Stainton Rogers, R., Stenner, P., Gleeson, K. and Stainton Rogers, W. (1995) *Social Psychology: A Critical Agenda*, Oxford: Polity Press.

Stohl, C. and Cheney, G. (2001) 'Participatory processes/paradoxical practices: Communication and the dilemmas of organizational democracy', *Management Communication Quarterly*, Vol. 14, No. 3, 349–407.

Taylor, J. R. (1999) 'The other side of rationality: Socially distributed cognition', *Management Communication Quarterly: An International Journal*, Vol. 13, No. 2, 321.

Varey, R. J. (2000) 'A critical review of conceptions of communication evident in contemporary business and management literature', *Journal of Communication Management*, Vol. 4, No. 4, 328–340.

Vickers, G. (1968) *Value Systems and Social Process*, London: Tavistock Publications.

Vickers, G. (1984) *Human Systems Are Different*, London: Harper & Row.

Weick, K. E. (1979) *The Social Psychology of Organizing*, Reading, MA: McGraw-Hill.

Weick, K. E. (1995) *Sensemaking in Organizations: Foundations for Organizational Science*, London: Sage Publications.

Chapter 4

RELATIONSHIP MARKETING AS MANAGING TRADING RELATIONSHIPS

A new era of buyer–seller interaction

Make a customer, not a sale
Katherine Barchetti, US clothes retailer, *The Independent on Sunday*, 1995

Keep care of the shop and the shop will keep care of you
Benjamin Franklin

When the terrain you traverse differs from the map, change the map!*

Introduction

Dialogical trading is two parties reasoning together to understand a problem and find a solution. Both parties have to be willing to listen to the other and must have an ability to discuss and communicate – in a purposive conversation. This requires mediated message-making (expressing) and interaction (discussing). However, a pair of monologues is far from the same as a dialogue.

Creating a dialogue between buyer and seller takes much more effort than merely prompting a response to an offer. Objective informing and persuasion efforts by a seller cannot be enough. Both parties have to be motivated to dialogue. Further, two distinct communication sources can be discerned (Grönroos, 2000). Planned communication arises through intentional efforts to use media to send messages. Interaction with other parties is also communicative. Relationship Marketing requires the integration of both in to a systematically implemented Corporate Communication Managing System. What is required is a process of managing that provides planned and planned-for interaction, while taking account of unplanned communication. In this way, the Relationship Marketing process produces credibility and likeability through aligning the

---

*Inspired by Gummesson (1999, p. 3).

saying of promise-making messages and the *doing* of respondability (receptiveness to customers' messages and promise-keeping).

Why is communication management a strategic management issue? Because this is a real source of competitive strength – investing in unbreakable relationships with customers, instead of the pursuit of converting buyers and consumers into customers (to refill a continuously leaking bucket). Sustainable prosperity in trading comes from selling more products to customers, instead of trying to find customers for more products.

Prospective customers and newly recruited customers are often, unwisely, treated no differently from seasoned customers. Recently, for example, the financial services ombudsman has chastised a small number of major UK banks and building societies. They have been treating some of their customers unfairly by offering mortgage discounts to new customers that were denied to established account holders.

Relationship Management

It is wrong to take 'satisfied' customer to necessarily mean 'loyal' customer. It is increasing value, as defined by the customer, that increases loyalty (perhaps commitment is a better term?). This requires of managers:

- mastery of the basic business;
- promises and provision of that which is valued;
- the realization that some actions are irritating and can be innovated into value;
- the acceptance that some actions are not important to the customer.

Heskett et al. (1994) asked why do customers defect to another supplier or are indifferent. Their conclusion is explained by Barnes's work on emotions. It is the way they feel that they are treated by the seller. This can be reviewed by considering how we define the nature of management.

The typical explanation of human behaviour that is used in the management field is that of goal-seeking and that people manage problem-solving through decision-making (Simon, 1960). These problems are indicated by gaps between performance and goals. Therefore, marketing aids problem-solving.

Vickers (1965), on the other hand, took a fundamentally different view on human action and rejected the goal-seeking model as unable to match the richness of life. Building on systems ideas, he proposed that personal or collective human regulators choose one of several possible mixes of courses of action. The standards by which these are judged are generated internally by the previous history of the social system and interactions with the environment. Rather than striving for goal attainment, the actions taken are to maintain or elude relationships. Therefore, according to Vickers, goal-seeking is only an occasional special case of managing relationships. As we saw in Chapter 3, the social system is 'appreciative', with a core activity of debating possible courses of action and the relationships they might affect.

Value can be created through managed relationships. Customer Relationship Management (CRM) is expected to be a specialized application of Relationship Marketing principles – but, it appears that many CRM systems are designed on the premise that RM is merely a component. We will return to this problem later in this chapter and in the next.

Relationship Marketing, as we are discussing here, is concerned with the co-creation of value from co-operative interaction. This is founded on personal commitment leading to mutual obligation. Alternatively, Transaction Marketing seeks to extract value from transactions.

Business-to-consumer trading differs from business-to-business in a number of ways (Table 4.1 is a summary of the discussion by Gordon, 1998). This suggests some significant differences in Relationship Marketing practices, driven by the same underlying principles.

The Relational Management of Commercial Trading

The actual mode of interaction of seller and buyer may be transactional or relational. Furthermore, each may have an intended mode of interaction, and must decide or choose their preferred mode in each case. Trading relationships may be latent or active. The latent relationship can be activated by either seller or buyer (the concept of *reverse marketing* explains this). Active engagement in a relationship arises from a relational intent, whereas passive attachment is the manifestation of a transactional intent.

The job of the Relationship Marketer (either seller or buyer) is to match the seller's marketing efforts to the buyer's desired/actual mode of exchange interaction, and trading conditions. The degree of alignment decisively impacts on the respective judgements of value of the parties. Grönroos has suggested a Relationship Configuration Matrix as a tool for analysing the current nature of the relationship with a customer (Grönroos, 1997).

TABLE 4.1 Comparison of consumer and producer markets (based on Gordon, 1998).

	Consumer	*Producer*
Goods and services	Buyer and consumer are one and the same or very close, usually through kinship or friendship – offers and needs are (relatively) simple	Buying is done by people in various roles for different reasons – offers and needs can be complex
Market structure	Numerous consumers	Concentrated end-user demand – fewer relationships
Distribution channels	Several intermediaries (before the advent of the Internet)	Direct trading
Decision-making criteria	Largely emotional	Claimed to be largely rational economic
Decision-making process	Buying for and with users – product choices	Decision-making unit, competitive tendering
Buyer–seller relationship	Distant, transitory	Close, personal
Reciprocity	Little	Common
Mutual value creation	Technology-facilitated personalization and customization	Considerable (untapped) potential
Transactional trading	Common among high-frequency and low-involvement purchases	Added value from skills and experience for solving problems
Brand equity	Added value of function and emotional association very significant	Functional performance is supposed to dominate

Fassot (2001) has studied the management of commercial relationships mediated by electronic systems of communication, defining eCRM as the planning and control of Relationship Marketing via the Internet. Four possible situations can arise when expectations are aligned or misaligned:

- the customer and supplier each pursue no more than repeat buying – this is a *functional relationship*;
- when the customer seeks a genuine relationship but the supplier seeks only repeat buying, a *cold relationship* results, since the emotional support sought is absent;
- when the supplier seeks a genuine relationship with a customer who pursues only repeat buying, a *troublesome relationship* arises since the relational offer merely irritates – each wants different, incompatible processes and outcomes;

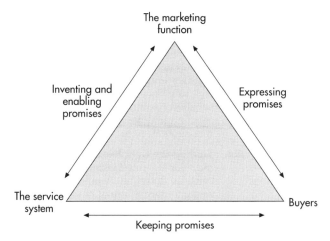

The marketing
function

Inventing and
enabling
promises

Expressing
promises

The service
system

Buyers

Keeping promises

FIGURE 4.1   The Relational Marketing Triangle (adapted from Grönroos, 1996).

● when both pursue a genuine relationship, the relationship produced is a *close relationship*, co-operative, mutual development.

This matching or mismatching of expectations on mode of interaction arises in the employment relationship. Is it conceivable that employees who are treated trans-actionally by their employer can be expected fully to understand and be motivated to enact a relational mode of interaction with customers? So, some alignment of internal mode of interaction and external mode of interaction is necessary. This idea of expectation vs. enacted mode of governance is examined in the concept of a psychological contract (see Rousseau, 1995, for example).

We can also see from Grönroos's Relational Marketing Triangle (1996) that the system of governance applied to employees and customers is not independent (Figure 4.1).

Return on Relationship

Morally, 'good relations' are right when people treat each other with respect and consideration, and trust results. In commercial relationships, a financial return can be realized from investments in managing the intensity of relationships (from none, to highly intense) to be appropriate for the situation. Gummesson (1999) provides a comprehensive discussion of the impact of Relationship Marketing on revenue, cost, capital employed, and profits. Here, a summary of the essential ideas is presented to show how a payback for the deployment of resources can be realized.

> ... *return on relationships (ROR) is the long-term net financial outcome caused by the establishment and maintenance of an organization's network of relationships.*
>
> (Gummesson, 1999, p. 183)

TABLE 4.2 Ways to determine return on relationship.

Approach	Outline rationale
Customer satisfaction and ROR	The accepted logic is that good internal quality satisfies employees who give good external service that satisfies customers profitably – but not all satisfied customers remain loyal, and the least satisfied may be the most profitable! In a network, managers have to ask 'what's in it for each member?'
Duration, retention, and defection	Finding the right balance between initiating and maintaining relationships. Indifference is the biggest cause of defection – employees and investors, as well as customers. Share of customer's spend, rather than market share.
Intellectual Capital and the Balanced Scorecard	Performance indicators: financial, customer, internal business processes, and learning and growth. Intellectual capital of people (knowledge, motivation, personal relationship network, interpersonal qualities) and structure (business relationships, contracts, systems, reputation, and so on)
Customer interaction, quality, productivity, and profits	The meeting of measures of revenue, cost, and profit – the problem is evaluating the role of the customer and balancing revenue, cost and capital employed (level of service)
Return on the unmeasurable	Avoiding the detrimental fetish of counting what can be counted and missing what matters, by taking measurement (an image of reality) as reality itself

Drawing on Gummesson's state-of-the-art review, five management 'tools' can be suggested (Table 4.2).

Gummesson points out that return on relationship is not only to be applied to customer–supplier relationships obviously, but also to non-market relationships that are antecedents to successful market relationships.

The Value of the Relationship

What can a customer gain from a relationship with a supplier?

Managing customer relationships is not merely a matter of initiating and trading. Based on lifetime value (i.e. the profitability of the trading relationship in the long term), customers should be rewarded, disciplined, or sacked. The task is to prioritize the value provided in line with the value received. Therefore, some customers will be attractive and appealing, while others will be repulsive. The latter should be encouraged to defect to competing sellers (Figure 4.2).

Of course, it is risky to predict customer relationship value. A current low spender may be uncommitted and a candidate for investment in making the relationship grow, or he or she may be incapable of higher spend (and thus be a candidate for termination of the relationship).

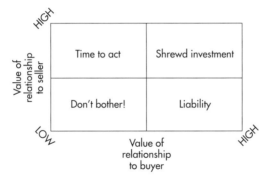

FIGURE 4.2   Relationship portfolio matrix.

The Relationship Marketing Audit and Plan

The marketing plan must be an integral part of the overall business plan, since Relationship Marketing is really marketing-oriented management. Gummesson suggests that a starting point for the journey toward this sophisticated way for managing is to add Relationship Marketing features in to the traditional marketing plan.

Therefore, the RM-enabling plan will have the following additional content:

- a definition and review of the relationship portfolio, and of the statement of relationships to be initiated, maintained, or terminated;
- additional goals for Return on Relationship (retention rate and share of customer spend, etc.);
- interaction activities;
- tools for evaluating processes, systems, and procedures.

The evaluation of a Relationship Marketing strategy is necessary to capitalize on opportunities, while correcting errors, omissions, and failures.

A marketing audit is a comprehensive, systematic, independent, and periodic examination of the marketing environment, objectives, strategies, and activities, to determine problem areas and opportunities, and to recommend a plan of action to improve overall marketing performance. This must include a review of the relationship portfolio, the handling of specific core relationships, and the assessment of Return on Relationship.

> *Of course, the special nature of evaluation ensures that this essential element of the planning, implementation, and control cycle is not easy. In any evaluation, there is the risk of revealing inadequacy. This may be threatening to colleagues, but is arguably a duty of managers if they are to manage. The intentions of the evaluator can be misconstrued. The findings can be misused or ignored. This is a question of managerial politics, research ethics, and research practices and skills (permissions, clearances, negotiations, etc.). An interested party (with an agenda that may not be made explicit) always sponsors the evaluation work.*

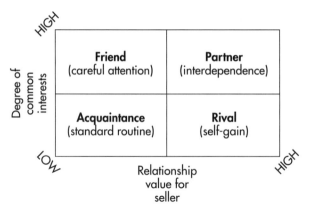

FIGURE 4.3   Relationship type.

A range of customer value positions may be identified through an audit of the customer base to reveal level of positive or negative association (see Etzioni's orientations, Chapter 3).

Ambivalent Terrorist Opponent Defector Indifferent Supporter Affectionate Ambassador Evangelist

Another basis for mapping relationship types is to consider the degree of common interests (Figure 4.3).

This can be developed further (Krapfel et al., 1991). The mode of management required can be defined as the balance of degree of common interests with assumed power position (of seller relative to the buyer) (Figure 4.4).

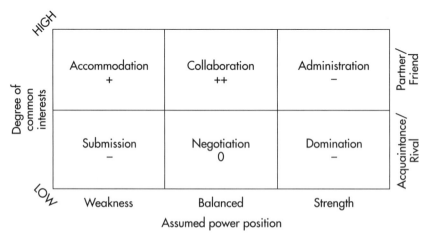

FIGURE 4.4   Management mode (based on Krapfel et al., 1991).
(Degree of openness in communication and information, from $++$, $+$, 0, $-$ to $--$).

A strategic Relationship Marketing process would type, map, match, and signal through dyadic interaction. Customer base profiling allows the manager to select priority customers, then develop and align capabilities with their expectations, in order to create desirable value. The relational marketer has to ask, 'which relationships, with which customers, do we need for sustainable business success?' The marketing task is then to facilitate the development of association from initial awareness, to interest, to evaluation, to trial purchase, to adoption, to commitment. Relationships are then characterized as: prospect, tester, shopper, account, patron, and advocates, as the level of commitment increases.

The Use of Market Data in Relationship Marketing Decision-making

In segmenting markets and prioritizing your customer portfolio, judgement is critical. Try these two tests.

Question 1

If you knew a woman who was pregnant, who had eight kids already, three of whom were deaf, two were blind, one mentally retarded, and she had syphilis, would you recommend that she have an abortion?

Question 2

It is time to elect a new world leader, and your vote counts. Here are the facts about the three leading candidates.

Candidate A associates with crooked politicians, and consults with astrologists. He's had two mistresses. He also chain-smokes and drinks up to 10 martinis each day.

Candidate B was kicked out of office twice, sleeps until noon, used opium in college, and drinks a quart of whisky every evening.

Candidate C is a decorated war hero. He's a vegetarian, doesn't smoke, drinks an occasional beer, and hasn't had any extramarital affairs.

Which of these candidates would be your choice?

Answers on page 137.

When you have answered both questions, take a look at page 138 for the answers.

Managers may well define customers as 'partners', but will nonetheless prohibit relationships that they determine are unprofitable or otherwise undesirable. The consumer, on the other hand, is far less able to enact such exclusions. Can the trading relationship really be mutual? The terms and conditions of a trading relationship are almost never negotiated, but rather are imposed by the corporation (see Gabriel and Lang's, 1995, discussion of consumer as victim). Once the relationship (inevitably) produces conflict, legislative authority and economic power lie with the corporation in resolving disagreements in their own favour.

A recent study of service quality management in a UK call centre (Gilmore, 2001) found that company policies and measurements concentrated on the number of calls answered, the speed of response, the length of call, standard responses, and the number of problems solved in a pre-specified time period. There was no attention to seeing problems through to full resolution, empathy, courtesy, response to individual customer problem, accessibility to relevant help, and so on. The result was call centre agent stress and frustration – presumably the same might also be found among at least some customers.

The Marketing Relationship

The first sale is different in character from a repeat sale. The task is to initiate a relationship, rather than to maintain and develop a relationship by reciprocating trust and attraction to foster 'devotion' – what Godin (1999) terms a 'commercial friendship'. This develops through initial interaction, into relating, and comes to an end in departing and terminating. Routine exchanges require little attention, whereas other exchanges require extensive problem-solving (Howard and Sheth, 1969).

In Relationship Marketing, exchange is not a single act, but rather a process that does not always start, nor end, with a purchase. What is required is not 'push' or 'interruption' marketing, but 'pull' or 'permission' marketing (Godin, 1999). The customer is an integral part of the marketing and value delivery process, not subject to it.

The *exchange control process* is important – parties to an exchange attempt to take control of the process for their own benefit – marketing is the management of exchange by both parties. Therefore, the contemporary challenge is to provide real-time customized assistance in the absence of a personal interaction ('e-care').

Peppers (Peppers and Rogers, 1993) has simplified the problem that Relationship Marketing addresses. Adoption would shift the role of seller from salespeople who find customers for their products, to relationship managers who find products for their customers.

The development of a relationship strategy is a complex and asymmetrical process, the effectiveness of which depends mainly on the seller.

Perrien and Ricard (1995) found, in their study of commercial banking in Canada in the early 1990s, that sellers (banks, in this case) regarded relationship marketing as a strategic issue because of the impact on organization structure, the decision-making process, and human resources management. Buyers (in this case, medium-sized companies), on the other hand, considered relationship marketing to be merely a communication process that should enhance the relevance of the seller's offerings. Automated banking systems save on the costs of providing physical resources, but rob the customer and staff of personal customer service situations.

Exchange episodes are embedded in a relationship framework or context. Partners adapt to one another and accommodate differences to produce beneficial outcomes. The strategic relationship management problem is to move beyond managing single, isolated relationships to managing a portfolio of selected

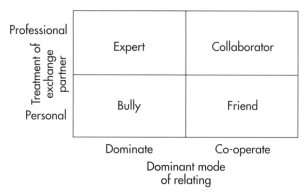

FIGURE 4.5   Relational stance (adapted from Krapfel el al., 1991).

relationships. The associated problem is one of resource allocations. Over time, attention has to be paid to yesterday's customers, today's customers, and tomorrow's customers. The central issue is lifetime value of the relationship. The relational stance (Figure 4.5) adopted by either party has implications for the relationship.

There are implications in terms of:

- current relationships;
- each buyer's assessment of his or her relationship;
- knowledge of buyers' relational preferences;
- the position of competitors;
- the skills of key managers;
- the skills of those who initiate and maintain relationships;
- the appropriate position of the business;
- the number of one-time-only sales;
- the proportion of business conducted in relationships;
- the most profitable mix.

Work by McDonald and Wilson (1999) suggests that a model of the life cycle of an exchange episode can be helpful to resource allocation decisions (Figure 4.6).

Brodie et al. (1997) propose a useful continuum of relational development stages, to which I have added an indication of the central concern for the marketing manager (Figure 4.7).

Two Functions of Marketing

Interactive marketing requires the planning, motivating, and managing of buyer–seller interactions with customers; that is, service promise-keeping that ensures customer retention is as important as the promise-making *traditional (external) marketing* activities such as market research, advertising, personal selling, publicity, sales promotion, and pricing, which largely focus on recruiting new customers. Enduring customer relationships are sought by attending to the co-production and consumption process to increase propensity to repeat-purchase,

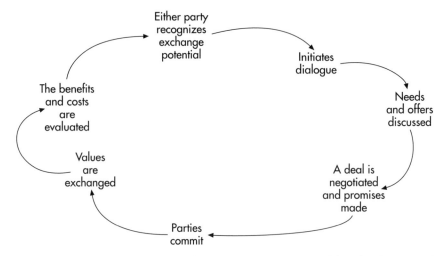

FIGURE 4.6   Exchange episode lifecycle (based on McDonald and Wilson, 1999).

Transaction	Interaction	Network	Passive relationship	Active relationship
Databasing	Conversing	Connecting	Coaxing	Innovating
to promote response	to learn	to build ties	to engage	to co-produce and share value

FIGURE 4.7   The evolutionary forms of a trading relationship
(based on Brodie et al., 1997).

rather than during the purchase process which is the domain of the traditional marketing approach. Interactive marketing is therefore required for relationship marketing. The customer is actively involved in the production/performance and delivery of products (goods and services).

The elaborated definition of marketing that is so helpfully promoted by Grönroos (2000) requires responsive and responsible systems for communicative interaction.

The two functions of marketing are outlined in Figure 4.8.

Table 4.3 outlines the purpose, aim, and mode of communicating of the two functions.

As I have said before, Relationship Marketing is a continuous process. Actually I wish to describe it as three interlocking processes of trading relationships that have to be managed together (Grönroos, 1999):

1   The value creation process.
2   The interaction process.
3   The planned communication process.

In relational marketing, the offering is developed through interaction. Product

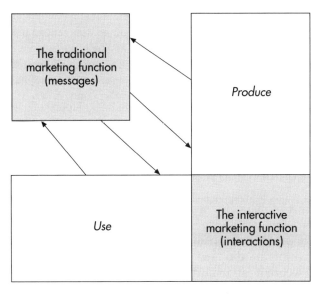

FIGURE 4.8   The two marketing functions (adapted from Grönroos, 2000, p. 247).

TABLE 4.3 When the functions are necessary.

Create interest	Promotional advertising and publicity	Attract by asserting, displaying, inviting, etc.	Traditional marketing
Make, give, and accept promises	Negotiative exchange	Persuade and commit	Integrated, traditional, and interactive marketing
Enable and keep promises to produce value in interaction	Consummation and commitment	Co-operate	Interactive marketing

exchange is the core of transactive marketing, whereas the interaction process is the core of interactive/relational marketing. In product markets, consumption is taken to be of outcomes, whereas in service markets it is the process that is consumed (i.e. the production process is part of the service).

FedEx

Social life is increasingly penetrated by home-delivery and on-line shopping. Federal Express is one of the huge network systems that reliably co-ordinate the movement of packages from supplier to buyer.

The FedEx website allows customers to track their packages, and is designed to handle a high volume of inquiries. Customers perform part of the service for themselves, reducing the number of customer service representatives needed. This also helps to reduce the appearance of risk associated with actions distanced in time and space and the opacity of the expert system to which parcels are entrusted. The system simulates transparency, providing information on departure, location, arrival, recipient signature, etc. Customers are assured by being allowed to 'see' where their package is, that the system is properly working, and that the parcel will finally arrive at its proper destination (based on Ritzer and Stillman, 2001).

The Internal Relationship Marketing System

One crucial aspect of managing marketing relationally is the employer's engagement with those who create value for which selected customers repeatedly pay. Peter Thompson, director of consulting services at BTexact, is clear that 'customer loyalty and retention are the new holy grail for business, however all too often efforts made to secure it fail to address the real issues. Organisations [*sic*] need to brand positively themselves both inside and outside. For a customer to experience excellent customer service, the employee must exude the positive energy and assurance than can come only from an inner feeling of company loyalty and self belief, while being supported by efficiently provisioned, customer-oriented information' (quoted from a company press release).

A particular form of *psychological contract* is required. This was initially explored in Chapter 3 where we considered Etzioni's explanation of involvement and participation.

Corporations as value creation systems cannot keep the promises of customer-oriented service unless the customer orientation is not confined to the marketing department – the function of customer service is a systemic requirement. So, what effort is expended by managers to produce genuine behaviour from employees?

Professor Chris Argyris is credited with the first published discussion of a 'psychological contract' (Argyris, 1960). This described and explained an unwritten social contract between employees and managers that was concerned with respective beliefs and expectations of each other in the workplace.

Since then, the psychological contract has become a central concept of employee–employer relations, and is discussed in pretty well every textbook on organizational behaviour and (less so) on human resource management. It is rarely considered in marketing management textbooks.

Levinson et al. (1962) considered the psychological contract to be the sum of mutual expectations of employers and employees. The title of their book is revealing of their concerns: *Men, Management and Mental Health*.

Many writers have assumed an exchange relationship in the workplace. This causes some difficulty because expectations at different levels (organizational and individual) are compared, and it is hard to imagine that there can be any single set of expectations in an organization constituted by a set of actors whose expectations are diversely different. Rousseau's solution has been to conceive the psychological contract as between employer and employee (Rousseau, 1995).

Leading researcher in this field, Professor David Guest (Guest et al., 1996) has defined the 'psychological contract' as the unwritten and implicit (i.e. unspoken) set of mutual expectations, promises, and obligations made between an employer and each employee. Such a contract is required in the informal process of committing.

The psychological contract reduces insecurity by 'filling in' the gaps in the relationship not covered by a formal written employment contract. Reciprocal obligations are the entitlements and benefits each party can expect to receive from the other, and what each is obliged to give the other in exchange for securing their contribution (Fulop and Linstead, 1999).

Katz and Kahn (1964) explained that every social role carries a set of implicit expectations of others' behaviours that are not defined or negotiated in a formal employment contract.

> *From the employee's point of view, the psychological contract is the agreement that they think they have [personally] with their employer about what they will contribute to their employer via their work, and what they can expect in return.*
> (Arnold, 1997, p. 38)

From the employer's point of view, the psychological contract may be defined as a 'commitment on the part of the organization to care for the personal and social needs of the employees who build up expectations such that those needs will be met ... in return, the company expects that for their part, the employees will remain loyal, well motivated and hardworking' (Schein, 1980).

Much of the literature on internal marketing has arisen from the field of retail service management, particularly in the USA where it has been applied to bank, health care, and professional services marketing as an approach to improving service quality and profitability.

Many writers have adopted this approach since the logic it offers is clear and attractive. However, there has been little examination of some of the major assumptions upon which this concept has been applied. Where critique has arisen, this has been concerned largely with imperialism or encroachment of marketing specialists into other management territory, such as HRM.

Re-examination of the early literature on internal marketing reveals a pervasive perspective on internal marketing, which is narrow and observably unhelpful due to its lack of clarity and poor fit with the realities of organization and management. Conceptual development would be a greater contribution at this point in the evolution of the field than would continued attempts to operationalize 'best practices'. We have yet to answer the moral and political questions satisfactorily about 'why?', so it is premature as yet to put all effort into working out 'how?'

A number of aspects of the popularized concept of 'internal marketing' have been re-examined to consider their appropriateness, and some significant flaws in the commonly held notion are revealed (Varey, 1996). Further work has examined the problem of the survival of an outmoded conception of communication in the marketing literature, particularly textbooks that reproduce the orthodoxy. A reconceptualization is suggested as a major development of internal marketing into a market-based management system.

It no longer makes sense to treat internal marketing as a specialist functional approach. It really represents the convergence of a number of previously separate management technologies, such as human resource development, employee relations, strategic management, quality management, corporate communications, and macromarketing. It is recognized, increasingly, that managing a business effectively requires the close integration of these many functional specialisms, and that management is a continual and complex process and cannot be seen as a sequence of discrete steps or a set of discrete functions. The work of the manager is not compartmentalized into discrete areas but is a portfolio of skills which are not functionally distinguishable and which cut across traditional functions – the manager as negotiator, resource allocator, information disseminator, etc.

It is proposed that the basic ideas that have led to the proliferation of writing on internal marketing are fundamentally sound. However, it is suggested that in order to take into account the real problems of achieving a genuine 'value-for-stakeholders' orientation, be it through marketing orientation, TQM, stakeholder analysis, Corporate Communication (the emerging discipline of managed, integrated business communication), or some other managerial approach, there is a need for managers to develop generalist skills and competencies based on the application of sound macromarketing principles throughout the organization. A particular form of internal marketing can provide the mechanism for the major reorientation needed in so many corporations. However, the view that internal marketing is solely the domain of marketing, or human resource specialists applying a micromarketing concept and associated tools (the ubiquitous 4Ps), is too narrow and does not take into account the needs of all local stakeholders. Gummesson (1991) points out the 'part-time marketer' role of service providers. In this respect, current interpretations of the internal marketing concept are too 'product'-oriented, being based on the traditional conception of marketing, rather than being marketing-oriented. Marketing thinkers must put their own house in order on this matter before they can hope to demonstrate the true worth of the internal marketing concept as a business management paradigm.

Major change programmes and plans clearly present problems, and Mastenbroek (1991, p. 243) has suggested that continual internal and external marketing are more effective in bringing about organizational change than any short-lived programme of attention. This is supported by Johnson and Scholes (1989, p. 314) who argue that the consolidation of acceptance of significant change is vital and is achieved through communication:

> ... it is the political and cultural barriers to change that may well provide the major stumbling blocks to the implementation of strategic change.
> (Johnson and Scholes, 1989, p. 46)

The terminology is yet to develop fully to the point where a single clear understanding of the underlying principles of internal marketing is widespread among managers. Some strong resistance to the use of the term 'internal marketing' has been experienced among academics and practitioners, as it suggests that the mechanism of change management being described is the exclusive property of marketers, or there is a narrow perspective on the purpose and form of 'marketing'. The terms *Internal Relationship Marketing*, *Internal Relationship Management*, or *Internal Social Process Management* are proposed as a development of other terms used by writers elsewhere. These new terms recognize the applicability of the marketing concept through the identification of (intraorganizational) exchanges in working relationships and between the organization and its customers, since all employees are customers of managers who wish to carry out the firm's objectives. It also recognizes differing goals of the parties to these exchanges, within the overall organizational goals of survival and prosperity – to be accomplished through profitable, long-run customer satisfaction and loyalty, requiring demonstrated customer orientation. This is pursued in a planned manner by all organization members as a means to achieving differentiation of the corporation for the purposes of attaining sustainable competitive advantage. Ulrich (1989) has argued that customer satisfaction is not sufficient and that differentiation must be sought in the conscious development of customer commitment; that is, loyalty and devotion that transcends short-term 'feel good' relationships by building interdependencies, shared values, and mutually beneficial strategies.

As yet, there is little empirical basis for the required theory of internal marketing as a change management concept. At the same time, there is empirical data to show that internal marketing, in various forms, is being practised as a viable response by managers to the real problems of achieving the objectives required by strategic decision-making. Internal marketing cannot be viewed as simply the application of (traditional mass-market) marketing concepts within the organization, nor is it the use of modified human resource management principles. It is, conceptually, a separate phenomenon that warrants further investigation and development. Further, much of the literature disregards the difficulty of the political processes (i.e. differing ideas, beliefs, and values held by managers, supervisors, and front-line service providers: Dawson, 1994). This literature is too prescriptive and too narrow in trying to apply the marketing concept as it has developed as a rational economist's response to (external) market relationships.

Ballantyne (2000) highlights the need for less emphasis on internal Transaction Management, and for more effort to establish an internal Relationship Marketing way of working. But, does a 'happy' workforce necessarily produce satisfied customers?

The Service Quality Value Chain

It can be argued that a service product is all the actions and interactions that customers/visitors believe they have purchased. *Internal service quality* is necessary for superior *external* service quality. Heskett (1992), among others, has provided a model of a *service profit chain* that can be managed, which explains linkages between internal service quality, employee satisfaction, their productivity, and external customer/visitor satisfaction and corporate performance. Johnson and Gustafsson (2000) provide an empirically tested service quality chain model and a systematic process for measuring service performance and for the related decision-making. They have developed a simple logic that provides a 5-stage process for creating an integrated customer satisfaction measurement and management system that can be used to increase trading loyalty profitably. The managerial framework presented is straightforward: quality influences satisfaction, which influences loyalty, and this impacts on profits or visitor numbers (not all visitor attractions are profit-driven). Performance must be benchmarked so that quality improvements can be prioritized and necessary resource allocation changes made.

Internal marketing can be compared to the process management concept within total quality management (TQM). The chain of internal customers and suppliers, where every employee is an internal 'part-time marketer' (Gummesson, 1991), facilitates the linkages between (otherwise) discrete functional groups (e.g. live interpreters and curators, or front-of-house staff and conservators). Internal marketing, then, is a management responsibility in which part-time marketers are both valued and trained (Grönroos, 1991). The concept of the boundary-spanning roles of certain employees, especially in service corporations, has been developed by Bowen and Schneider (1985). Some persons, and especially those working at the 'front line', have a strategic position as information gatherers and processors who can feed new information into management decision-making on service design and delivery, and as external representatives whose behaviour shapes the customers' experience of the service (how it happens – the functional quality) and attitudes about the service (how good it is – the outcome – technical quality). The nature of mutual support between managers and boundary-spanning-role employees will affect service quality and the corporation's overall business effectiveness. The participation of boundary-spanning-role employees in decision-making about overall goals and how they are to be attained, which affects service quality, will help to ensure that they will act as knowledgeable and willing implementers of change in a volatile, international leisure and tourism business.

Mohan-Neill (1991) provides a rationale for internal marketing in service industries that is similar to the service–profit chain and shows the link between internal marketing, business performance, and competitive advantage (Table 4.4).

TABLE 4.4 The logic of internal marketing impact (based on Mohan-Neill, 1991).

Internal marketing activity at the level of the
corporation/Attraction to augment the core product

Greater loyalty and motivation, and reduced turnover among employees
(as internal customers)

Improved service quality at the service encounter

Increased satisfaction of external customers/visitors/guests

Increased profitability and other performance measures
– a competitive advantage is secured and maintained

Part-time Marketers in an Internal Customer–Supplier Chain

A recent study (Piercy, 1995) demonstrates the considerable problems of implementing a customer satisfaction focus in a marketing strategy, and argues for an internal marketing strategy to overcome a range of internal barriers. Shaw (1978) argued that employees need to be 'sold' on the service they provide before they will commit to the employer's goals.

Customer care programmes have been widely adopted as, often superficial, attempts to improve customer service. From an internal marketing perspective, customer care programmes would 'sell' trading with an external customer as a 'product' to be 'bought' by employees who would then pay attention to the needs and desires of each of their customers (Piercy, 1995). A large and growing number of management writers have suggested that if the employees of the corporation are viewed and treated as internal customers, then good service will be more likely and possible for external customers. This stems from effective marketing behaviour by customer-oriented and sales-minded people who may be 'non-professional marketers' or 'part-time marketers'. Employees capable and willing to give excellent service must be attracted, recruited, developed, motivated, and retained, by treating them well and making them feel important. This is inherently problematic given the nature of the typical workforce of many visitor attractions. Grönroos (1982) takes this further by specifying the need for five principles of internal marketing, all of which highlight interpersonal communication issues:

- personnel are the first market of the service business;
- managers must ensure that staff understand what is expected of them, why they are expected to perform in a certain way, and that they actively support the service 'idea' (or concept) of the corporation;
- staff must be mentally prepared for, and accept, the stipulated approach to service provision in order to support the corporation's service guarantee in contact with their customers;
- the service must be fully developed and accepted by employees before it is launched;
- internal information channels must work, and personal selling is needed within the corporation's operations.

Wasmer and Bruner (1991) have modelled the relationships which the employee, who personally interacts with the customer and performs the act of service, has with his/her employer as well as the (external) customer. They view these relationships as 'flows' (Figure 4.9). An effective system removes or minimizes gaps in these 'flows'.

Schlesinger and Heskett (1991) described a 'cycle of failure' as prevalent in poor performing corporations, while the outstanding corporations pursue a 'cycle of success' by ensuring they become *preferred employers* capable of being seen as *preferred service producers*. All customer-contact people must be well attuned to the mission, goals, strategies, and systems of the corporation (Gummesson, 1987). A suitable customer service climate or thematic coherence in management actions is necessary to model a good service experience to employees who will then do the many necessary things right, *and* do the right things to create a quality service

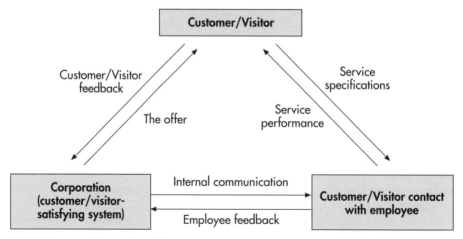

FIGURE 4.9   Relationship 'flows' between service deliverer, employer, and customer (based on Wasmer and Bruner, 1991).

experience for consumers. Internal marketing aims to identify and satisfy their needs as individual people and as service producers (i.e. to match individual and group needs to those of the corporation). Internal marketing is then the process of 'selling' the concept of customer service to employees so that they internalize an appropriate set of values. The strategy therefore aims to change attitudes and behaviour and to create shared attitudes to service quality (i.e. a culture change: Wasmer and Bruner, 1991).

Robert Desatnick is cited by Davidow and Uttal (1989) in observing that:

> ... *managing a corporation's human resources equates with managing its customer services ... employee relations equals customer relations. The two are inseparable.*
>
> (p. 122)

Managers are thus seen as providers of support services to their workers in an 'inverted hierarchy' in order to facilitate appropriate behaviour for the satisfaction of external customers through service. Recent emphasis on 'relationship marketing' has led to the recognition that customer experience of service encounters can be a strategic issue which, if managed, can be a source of competitive advantage, even when product quality is on a par with competitors (Grönroos, 1991). Internal functional interfaces are then of strategic importance, and will depend on the marketing orientation and skills of 'part-time marketers' within the corporation. Therefore, service encounter management can be seen as a form of marketing competence or 'core' capability. Gummesson coined the phrase 'part-time marketers' to describe all members of the corporation who carry out marketing activities but who are not formally members of the sales or marketing department. They therefore may not identify readily with their customer service role. Gummesson's 'point of marketing' is the interaction between buyer and supplier at a point in time; that is it is an opportunity to contribute to the building of relationships, without necessarily a sale taking place at each contact. This is a development of the 'moment of truth' concept (Carlzon, 1987 – this term was first coined by Koestler, 1969, to describe the point at which a sudden new insight emerges – the 'shock of recognition') or service encounter, and can be identified directly with the relationship marketing concept.

Barnes (1989) has pointed out that managers and service-support people are also internal customers as well as those employees who deliver service to external customers by *interacting* with them. This theme has received considerable attention from service quality specialists, many of whom have urged the recognition of an internal customer–supplier chain as an enabler of good (external) customer service. Some have even offered means to measure internal customer transaction satisfaction (see Gulledge, 1991, for example). Rosenbluth and Peters (1992) go as far as to argue that the needs of the external customer are secondary to those of employees, suggesting the latter's needs will be met *only when* particular employee needs are met.

The Corporate Communication Managing System

Some 30 years have passed since Bower (1966) offered the simple programmed management system to stimulate the inspiration of individuals to give their best efforts toward achieving group objectives, while requiring them to adhere to corporate philosophy and to follow strategic plans, policies, and procedures in accordance with established standards.

Bower's wide consulting experience with McKinsey & Co. had revealed all too many instances of a lack of will to manage and the absence of effective, basic managing processes. Too much effort was being put by senior executives into operating work, to the neglect of developing managing processes by which all members of the organization can contribute to achieving the objectives of the enterprise and assuring its success.

Bower identified the classical managing processes – the way things get done effectively through group action:

- setting objectives;
- planning strategy;
- establishing goals;
- developing a corporate philosophy;
- establishing policies;
- planning the organization structure;
- providing personnel;
- establishing procedures;
- providing facilities;
- providing capital;
- setting standards;
- establishing management programmes and operational plans;
- providing control information;
- activating people.

It is hard to see these as anything other than managing processes for which there are a set of patterned relations among these structural elements so that changes in one element set up pressures for adjustment or other types of change in the other functions. In other words, this is a managing system. Bower observed that failure to establish and maintain effective processes was often because of a lack of *will to manage* among managers. Bower also provides the link to communication (1966, p. 16):

> No business, regardless of type or size, can maximize its success in the long run unless its managing processes deal effectively with the ambitions, abilities, strengths, indifferences, inertias, weaknesses, fears, and foibles of (its) people.

In terms of the membership of the enterprise, the function of the management system is to get people to plan, decide, and act effectively, in the interest of the enterprise, because they like and want to. The system must help them determine what activities to perform and how to perform these activities well. The system should also help the corporation attract and retain high-calibre people. As far as the system concerns other people not employed by the corporation, decisions and actions are made consciously within the web that includes other (external) stakeholders.

The corporate enterprise has two primary communication subsystems that are interrelated. The internal system directs activities of organizing to accomplish goals that are based on the gathering and interpretation of data on expectations and attitudes, and on conditions, from the corporation's relevant environment through external channels of communication. External channels of communication are also used to present relevant information about the internal processes of the corporation to the relevant external environment to attempt to influence the behaviour of the various publics. Internal communication processes are directed toward establishment of structure and stability in organizing, while external communication processes are directed toward innovation by facilitating identification of directions for corporate development (Kreps, 1990). Managers and leaders seek co-operation for a productive balance between stability and innovation.

Traditionally, departments and narrow specialist groups operating in institutional 'silos' are seen as in competition: for supremacy, to protect their 'turf', to secure credibility, for 'a seat at the Boardroom table'; to secure 'the ear of the dominant coalition', or simply for resources. However, a model of integrated communication systems seeks to build bridges between the 'islands of communication', and eventually to establish new task groupings, perhaps by way of cross-functional working in the interim. As corporations re-engineer working arrangements and formal structure around business processes, so they should re-engineer their communications management into a truly corporate (sub)system for managing. Kreps (1990) sees divisions between communication systems as artificial and traditionalist, and no longer relevant.

Departments should not be allowed to seek independence and the concern of managers should not be encroachment, but how to remove barriers to real co-operative working so that communication outcomes really can add value to business enterprise. The model we seek to build and deploy does not promote the engagement of non-specialists in competition to manage traditional com-

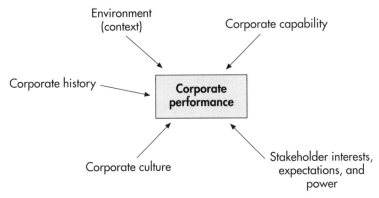

FIGURE 4.10 Determinants of corporate performance (derived from Brown, 1995).

munication departments, but rather seeks to foster greater recognition of corporate dependencies and shared organizational (business) goals, and to make stronger, direct linkages between those who need to communicate and those who are charged with enabling and facilitating these interactions. A value-creation perspective on the departmentalization issue is required if the power-control assumptions and desires of the traditionalist manager are to be overcome for the benefit of the corporate community. This will require that managers recognize the Corporate Communication managing system as central to the work of the enterprise community. The Corporate Communication approach enables the reconciliation of social and economic interests, for business is in reality a socio-economic institution upon which we are all dependent, and may allow the vista of a 'life ethic' to temper the debilitating effects of the mutation of citizens into consumers.

The interests of the few (corporate owners, managers, and their customers) are no longer given greater value than the interests of the many (all other stakeholders). Arrogant managers who do not value relationships and stakeholders' interests (or even stakeholders themselves), and do not value leadership and other change-oriented ways of working (Brown, 1995) will find it more difficult to keep their licence to operate (Figure 4.10), and to retain staff (except the arrogant ones!).

Democracy as a system of values

A climate of beliefs governing behaviour that people are compelled by their own expectations to affirm in deeds as well as words:

- communication is full and free regardless of rank and power;
- consensus is relied upon for the resolution of conflict, in place of coercion or compromise;
- influence comes from technical competence and knowledge, and personal whims or prerogatives of power;
- expression of emotions is encouraged;
- human bias is evident in accepting the inevitability of conflict between corporate and personal interests, allowing coping and mediation on rational grounds.

(based on Bennis, 1993)

Carroll's (1993) stakeholder view of the firm requires that managers see stakeholders' groups and their subgroups, at least until the legitimacy of claims and respective power have been examined, as both:

1   Those who the management group thinks has some stake (an interest, right, or ownership) in the firm.
2   Those groups that themselves think they have some stake in the firm.

It is then necessary to examine the nature of each relationship, as well as recognizing that some stakeholder groups also have relationships with each other. Stakeholder expectations cannot be ignored, but can be missed and/or misinterpreted.

The corporation becomes defined by its links to its stakeholders and binds them into constructive relationships, not always based on agreement, through the design of its communication systems.

Those who have shaped their network of relationships, and the processes through which they enact their value-creating projects, have better understood the nature of information, knowledge, and relation, and in doing so have abandoned the older models of organization.

In this book we have adopted a human system perspective on corporate life. The corporation is a social system or society. The corporation is seen as a set of nested systems, each dealing with an external sector of the environment.

The corporation can be conceived as a dynamic 'communicational' whole (a system). We can gain by adopting such a network-based model of management to replace the now outmoded notion of compartmentalized organization of work.

Our use of our language has such a powerful influence on our thinking that we can make the necessary shift in our expectations and strategies largely by using different terminology. Instead of speaking of the 'organization' (as though it were a machine), we can talk about the *enterprise ecology* we value and desire. By this I choose to mean value-creating activity managed in relation to the surroundings. Prosperity of the people who are interdependent is the central goal, and this is gauged in more than economic terms since overall quality of working life and contribution to a corporate community is beneficial to all participants.

In the natural run of things, the various *zones of meaning* (Heath, 1994) become differentiated and idiosyncratic. The corporation is the entire set of relationships it has with itself and its stakeholders (Mitroff, 1983). Organizing, then, is negotiation – the corporation is a network of ongoing negotiated enactments of stakeholder interests (Putnam, 1982).

The corporation is a network of coupled zones of meaning (i.e. an interpretive system. The management task is to strengthen the coupling, to enable the negotiation of zones of meaning or 'life spaces' (a term used by Kurt Lewin, 1951) into compatibility to ensure sufficient co-operation for the achievement of personal and corporate enterprise goals.

Making sense of what is going on around us is necessary for us to act toward the realization of our desired state. Meanings must be the product of narratives enacted by managers with employees (Smircich, 1983). There must be voice-to-voice dialectic. Democratic communication is about the formation of knowledge, experience, and identity, and not merely their expression (Deetz, 1992). Shared understanding may not be necessary. Managing business enterprise is concerned with the purposive deployment of frames of meaning, through active and selective interpretation of events, expectations, and intentions. We try to bring people together to co-operate in executing collective tasks and must face a variety of 'fields of experience' or 'personal cultures'. The humane way to get the job done is not through people but with people. Our communication must create productive *interaction*.

Strategic management of corporate communication

The management of corporate communication:

- is linked to strategic planning;
- contributes to corporate performance;
- is diffused throughout line management;
- has a long-term, proactive, and accommodating focus;
- systematically plans and evaluates

(adapted from Fleisher, 1998)

Management efforts should foster boundary-spanning to facilitate the flow of vital information and a sense of meaning that fosters cohesiveness. To survive and prosper, a corporation needs a shared appreciative system or a set of compatible appreciative systems (Vickers, 1984) that can turn data about phenomena, events, relationships, and expectations into decisions on how to act.

Common starting points (Riel, 1995) provide the structure for sufficient co-ordination and coherence in working to ensure that enough of the communication that is desired, and takes place, is:

> ... *harmonised as effectively and efficiently as possible, so as to create a favourable basis for relationships with groups upon which the company is dependent*
>
> (p. 1)

We have seen that the price to pay in pursuing a narrow, closed, mechanistically controlled environment is too high for the people who desire the creation and delivery of valued contributions to personal goals. A 'reputation czar' (Fombrun, 1995) takes overall responsibility for communication system performance and building communicative competence at corporate, process, and performer levels.

By seeking productive participatory processes we can gain the benefits that authentic, ethical communication experiences bring to people. Otherwise we lose the possibility of creating and experiencing opportunities to be who we are.

Summary

Relationship Marketing is not merely a way to deal with customers. Rather, it implies a corporate commitment with considerations of organization structure, the decision-making processes, and the management of human resources. The aim is to organize and co-ordinate a complex set of actions for value-creating planned (contrived) and unplanned (natural) interaction.

Dialogical trading arises in a *relationship of learning*.

Relationship Marketing is more than the pursuit of consistency among 'marketing communication' objectives, activities, and resources. Relationship Marketing is more than Integrated Marketing Communications. However, IMC is an important aspect of a Relationship Marketing strategy that needs to be integrated in to the Corporate Communication Managing System.

The entire production system has to become dialogical so that inquiry informs value analysis as the regulator of the integrated value production processes.

New methods of trading enabled by connection to the developing Internet allow 'interactive marketing' as a way of broadening and deepening the trading relationship. This is limited by the organization of the seller's work processes. The marketing department is usually responsible for the corporate website strategy, but so may be the IT department. CRM adoption must lead to the redesign of the organization of the seller.

There is a paradox to be faced: In developing e-commerce:

We've created this empowered, impatient customer who has a short attention span, a lot of choices, and a low barrier to switching.
$\qquad$ (Windham, 2001)

What better justification for managing the way we treat our customers?

It is not uncommon to hear managers and marketers talking of 'pursuing customers' and 'aggressively pursuing customers'. Prus (1989) even published a research-based book on the subject. It seems highly inappropriate to me to talk in terms of chasing customers who are running away in an attempt to catch them. Should not the tenor of marketing be the authentic attraction of willing customers and the truthful recognition of dependency conditions?

To practise this requires a shift in thinking from demand management and product profitability management, to *interaction management* and *customer profitability management*. Product managers then become customer relationship managers, requiring expertise in account management, human resource management, and corporate strategy. The Customer Relationship Management system provides the 'connections' to allow either party to initiate the marketing process and the other to respond responsibly. The Relational Marketing process supports the continual co-creation of appreciated value for participants. Relational Marketing subsumes Transactional Marketing – the latter is a special case of the former.

Interaction management and integrated brand management require cross-functional (boundary spanning) management to accomplish strategic consistency (i.e. the integration of corporate functions). This requires ubiquitous information and a corporate memory. It is to this that we turn in Chapter 5, where we examine the CRM system. Is CRM a system of governance, or a tool deployed with a 'marketing mix' mentality?

References

Argyris, C. (1960) *Understanding Organisational Behaviour*, London: Tavistock Publications.

Arnold, J. (1997) *Managing Careers in the 21st Century*, London: Paul Chapman Publishing.

Ballantyne, D. (2000) 'Dialogue and knowledge generation: Two sides of the same coin in relationship marketing', *Proceedings of the 2nd WWW Conference on Relationship Marketing, Monash University*, Bradford: MCB University Press, online @ www.mcb.co.uk/services/conferen/nov99/rm/paper3.html

Barnes, J. G. (1989) 'The internal marketing programme: If the staff won't buy it, why should the customer?', *Proceedings of the Marketing Education Group Conference*, Glasgow: Glasgow Business School.

Bennis, W. (1993) *An Invented Life: Reflections on Leadership and Change*, London: Century Books.

Bowen, D. E. and Schneider, B. (1985) 'Boundary-spanning-role employees and the service encounter: Some guidelines for management and research', In J. A. Czepiel, M. R. Solomon, and C. F. Surprenant (eds) *The Service Encounter*, Lexington, MA: Lexington Books.

Bower, M. (1966) *The Will to Manage*, New York: McGraw-Hill.

Brodie, R. J., Coviello, N. E., Brookes, W., and Little, V. (1997) 'Towards a paradigm shift in marketing? An examination of current marketing practices', *Journal of Marketing Management*, Vol. 13, 383–406.

Brown, A. (1995) *Organisational Culture*, London: Pitman Publishing.

Carlzon, J. (1987) *Moments of Truth: New Strategies for Today's Customer-driven Economy*, Cambridge, MA: Ballinger Publishing.

Carroll, A. B. (1993) *Business and Society: Ethics and Stakeholder Management*, 2nd edn, Cincinatti, OH: South-Western Publishing/International Thomson.

Davidow, W. H. and Uttal, B. (1989) *Total Customer Service: The Ultimate Weapon*, New York: HarperCollins.

Dawson, P. (1994) *Organisational Change: A Processual Approach*, London: Paul Chapman Publishing.

Deetz, S. A. (1992) *Democracy in an Age of Corporate Colonization: Developments in Communication and the Politics of Everyday Life*, Albany, NY: State University of New York Press.

Fassot, G. (2001) 'Towards a conceptual framework for e-CRM', *Proceedings of the 9th International Colloquium in Relationship Marketing, John Molson School of Business, Concordia University, Montreal, Canada, 24–26 September*.

Fleisher, C. S. (1998) 'A benchmarked assessment of the strategic management of corporate communications', *Journal of Marketing Communications*, Vol. 4, 163–176.

Fombrun, C. J. (1995) *Reputation: Realizing Value from the Corporate Image*, Boston: Harvard Business School Press.

Fulop, L. and Linstead, S. (eds) (1999) *Management: A Critical Text*, London: Macmillan Business.

Gabriel, Y. and Lang, T. (1995) *The Unmanageable Consumer: Contemporary Consumption and its Fragmentation*, London: Sage Publications.

Gilmore, A. (2001) 'Call centre management: Is service quality a priority?', *Managing Service Quality*, Vol. 11, No. 3, 153–159.

Godin, S. (1999) *Permission Marketing: Turning Strangers into Friends, and Friends into Customers*, New York: Simon & Schuster.

Gordon, I. (1998) *Relationship Marketing: New Strategies, Techniques and Technologies to Win Customers You Want and Keep Them Forever*, Toronto: John Wiley & Sons.

Grönroos, C. (1982) *Strategic Management and Marketing in the Service Sector*, Helsinki, Finland: Hanken School of Economics & Business Administration.

Grönroos, C. (1991) 'The marketing strategy continuum: Towards a marketing concept for the 1990s', *Management Decision*, Vol. 29, No. 1, 7–13.

Grönroos, C. (1996) 'Relationship marketing logic', *Asia-Australia Marketing Journal*, Vol. 4, No. 1, 7–18.

Grönroos, C. (1997) 'Value-driven Relational Marketing: From products to resources and competencies', *Journal of Marketing Management*, Vol. 13, 407–419.

Grönroos, C. (1999) 'The relationship marketing process: Interaction, communication, dialogue, value', *Proceedings of the 2nd WWW Conference on Relationship Marketing, Monash University*, Bradford, UK: MCB University Press, online @ www.mcb.co.uk/services/conferen/nov99/rm

Grönroos, C. (2000) *Service Management and Marketing: A Customer Relationship Management Approach*, 2nd edn, Chichester, UK: John Wiley & Sons.

Guest, D. E., Conway, N., Brier, R., and Dickman, M. (1996) *The State of the Psychological Contract in Employment: Issues in People Management*, London: Institute of Personnel and Development.

Gulledge, L. G. (1991) 'Satisfying the internal customer', *Bank Marketing*, Vol. 23, No. 4, April, 46–48.

Gummesson, E. (1987) 'Using internal marketing to develop a new culture – The case of Ericsson quality', *Journal of Business & Industrial Marketing*, Vol. 2, No. 3, 23–28.

Gummesson, E. (1991) 'Marketing-orientation revisited: The crucial role of the part-time marketer', *European Journal of Marketing*, Vol. 25, No. 2, 60–75.

Gummesson, E. (1999) *Total relationship Marketing: Rethinking Marketing Management – From 4Ps to 30Rs*, Oxford: Butterworth-Heinemann.

Heath, R. L. (1994) *Management of Corporate Communication: From Interpersonal Contacts to External Affairs*, Hillsdale, NJ: Lawrence Erlbaum Associates.

Henderson, C. (2000) 'Relationship marketing: I want to be your friend', *Revolution Asia*, 31 December [@ www.revolutionmagazine.com]

Heskett, J. L. (1992) 'A service sector paradigm for management: The service sector profit chain', *Proceedings of the Service Sector Management Research Workshop*, Bedford, UK: Cranfield School of Management.

Heskett, J. L., Jones, T. O., Loveman, G. W., Sasser, W. E., and Schlesinger, L. A. (1994) 'Putting the service profit chain to work', *Harvard Business Review*, March–April, 164–174.

Howard, J. A. and Sheth, J. N. (1969) *The Theory of Buyer Behavior*, New York: John Wiley & Sons.

Johnson, M. D. and Gustafsson, A. (2000) *Improving Customer Satisfaction, Loyalty, and Profit*, San Francisco: Jossey-Bass.

Johnson, G. and Scholes, K. (1989) *Exploring Corporate Strategy: Text and Cases*, London: Prentice Hall.

Katz, D. and Kahn, R. L. (1964) *The Social Psychology of Organizations*, New York: John Wiley & Sons.

Koestler, A. (1969) *The Act of Creation*, London: Pan Piper.

Krapfel, R. E., Salmond, D., and Spekman, R. (1991) 'A strategic approach to managing buyer–seller relationships', *European Journal of Marketing*, Vol. 25, No. 9, 22–37.

Kreps, G. L. (1990) *Organisational Communication: Theory and Practice*, 2nd edn, New York: Longman/The Guilford Press.

Levinson, H., Price, C. R., Munden, K. J., Manhl, H. J., and Solley, C. M. (1962) *Men, Management and Mental Health*, Cambridge, MA: Harvard University Press.

Lewin, K. (1951) *Field Theory in Social Science*, New York: Harper & Brothers.

Mastenbroek, W. F. G. (ed.) (1991) *Managing for Quality in the Service Sector*, Oxford: Blackwell.

McDonald, M. and Wilson, H. (1999) *e-Marketing: Improving Marketing Effectiveness in a*

Digital World, London: FT Management Briefing/Cranfield University School of Management.

Mitroff, I. I. (1983) *Stakeholders of the Organizational Mind: Toward a New View of Organizational Policy Making*, San Francisco: Jossey-Bass.

Mohan-Neill, S. I. (1991) Adoption of innovations: Influence of objective and subjective context on choice of child care services, unpublished doctoral thesis, University of Illinois at Chicago.

Peppers, D. and Rogers, M. (1993) *The One-to-One Future: Building Business Relationships One Customer at a Time*, London: Piatkus Books.

Perrien, J. and Ricard, L. (1995) 'The meaning of a marketing relationship: A pilot study', *Industrial Marketing Management*, Vol. 24, No. 1, 37–43.

Piercy, N. (1995) 'Customer satisfaction and the internal market: Marketing your customers to your employees', *Journal of Marketing Practice*, Vol. 1, No. 1, 22–44.

Prus, R. C. (1989) *Pursuing Customers: An Ethnography of Marketing Activities*, Newbury Park, CA: Sage Publications.

Putnam, L. L. (1982) 'Paradigms for organizational communication research: An overview and synthesis', *The Western Journal of Speech Communication*, Vol. 46, 192–206.

Riel, C. B. M. van (1995) *Principles of Corporate Communication*, London: Prentice Hall.

Ritzer, G. and Stillman, T. (2001) 'From person- to system-oriented service', in A. Sturdy, I. Grugulis, and H. Willmott (eds) *Customer Service: Empowerment and Entrapment*, London: Palgrave, pp. 102–116.

Rosenbluth, H. and Peters, D. (1992) *The Customer Comes Second: And Other Secrets of Exceptional Service*, New York: Wm M. Morrow & Co.

Rousseau, D. M. (1995) *Psychological Contracts in Organisations: Understanding Written and Unwritten Agreements*, London: Sage Publications.

Schein, E. H. (1980) *Organizational Psychology*, 3rd edn, New York: Prentice Hall.

Schlesinger, L. A. and Heskett, J. L. (1991) 'Breaking the cycle of failure in services', *Sloan Management Review*, Vol. 32, No. 3, 17–28.

Shaw, J. C. (1978) *The Quality–Productivity Connection in Service Sector Management*, New York: Van Nostrand Reinhold.

Simon, H. A. (1960) *The New Science of Management Decisions*, New York: Harper Brothers.

Smircich, L. (1983) 'Implications for management theory', in L. L. Putnam and M. E. Pacanowsky (eds) *Communication and Organizations: An Interpretive Approach*, Newbury Park, CA: Sage Publications, pp. 221–241.

Ulrich, D. (1989) 'Tie the corporate knot: Gaining complete customer commitment', *Sloan Management Review*, Summer, 19–27.

Varey, R. J. (1996) A broadened concept of internal marketing, unpublished PhD thesis, Manchester School of Management.

Vickers, G. (1965) *The Art of Judgment: A Study of Policy Making*, London: Chapman & Hall.

Vickers, G. (1984) *Human Systems Are Different*, London: Harper & Row.

Wasmer, D. J. and Bruner, G. C. (1991) 'Using organisational culture to design internal marketing strategies', *Journal of Services Marketing*, Vol. 5, No. 1, 35–46.

Windham, L. (2001) *The Soul of the New Consumer: The Attitudes, Behaviours and Preferences of e-Customers*, New York: Allworth Press.

Answers

How, in your judgement, do you change the map when the terrain differs from the map?

Question 1

If you said 'yes' to the abortion question, you just killed Ludwig von Beethoven.

Question 2

- Candidate A is Franklin D. Roosevelt;
- Candidate B is Winston Churchill;
- Candidate C is Adolf Hitler.

Surprising, isn't it? Makes a person think before judging someone.

Chapter 5

THE CUSTOMER RELATIONSHIP MANAGEMENT SYSTEM

In the world of e-commerce, taking an IT-first approach is like putting lipstick on a pig

(inspiration unknown)

30% of supposedly 'loyal' customers find an alternative supplier because of bad service, whilst 70% of customers do so because they experience indifference from a service provider
Ignored marketing folklore

If CRM is so difficult and over 50% of CRM projects fail, why should we bother?
Report on CRM, Nicola Millard, BTexact Technologies

People seldom improve when they have no model but themselves
Anon

Introduction

Customer Relationship Management has become a global mega-business. The Gartner Group estimated spending to be around $23 billion in 2000, rising to $76 billion per annum by 2005.

In recent years, the likelihood of a seller employing a service manager in a call centre has increased dramatically. What does this mean for buyers and consumers? As satisfactory service is becoming harder to find, despite TQM, BPR, and CRM, we ask: 'who wants social interaction as the means of consumption?' Perhaps the logic upon which these management strategies are premised is flawed. ICT offers low-cost communication through automation and connectivity. New technologies are (too) often adopted for cost-cutting, rather than to enable organization around selected customer value-creation meta-processes (relationships). ICT can be used as a buyer–seller link and/or as a buyer–seller buffer (to keep customers at arm's length from the production system). Is the cost, to buyers, of greater product choice, through more information, the decline of social interaction? Is more 'communication' leading to less 'communicating'? Do we care?

In addition to this concern with the effects of 'systemizing' buyer–seller interaction, we find evidence that the full potential performance and benefits of the underlying technologies (enterprise resource planning (ERP), EDI, and so on) of CRM have yet to be realized. In a recent study by the Hewson Group, the term CRM was correctly used, in their view, in only 18% of the 500 project cases studied.

In this chapter, we will examine, from the point of view of communicating and relating, some principles for the design and deployment of a customer relationship management system. This will be followed, in Chapter 6, with some case studies to illustrate practices as a test of the theoretical explanation and critique.

Mini-case: trust, respect, and loyalty – the Cathay Pacific service

Cathay Pacific have practised relationship management for decades, since building a meaningful trading relationship requires trust and respect. Recently, new technology has made it possible to re-create 'truly intimate relationships' with customers.

A dialogue is created each time a customer interacts with the company's systems. From every 'touch point', data is stored about flying history, lifetime revenue, frequent flyer status, complaints, feedback, and other variables of the trading relationship. Data analysis provides customer value modelling, and segmentation by lifestyle, psychographics, and demographics. In this way, 'tribes' are defined and members identified. Various market research analyses are used, including focus groups and conjoint analysis, to discern motivations and sources of satisfaction for each tribe. The management objective is to identify the most profitable customers and to tailor products to their needs and wants.

The website (www.cathaypacific.com) provides online flight booking, vacation planning, and frequent-flyer mile checking and other information about the customer's account status, including recent transactions. The customer's preferred channel of communication is used to provide personalized news and messaging, notify schedule changes, award air mile points, and so on (for more see Henderson, 2000).

A Model of Buyer–Seller Interaction Cycles

The customer and supplier interact, thereby developing a relationship which is mediated by a corporate brand. Dialogue, as a basic joining element, is introduced to make the customer–supplier relationship more effective and productive. Interacting partners participating in dialogue are independent systems, each with core values, beliefs, traditions, visions, and interests. Through dialogue they discuss, and the input and output of both enhances a successful communication process. Change in values, strategies, and lifestyles, from one end of the dialogue process, and products and services, at the other end, are the outcomes from which both participants can benefit. The level of communication might cover core values and a search for understanding, as well as the need for a new modification of an existing product. Dialogue does not only mean a request for a new product from a customer and the response of production and an offer of this product from the suppliers, it also arises at the initiation and choice of either party – the dialogue can be initiated by anyone. Change inside the systems that might take place as result of dialogue depends on the willingness of the communicators to implement and accept change. It comes as a result of an evaluation process, and also depends on flexibility and a recognized need to adapt.

This dialogue is not a 'one cycle action' but is a constant communication process where both sides are in continuous interaction. Both participants are not only interacting with each another but also are connected with the outer environment and are operating in a constant information exchange process.

A corporate brand is a dynamic formation that binds together and reflects the corporation with all its constituting elements, systems, and subsystems. A corporate brand serves as a communication mediator and reference point for stakeholders of the corporation – meaning is co-created through the dialogue process by two interacting systems – the consumer and the supplier.

Seller–buyer interaction takes place at three communication levels.

1. The General Communication Environment Level

The corporation and the customers interact in an environment that includes media, competitors, potential customers, other audiences, social groups, and so on. Each is constantly monitoring information that is coming in from the general environment to help evaluate decisions and opportunities that might arise (appreciation).

2. Dialogue Communication Level

At this level the corporation and customers are interacting in a dialogue. This level allows the formation of the corporation's basic business foundation and justifies its existence. By engagement in dialogue the customer is rewarded with an opportunity to satisfy their needs and interests. This is where both parties are engaged in proposal expression and evaluation. The customer expresses his or her interests and ideas, the corporation evaluates this, and, in a positive outcome, in response offers products that are then evaluated by the customer. The dialogue process also involves reconsideration of basic values and interests of the parties involved if such a request is expressed by a participant. Dialogue occurs at the level that is initiated by one of the participants, and either can be initiators. The positive outcome is a co-creation of values that are mutually beneficial and are recognized and accepted by both sides. A change process might be initiated as the response to a request expressed by the other party; however, after evaluation the responding system might remain constant if it does not accept the expressed proposal from the other participant. In an ideal situation, the interaction process ensures a constant and balanced development process for those involved.

3. Corporate Brand Communication Level

At this level, the corporation and customer have finalized their dialogue and have come to a mutually beneficial understanding: values are co-created during the dialogue process and both sides have accepted them as beneficial. A mutually agreed meaning of those values has been created and converted into shared meaning that becomes part of the corporate brand. The corporate brand at this level acts as a formation that contains all elements that are the outcome of the dialogue and are recognized by both sides – commonly agreed meanings are attached to those elements.

So, in the widest sense, a corporate brand acts as a communication medium between a corporation and a customer, and contains the result of this communication process – shared meaning of co-created values.

To operate the dialogue model as a working process, the corporation should develop an extensive receptory system and ensure that each valued customer becomes a partner in dialogue. Each customer has to be sure that their expressions will be highly appreciated through interpretation and evaluation. Dialogue lets the corporation and customers build a common communication environment that is recognized and familiar. Recognition, familiarity, and honesty leads to trust-building and customer confidence that ensures a successful communication process.

The Corporate Brand Dialogue Box Graphical Model

The presented graphical model (Figure 5.1) can be divided into four conceptual quadrants:

1   Seller evaluate/formulate.
2   Seller respond/offer.
3   Buyer evaluate/formulate.
4   Buyer request/express.

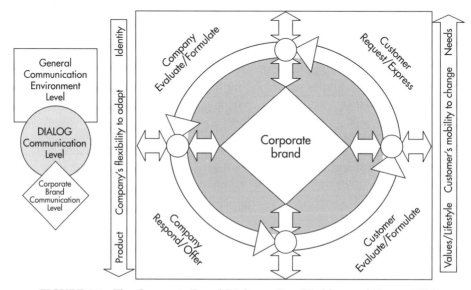

FIGURE 5.1   The Corporate Brand Dialogue Box (Karklins and Varey, 2001).

All quadrants represent the seller's and buyer's activities during the communication process taking place at all three communication levels. Quadrants 1 and 3 represent conceptual evaluation (appreciation) and the manifestation of interest, while Quadrants 2 and 4 represent implementation of interests by transformation into concrete actions.

Customer Relationship Management (CRM)

An IT system for CRM is central to most e-commerce plans. This has been developed from earlier management (or marketing) information systems to provide a central customer information system and decision support. E-commerce facilities allow consumers to establish direct contact with front line service providers, and vice versa. Further, the back office is brought to the fore by recording trading histories, consumer preferences, and buying habits. The inherently interactive nature of the CRM system is capable of enabling marketers to implement effective customer retention strategies by monitoring, rewarding, and reminding them about goods and services. Consumers can directly voice concerns, complaints, and suggestions, while the provider can respond directly and specifically to each person.

A full-blown eCRM system integrates internal and external communication channels, sales management, marketing management, and the rest of the corporate management system.

Communication (call) centre(s)

To handle incoming telephone calls and e-mail

Databases

To help track and learn from sales leads, forecast sales and revenues, record enquiry and purchase transactions, and evaluate response to marketing actions

Data warehousing

To process and analyse data and retain data history to identify patterns and details

Internet website

To allow customers to interact with databases for online shopping, customer service e-mail, etc.

To what extent, however, does ICT enable and facilitate engagement, leading to interaction, resulting in collaboration?

Spending time with customers

Renault operate a customer relationship management programme called Collection Partenaire that is designed to give customers an overall, personalized, and unique buying experience that will differentiate the company. The programme provides resources for a personalized proposal, matched to needs, so that technical solutions are transformed into meeting personal requirements. This is intended to turn away from undifferentiated mass-marketing based on an industrial model of doing business, to a customer-oriented value-adding supply strategy. Customers are treated as partners rather than as targets. Technology is being deployed to provide access to information and enable proactive behaviour, such as interactive selling using laptop computers. The ultimate aim is an integrated front office system to support a coherent strategy for engaging with customers to supplant the age-old supply strategy (based on a case study from Cap Gemini at www.crm-forum.com).

If customers are seen as passive, suppliers tend to 'push' information and entertainment at them to provoke a response. Active customers, on the other hand, are provided with information that can be found with search engines. *Broadcasting* is sent by one (the marketer) to many (customers, buyers, consumers) (Figure 5.2). *Narrowcasting* is sent by the marketer to a few selected receivers. *Pointcasting* is two marketers (seller–buyer) conversing. The choice is driven by the seller's cost constraints and the notion of cost-effectiveness (lowest cost to accomplish a communication objective – there is usually a problem here of how to measure this). Advertising and CRM can be used to support each other – indeed, the CRM process usually starts with some form of advertising. Of course, sometimes it is the buyer who initiates communicating activity. How does the seller handle this?

The essential marketing activity is the establishment of real dialogues as the link between the production sphere and the consumption sphere. When mediated by information and communication technologies, what happens is that second-level effects are produced (Christensen, 2000; Sproull and Kiesler, 1991). These change the behaviour of the communicators. They pay attention to different things, organize and interpret their relationships differently, and expect different outcomes from their own actions.

Increasingly, service is produced outside a face-to-face interpersonal interaction. 'Good' ICT emulates the face-to-face conversation, allowing the establish-

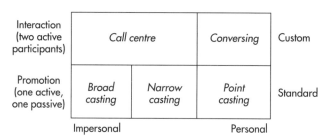

FIGURE 5.2 ICT use.

TABLE 5.1 Different relationship potentials.

Face-to-face interaction	e-Commerce interaction
Affiliation potential is natural	Desired rational development is absent (close affiliation missing)
Intimacy potential is natural	The degree of intimacy is constrained by the nature of the transaction and the prescribed customer–machine interaction
Social outcome potential is natural	E-commerce relationships are not designed to move beyond economic transactions

ment of real dialogues between sellers and buyers (buyers and sellers). The typical customer service encounter, however, is not truly a dyadic interaction of buyer and seller, since the seller is always able to retain greater agency than is the buyer.

At the time of writing, recent advents in partner relationship management applications technology include:

- web-based customer interaction (WCI) (e.g. chat rooms, email management, etc.);
- e-centres – web-enabled call centres;
- virtual customer service representatives;
- eCRM (Internet and Intranet) using online customer interface management (CIM);
- self-service technologies (SST).

When ICT mediates ('goes between') seller and buyer, how is the development of the relationship through attraction, engagement, interaction, and fulfilment accomplished? Table 5.1 summarizes some significant differences.

Both parties must ask: 'to what extent do I trust the other "party" (person, machine, system) to do what he, she, or it promises to do?' and 'who (what) is making the promise?'

Perhaps trust can be built through careful attention to both system design and behaviour. A personal relationship has to be structured to underpin a series of e-commerce transactions to allow knowledge-based or identification-based trust to develop. This has to be more than reassurance concerning data protection and system reliability, and requires that designers and users fully appreciate key interface factors at the human–computer interface.

The dimensions of communication behaviour analysed for a range of means of interaction by Lievrouw and Finn (1990) are summarized in Table 5.2.

When the purchaser experiences a high level of involvement, physical and psychic distance are transcended. Control is the relative dominance of the participants (ranging from sharing to dominating).

Higher levels of interaction require greater amounts of resources, but can produce greater benefits (Table 5.3).

TABLE 5.2 Dimensions of communication behaviour and means of interaction (adapted from Lievrouw and Finn, 1990).

Means of interaction	Degree of involvement	Locus of control	Temporality of interaction
Face-to-face	High	Equal	Simultaneous
Telephone	Medium	Equal	Simultaneous
Email	Low	Equal	Non-simultaneous
Mailing	Low	Equal	Non-simultaneous
Database	Low	'Receiver'	Non-simultaneous

TABLE 5.3 Levels of e-commerce (based on O'Connor and Galvin, 1998).

Publish	Engage	Trade	Integrate
Distribute (push) information via ICT, often some stakeholders' interests are excluded	Online technical support, with exchanges of information, discussion forums, and downloadable resources	Buy–sell transaction processing	Formalization of trading relationship bonds

In 1998, the World Wide Web carried some 300 million pages. By 2001, this had been expanded to 3 billion pages.

The limits of machine interactivity are predetermined by the producer's notion of what would be of interest to users. Users interact with ICT within a pre-specified set of options (partly specified by the technology, partly by the designers of the system). Yet, users can creatively interact in appropriating options and thus can move beyond the meanings the producer provided.

In the eCRM system, multiple 'contact points' (interactions, really) generate data. The databases draw from multiple data sources. Information is generated by both parties, but the CRM databases largely only capture what is specified from the seller's point of view. Professor Barnes's interest, emotions, is an example of 'missing' data. Further, customers may want consistent treatment, regardless of which point of contact they (choose to) encounter, and they may wish to specify how they are to be informed.

Therefore, the eCRM challenge is the integration of 'points of interaction' for marketing, sales, and service/care in the differing modes of relating. Conversation and consultation arise through 'interactive' media, while only presentation can be conducted through 'directive' media. In this way, ICT use generates 'feedback' – with an alternative meaning of this term. Feedback, in this carefully chosen sense, does not then mean an expressed opinion on an observed act or suggestion, but *reciprocal influence*. We are here recognizing not just a different quantity, quality, or speed of feedback from that traditionally claimed for 'interactive' media, but an alternative form, in which knowledge, meanings, and identities are co-produced by the participants.

Person or System as the Basis of Interaction?

Large-scale automation serves mass consumption. Such systematized service seems incompatible with Relationship Marketing aims. From a sociological perspective, Ritzer and Stillman (2001) distinguish person-oriented vs. system-oriented consumption forms to highlight the impact of non-social interaction on service.

The adoption of a system-oriented way of producing and delivering value is premised on a particular set of beliefs about modes of communication, and an instrumentally rational mindset, as we have seen in earlier chapters. Here we examine further the problem of designing and operating CRM as disembedded 'expert' service systems, and show that human relationships need to be re-embedded.

Buying–selling and customer service arise at the interface of systems of production (the seller's sphere of influence) and systems of consumption (the buyer's sphere of influence). The modern day emphasis on efficiency, mechanization, and the 'Taylorization' (control) of the workplace, have had a dramatic effect on the experience of buyers and consumers. Instrumentally rational production (that strives for efficiency, calculability, predictability, and control) accomplished through non-human technology reduces the buyer's experience to a standardized, impersonal 'battle of wits' (in which sellers have to meet the expectations of their managers, while buyers can choose to walk away). This is a fundamental tension.

Re-enchantment is a prevalent way of dealing with this managerially. Rationalized settings are made more appealing through the contrivance of spectacle and simulation. For example, many people experience first-line contact with a sales or service office through a multilevel, automated telephone system that plays popular music to entertain them as they are made to wait to engage with a person. Pubs and cafes provide manufactured themed enchantment to disguise the rationalized production and service routines (Ritzer (1993/2000) calls this effect 'McDonaldization') (Figure 5.3).

Person-oriented service is attentive and personalized in face-to-face relating and is found in less rationalized settings (family businesses, and so on), but less so as managers argue for economies of scale. Personal service requires experience,

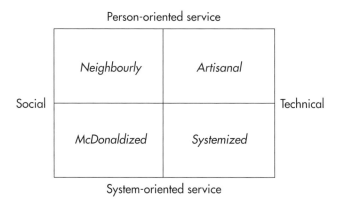

FIGURE 5.3   Types of service (Ritzer and Stillman, 2001, p. 107).

know-how, willingness, patience, and dedication to helping. This is skilled, time-consuming, and relatively expensive labour.

Through the use of non-human technology, *system-oriented* customer service deskills and ultimately replaces workers with technology. Intersubjective personal service is replaced with instrumentally rational, standardized, 'cost-effective' processes (e.g. inquiries are fielded by computers and touch-tone telephones).

Service encounters occur within human relationships (social) or these are reduced or eliminated (technical). The long-term trend, observe Ritzer and Stillman, is from neighbourly/artisanal service toward McDonaldized/system-ized service.

So, we should ask, does Relationship Marketing require person-oriented service? Is Customer Relationship Management fundamentally used to accomplish systemized, 'cost-effective' (automated) distancing of buyers from sellers? Are the promises of CRM benefits for buyers simply delusions if CRM is used to remove people from service settings?

In Chapter 6, we will consider a range of cases to see if we can convince ourselves that CRM can deliver the promises of benefits for consumers as well as suppliers.

In part, at least, might not the much reported dotcom failures (more than 200 in 2001, with $1.5 billion in investment) be explained by an unwillingness of consumers to relinquish human relationships in surrendering their trading encounters, at the behest of suppliers (and for their convenience), to layers of disembedded systems (Ritzer and Stillman, 2001)? System-oriented trading provides benefits to producers/suppliers that are distinctly disadvantageous for buyers/consumers. In system-oriented service, how is trust (rooted in face-to-face interaction) to be established and maintained? Ritzer and Stillman suggest that such systems have to be made more knowable and transparent. Further, as we will see in the next chapter, buyers/consumers have little voice in the colonization of trading encounters by technologies of 'information' and 'communication'.

The Emotionally Intelligent Interface

The World Wide Web is a catalyst for trading and communicative interaction, but use reduces loyalty, because it makes product-finding easier.

We are witnessing the evolution of exchange party interfaces as we see traditional 'brick-and-mortar' and 'online' business systems converge into a hybrid 'click-and-mortar' system with multiple, electronic and physical, interpersonal 'touchpoints' (Bergeron, 2001). The challenge is to integrate the subsystems to provide a seamless interface.

Bergeron (2001) has developed the concept of the Emotionally Intelligent Interface to assist with the development of highly responsive customer–supplier trading that is owned by those who interact and produce valuably. These events are not to be neglected, nor taken for granted, but require care and attention; each is a joint problem-solving episode, based on something in common and mutual (i.e. trust – forget the simplistic and incorrect term 'two-way' – this smacks

TABLE 5.4 Forces on a buyer–seller relationship.

For (+) – internal	*Against (−) – internal*
Emotional bond (trust, accountability, respect, etc.)	Employees coerced by managers to conduct customer relationships inauthentically
The extent to which the product is valued	Alienated employees
The amount of time and energy invested (information making, negotiating, critique, opportunity costs, etc.)	
For (+) – external	*Against (−) – external*
The difficulty in locating alternatives (the WWW reduces this)	The number of affordable alternative products
	Frustration experienced when doing business with the seller

of reciprocal manipulation, when we very specifically and carefully mean interaction).

Table 5.4 summarizes an attempt to identify forces that may bear on a buyer's relationship with a seller.

The aim of managing the EII (emotionally intelligent interface) for all interaction points is to provide the missing link of many so-called CRM systems – an ambassador (comprising caring customer service representatives supported by computer systems) that mediate customer–supplier dialogue through the CRM system in order positively to influence the buyer's emotional bond. This requires personal attention and intimacy to engage people in the necessary dialogue. The aim is to increase the emotional bond. This requires that all components are assembled and managed in a cohesive structure, and the emulation of the self-controlled, conscientious, empathic service orientation of the highly effective and efficient customer service representative (displaying anticipation, recognition, and fulfilment of customer needs).

Figure 5.4 is a summary of Bergeron's user interface hierarchy (2001, p. 87), outlining the levels of 'connection' with the user and the associated performance criteria.

It is the emotional bond that produces customer loyalty. The EII must be designed and managed to ensure that familiarity, personality, and consistency are developed, and that contact between people is not reduced to a cold datapoint. The prevailing source of frustration and disappointment is that so-called 'touchpoints' appear unco-ordinated and provide different and inconsistent levels of service. Some, thankfully, are personalized and active, offering assistance and advice by taking the customer's point of view. Others are passive and fixed and impose or rebuff the customer.

So what would an EII (at the contact point of customer service, e-commerce, call centre, and Internet) look like to a customer? Table 5.5 summarizes Bergeron's explanation.

| Emotionally intelligent – automated reps. and bots
Personal connectivity |
| Intelligent – voice recognition, expert system
Adaptability |
| Emotional – games
Fun |
| Logical front-end application (e.g. spreadsheet)
Ease of use and effectiveness |
| Graphical – windows, controls
Aesthetics and intuition |
| Physical – speech synthesis
Efficiency and feedback |
| Physical – mouse, keyboard
Efficiency and comfort |

FIGURE 5.4   User interface hierarchy (derived from Bergeron, 2001, p. 87).

Bergeron also compares the relative capacity for interactivity (defined as 'distance') and potential for EII of a range of ICT technologies (Figure 5.5).

According to Bergeron, leaders in developing emotionally intelligent interfaces are Nintendo, Sega, and Sony.

The Customer Information File

Although we are here not concerned with the technology of Relationship Marketing and Customer Relationship Marketing, we should consider that character of an effective database system that assists the Relationship Manager and Marketing Manager with relationship management through:

- identifying the most important customers;
- personalized interaction with customers;
- emulating dialogue;
- new product development.

Table 5.6 summarizes Gordon's suggestions for the information that might help.

I am struck by some questions here. Rather like a personnel file on an employee, the Data Protection Act applies to any such records. Should the customer be able to see what is recorded about their relationship with the seller? How might this help to build the relationship? What about emotions? How would that aspect of the relationship be recorded and taken into account in commitments to action?

TABLE 5.5 Characteristics of a productive*, emotionally intelligent interface
(based on Bergeron, 2001, p. 103).

Characteristic	Comment	Example of a common failure on so-called CRM systems
Respectful	Doesn't waste the customer's time and asks for information only when really needed – suggests a course of action, doesn't demand	Website repeatedly won't accept submission of a form until every field is completed
Helpful	Facilitates the task	Online bank system requires account number to be keyed in – then operator asks for the same details
Empathetic	Matches the interface to tastes and personality	
Socially adept	Limits information exchange to what is needed and can adapt to context	Asking for an email address that is not needed for a postal mailing
Truthful	Provides correct data (without obscuring or confusing) to influence behaviour	Website does not give any telephone number or mailing address – no people can be found!
Unambiguous	Gives single meanings to statements or requests	
Anticipatory	Can anticipate needs	'Registration' at first contact, then required to enter same details at all subsequent contacts
Persuasive	Applies social skills to persuade to a course of action	Website content does not engage attention or inspire further action
Responsive	Responds to customer's input	Never get a reply to an enquiry
Emotive	Responds in ways that positively influence the customer's emotions	Automated telephone answering system that offers multiple options, then gives an option that is unavailable

* Note that 'productive' here means value-creating for participants.

---

eCRM functionality

A suite of more than 30 modules is offered by System Access (www.systemaccess.com) in their NetSymbols retail and wholesale banking system. Modules include Customer Profile, Target Marketing, Alerts & Notifications, and Contact Management. This can be integrated on a server or Internet platform.

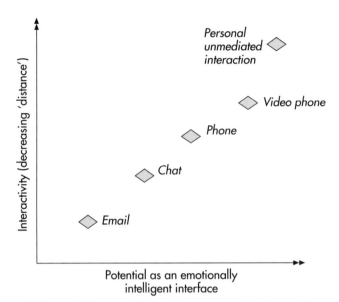

FIGURE 5.5 EII potential of various communication mediators (adapted from Bergeron, 2001, p. 184, fig. 7.2).

TABLE 5.6 Outline customer information files (based on Gordon, 1998, ch. 7).

Consumer customer file	Producer customer file
Identification	Identification
Customer rating	Customer rating
Background	Background
Pre-sale communication	Pre-sale interaction
Purchase behaviour	Purchases
Post-purchase behaviour	Decision makers
Predicted behaviour	Decision making
Creditworthiness	Influences
Attitudes and judgements	Post-purchase behaviour
	Channels
	Pricing
	Predicted behaviour
	Creditworthiness
	Selected relevant information

Summary of eCRM Principles

CRM is not simply an installed technology – it is an enacted model for a way of trading. Put simply, CRM is a highly structured, technology-enabled way of organizing the finding of goods and services for customers who you know, as a

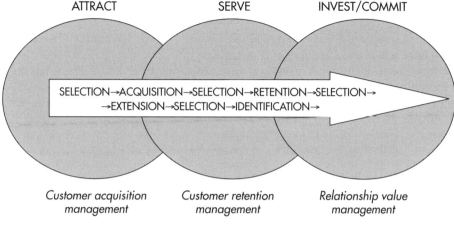

FIGURE 5.6   Relationship development progress.

value-creating alternative to attracting buyers you don't know to products they don't know.

Chaffey (2002) equates CRM with 'customer acquisition': 'CRM is one of the tactics aimed at fulfilling the objectives defined in the e-marketing plan' (p. 330). Of course, we have realized that CRM can be much more socially productive than this. Figure 5.6, on the other hand, illustrates the continuing progress of managed relationship development through the careful selection of those people with whom to trade in a profitable trading relationship.

The whole question of eCRM has to be about a better (extended) trading relationship, not a cheaper, easier one. It does not really make sense to make an effort to solve specific business problems with ICT until the CRM philosophy is formulated.

If we consider the emphasis to be on 'relationship', we can reassess the notion that data capture and database technology can allow a seller to 'know customers as individuals'. The data merely characterize a person as similar to or different from another. Such databases can help in reporting retention rates, segmentation, and root cause of defections, etc. This is an asymmetrical information distribution in the seller–buyer 'relationship'.

Buttle (1996), among others, has remarked that the voice of the customer is absent from much so-called relationship marketing. This seems to cast doubt on the very principle that such practices serve mutual interests in win–win outcomes. Of course, not all customers want personal attention, yet the impersonal approach must still allow their voice to be heard (in product decisions, trading arrangement decisions, and so on). eCRM robs interacters of human contact, conversational opportunities, and the possibility to 'read' a situation. Participants are not able to learn about each other's interests, expectations, assumptions, and so on, through a dialogical negotiation/conversation.

The duty of the Customer Relationship Manager is to manage customer profitability, share of spend, and selective retention of trading relationships. So, the salesperson has to become a customer relationship initiator. The attractors (i.e.

what motivates customers to trade with a supplier) are to be managed as investments, not as costs.

Philosophically, a buyer can only exist in the presence of a seller. These social roles only make sense if there is a purposive interaction encounter. The trading exchange relationship is a system of communicative interaction. There has to be communicative interaction. How can eCRM operate this? How can we avoid CRM being operated as no more than a sophisticated (i.e. complex, large-scale, expensive, ICT-intensive) form of database marketing that drives, rather than supports, service production and delivery? CRM is not merely a part of database marketing, but the latter is certainly a part of eCRM.

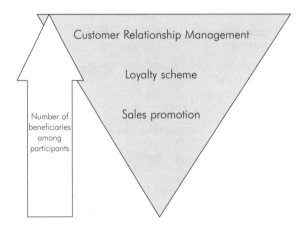

Christensen (1997) has noted the almost frantic 'ceremonial conformity' with which managers wish to demonstrate their adherence to prevailing norms on how to operate in markets. Perhaps CRM offers (yet) another form of reorganization to regain control in the face of disappearing, other ways to control? Now we turn to the evidence. Who is practising RM as *joined-up marketing* through a CRM system? To what extent can we discern a technology infrastructure for a strategically managed, value-making business system? Who recognizes that ICT is an enabler, not the cause, of good CRM? Have they really integrated marketing, sales, service, and IT? Does the way customers want to trade really drive the way the business is managed?

A CRM system should be capable of:

- enabling responsive and responsible interaction;
- allowing customers to manage their trading relationship;
- providing an integrated range of means of contact, such that interaction history is comprehensive and complete;
- supporting, intuitively, a range of modes and degrees of human interaction, supported by automated processes and tools;
- anticipating, capturing, and responding to human emotion – a 'human feel', thus acting as a gateway to the business, not a drawbridge;
- instilling confidence in users, by demonstrable response and ease of use;
- delivering consistency and coherency in offers, profile, and treatment;

- registering and understanding all interactions;
- mapping, integrally, to the way the business needs to operate, so that processes are relevant and understandable for staff and customers;
- supporting the management of knowledge;
- encouraging return and continuing interaction.

This is a tall order. Many systems have not yet met these requirements, though the promises are still being made.

References

Bergeron, B. (20001) *The Eternal E-Customer: How Emotionally Intelligent Interfaces Can Create Long-Lasting Customer Relationships*, New York: McGraw-Hill.

Buttle, F. (ed.) (1996) *Relationship Marketing: Theory and Practice*, London: Paul Chapman Publishing.

Chaffey, D. (2002) *E-Business and E-Commerce Management*, London: Prentice Hall.

Christensen, L. T. (1997) 'Marketing as auto-communication', *Consumption, Markets & Culture*, Vol. 1, No. 3, 197–227.

Christensen, L. T. (2000) 'Marketing and communication technology: Paradoxes and dialogics', *Consumption, Markets & Culture*, Vol. 4, No. 1, 1–21.

Gordon, I. (1998) *Relationship Marketing*, Toronto: John Wiley & Sons.

Henderson, C. (2000) 'Relationship Marketing: I want to be your friend', *Revolution Asia*, 31 December [www.revolutionmagazine.com].

www.hewson.co.uk

Karklins, G. and Varey, R. J. (2001) 'The corporate brand and corporate communication: The Corporate Brand Dialog Box (CBDB)', invited article for the special issue on corporate branding, *THEXIS*, the journal of the Research Institute for Media & Communications Management, Issue 4.2001, 38–41, Graduate School of Business, University of St Gallen, Switzerland.

Lievrouw, L. A. and Finn, T. A. (1990) 'Identifying the common dimensions of communication: The communication systems model', in B. D. Ruben and L. A. Lievrouw (eds) *Mediation, Information and Behaviour*, New Brunswick, NJ: Transaction Publishers, pp. 37–65.

Millard, N. (2001) *CRM Best Practice 2001*, Martlesham Heath, UK: BTexact Technologies (www.btexact.com).

O'Connor, J. and Galvin, E. (1998) *Creating Value Through eCommerce*, London: FT Management Briefings.

www.rightnowtech.com

Ritzer, G. (1993/2000) *The McDonaldization of Society: An Investigation into the Changing Character of Contemporary Social Life*, London: Sage.

Ritzer, G. and Stillman, T. (2001) 'From person- to system-oriented service', in A. Sturdy, I. Grugulis, and H. Willmott (eds) *Customer Service: Empowerment and Entrapment*, London: Palgrave, pp. 102–116.

Royal Mail @ www.royalmail.com/ebusiness

Sproull, L. and Kiesler, S. (1991) *Connections: New Ways of Working in the Networked Organization*, Cambridge, MA.: MIT Press.

Chapter 6

MANAGING CUSTOMER RELATIONSHIPS

The knowing buyer and the knowing seller

*Hello, are you a real person?**

Marriage is one long conversation, chequered by disputes. Two persons more and more adapt their notions to suit the other, and in the process of time, without sound of trumpets they conduct each other into new worlds of thought
Robert Louis Stevenson

Introduction

In this chapter we ask: Is CRM simply, as is suggested by many enthusiasts, the meeting of relationship marketing (strategy) and the marketing information system (technology)? Is the form of relationship marketing in which this is based no more than the manipulative pretence of friendship, or is it the authentic management of co-operative trading interaction? Do buyers (marketers and consumers) want managed trading relationships with suppliers? Managed by whom? Both parties to a commercial exchange are marketers – can they both manage their value acquisitions? How can the marketer as consumer manage his or her exchanges with providers (marketers as producers and/or sellers) when the media are controlled by the (dominant) party? Is CRM simply a call centre and a website? We are not concerned here with 'technology solutions' – is the typical CRM offer no more than an ICT solution in search of a problem?

CRM is generally explained by its commercial proponents as a business strategy (process) aimed at understanding and anticipating the needs of a corporation's current and potential customers, and/or a technology platform for linking people, resources, and processes across the whole business enterprise and beyond. From the technology perspective, CRM involves widely capturing customer data,

---

*Inspired by the title of Johnson's recent article (2001).

consolidating all internally and externally acquired customer-related data in a central database, analysing the consolidated data, distributing the results of the analysis to various customer 'touchpoints', and using this information when dealing with customers via any 'touchpoints'. Customers are thus linked into the business enterprise system in a way that suits them.

Contemporary CRM is data driven with a focus on behaviour, but little regard for buyer emotions. Patterns of potential buyer–seller purchase interactions are sought by matching buyer behaviour with classified prospect profiles, in order to target promotional expressions (offers/promises). In this way, the 'relationship' effort is driven by accounts of past behaviour and segmentation analyses. None of these data can inform the seller on why customers purchase.

We have seen that genuine relationships do not emerge as a product of Relationship Marketing programmes or of CRM systems, but through appropriate treatment of buyers by sellers. Mutual trust arises from the exchange of information, commitment, and satisfactory performance of the partners' respective roles. Barriers to committed trading relationships include:

- infrequent contact;
- absence of direct contact;
- insertion of technology into interactions;
- the anonymizing of the person as a customer ('help me, I've been digitized!').

Here we consider how theory helps to explain and guide practice in terms of:

1 The need/problem.
2 The product/solution.
3 CRM practice.
4 Developmental issues.

The chapter is presented in two parts. In Part I we further critique the concept and its application. In Part II we examine a number of situations in which Relationship Marketing is being applied through Customer Relationship Management systems to see what is actually being done.

In planning the writing of this book, I originally intended to present cases of relationship marketing application and customer relationship management application separately. Of course, as things move on at a seemingly frenetic pace I found that all significant cases of Relationship Marketing were supported by CRM.

Part I

The Meeting of Managerialistic Marketing and ICT

Fitchett and McDonagh (2001) have pointed out that the CRM logic boasts sophisticated consumers and enthusiastically embraces new technologies for rapid generation, storage, transmission, and analysis of market data.

In raising questions about the rhetoric of CRM, I outline reflections on the instrumentality of much of what is said and done about marketing, information systems, and CRM systems. The departure point is critical scepticism, motivated by concerns for the ethical status of the commercially valuable outcome of (at least) two conjoined, simplistic, and fundamentally dominatory conventional wisdoms. These stem from two managerialistically biased fields that share a common basis in a false rationality.

The combination of information systems and communication systems offers an infrastructure for operating a customer relationship management (CRM) strategy that integrates otherwise discrete production and support functions in the service of customers. There the rhetoric ends.

Many of the (complex, expensive, untested) e-CRM systems appear to be no more than automated customer response (sub)systems. As yet another configuration of ERP, process automation, call centre, and other ICT products, CRM has been created in the desire of the vendors to position themselves as locked-in, one-stop shops for marketing and service automation.

Our tricky practice-oriented question is this: 'Do customers benefit from the rather obvious increased convenience that these systems provide to adopters?' This prompts another difficult query: 'How do adopters benefit from using these e-CRM systems?' We can imagine that some customers will tolerate bad experiences in engaging with eCRM systems if they can recognize lower prices as compensation. This may not always be the case. Prices may not be reduced by such automation, and low price may not be the primary benefit sought.

We can choose the stance of reflection as critical sceptic. We discover, by critically examining the intellectual sources of the latest saviour ('strategic imperative') of enterprise management, that CRM principles are substantially unreflectively adopted in e-CRM as a reinvention of IT as information and communication systems, as technology-enabled relationship marketing, and in large-scale business process integration. Worse still, we find that the marketing and IS parents of the CRM child are themselves damaged. The progeny is, predictably and for the time being, an unhealthy mutant.

ICT can automate, on a large scale, the information basis of a control system. CRM, according to Brown (2000), is 'a business strategy that aims to understand, anticipate and manage the needs of an organisation's [sic] current and potential customers' (p. xiv). Further, CRM is 'the process of acquiring, retaining, and growing profitable customers. It requires a clear focus on the service attributes that represent value to the customer and that create loyalty' (p. 8). CRM organizes strategic customer care.

We therefore have yet another strategic imperative in the management of business! Brown's book on e-CRM (2000), providing as it does a recipe for exploiting the reinvented business systems services of the dominating consulting firms and their partnering IT vendors, is but one of a flood of products, courses, conferences, and publications that herald our managers' latest dissatisfactions and insecurities.

An example of the current rhetoric is drawn from a trade newsletter from a major systems vendor:

CRM: a radical change in business practice

The main asset of a company is its customers. Today, companies are active in a dynamic market facing deregulation, liberalization, globalization, and increasing competition. This makes the question of how to win new customers and how to keep them an essential one, meaning that companies are tending to switch from a product-oriented to a customer-oriented strategy. Information plays a major role and has become a strategic and competitive tool for management, resulting in the activity known as Customer Relationship Management (CRM).

Customer loyalty is the name of the game and loyal customers will be behind tomorrow's profitable companies. But keeping customers loyal means lots of individualized attention which may sometimes seem in contradiction to a mass market. And when that individualized attention is provided, the copycat pace is frantic; no good marketing idea remains privileged property today for more than a matter of moments and the effort required to stay ahead is enormous. The reaction, 'looking after customers is fine, but what about our margins', is understandable.

The key to this conundrum will be provided by the new information technologies. Don't imagine that traditional customer channels such as salesforces and agency networks will be swept away overnight by state-of-the-art, dehumanized IT. They won't. Increased customer attention will mean increased awareness of the customer as a better educated and more sophisticated player and people-to-people relationships will still be vital. But proactive marketing and after-marketing will focus on making the customer happy through the use of technology-based improved knowledge about him.

Data warehousing and analysis of our customer information will enable us to gain better access to the customer. At the same time, call centres and interactive Internet sites will give the customer better access to the company. Response times to the customer's requirements will accelerate phenomenally.

The cultural shift companies are going through here is really very exciting and so far we are only at the tip of the iceberg. Within a staggeringly short timescale, even within a couple of years, CRM will be a very different reality as software is developed that will be able to look after all of a company's front and back office information systems (extracts from *Market Trends*, Issue No. 2, July 1999, Cap Gemini).

Therefore, according to Brown (2000) for example, eCRM provides a universal corporate infrastructure that enables the strategic use of customer and prospect information, focuses on all transactions as investments in the relationship, provides information during all contacts for use throughout the 'organization', allows the customer to use preferred communication channels, and systematizes the common business processes and strategic data capture on all customer 'touchpoints'.

At present, I don't see the evolution of e-CRM as healthy. Through my reflection, I see the present manifestations, in e-CRM, of a convergence of relationship marketing and ICT as fundamentally flawed due to an overly rationalistic cost-reduction motive. When a major new capability is heralded, yet constructed in the unreflective feeding of one distorted/flawed discourse upon another, a recipe for disappointment (at least) and potential for a disaster might reasonably be anticipated. Is the mutant that is being created from the damaged marketing and ICT (both spawned of a limiting managerialistic rationalism) really what we, as citizens, want?

I propose that the root of the problem lies partly in the wholesale avoidance of the issue of the politics of management, which leads to an obscuring and diversionary way of thinking of 'interactive communication'. I offer a clarifying alternative terminology: communicative interaction that deals with the integrating and producing qualities of human communication (see Cooren, 2000, for a fascinating, detailed explanation of the organizing property of communicating). What would be required for e-CRM systems to be capable of enabling and supporting this mode of engagement among stakeholders to a managed enterprise? In pursuing a careful critical analysis, I am attempting to talk of the democratization that is both necessary and, I believe, feasible.

Part II

Just the facts
Start today and have global CRM in 90 days
Time is money

Oracle advertisement, *Financial Times*, 4 May 2001

As a fairly typical citizen and consumer (no more demanding than many), I have become increasingly disillusioned by my experiences of so-called customer service. Here are just a few recent examples of promises not being met and responsibility for consequences being ignored:

- an online credit card company takes three months to process a credit card application and issue a credit card, then twice sends a card with the wrong name on it;
- an automated credit card service phone line asks for my card number to be input through the keypad, then the first thing I am asked for by the operator on connection is my card number – twice!
- a credit card telephone transaction request to transfer funds is not actioned and interest charges are incurred;
- an online website bank account transactions are not actioned;
- an online shopping service company issues me with two membership cards with different account numbers;
- a cable TV provider's automated phone service has five layers of options on the helpline. The final selected option announces – 'sorry this service is not available'.

Why do ICT-enabled services not deliver on the promise of 'interactive communication'?

Case Studies of Relationship Marketing Implementation in Customer Relationship Management

Let us now examine some commercial situations in which relationship marketing and customer relationship management claims are made, as a test of the theories selected here to investigate and re-view Relationship Marketing in the era of ubiquitous ICT and the growth of social networks.

In selecting and compiling these case studies, I asked myself: 'How successful are these examples of implementations – in terms of the critical communication theory?' Don't take them as answers, but, rather, as discussion points.

E-commerce takes off at Airtours

Keywords: Internet integration; loyalty programme; CRM

The launch of mytravelco.com provides a global, branded, integrated travel service through which holiday and travel products can be bought by means of multiple channels including the Internet, interactive TV, WAP phones, telephone call centres, and high street offices.

The integration of customer relationship management and distribution systems is founded on strategic technology partnerships with BT, Oracle, Sun Microsystems, the Landmark travel channel, Lonely Planet, Telewest, and others. This recognizes that the distribution structure that puts value into the 'hands' of consumers and buyers is part of the total communication environment. Marketing communication management is a critical aspect of supply chain management, and not separate from it.

The mytravelco loyalty programme rewards customers with points throughout the holiday experience.

Chairman David Crossland believes that this £100M investment will 'revolutionize our relationships with our customers, enhance our revenues, and provide significant opportunities to further increase efficiency.'

(Details drawn from *The Happening*, the Airtours employee newsletter, Issue 14, July–August 2000, and www.airtours.com/emedia)

Access all areas at BUPA

Keywords: customer contact management; service strategy, CRM

In order to maintain their position as the leading private medical insurance services group, BUPA determined that they had to be able to offer customers an easy, accessible means of trading with them. This, it was realized, would require a speedy and personal service supported by appropriate technologies.

Service and sales would have to be facilitated with individual customers on a personal basis through all contact media. Recent research had shown that customers are increasingly sophisticated in their service and communication expectations. They expect to be able to get their enquiries answered quickly and are less tolerant of poor response. They will use the growing variety of means of communication and will take service to be of paramount importance in their assessment of value-for-money and other service criteria.

BUPA commissioned a development group to produce a service access strategy that would contribute to the customer focus aspects of the strategic business plan.

This required that all service development would be driven by customer demand and preference, while taking account of commercial and operational viability. Wherever possible, customer expectations would be exceeded within operating cost limits. Contact media should be integrated. Customer service records should be available in all parts of the service system. Business processes will be managed with an understanding of customer behaviour and preferences. Customer Relationship Management would be developed from the current call centre system to provide access management, with the trading relationship seen as the continuing service experience of each customer within which the style of service is tailored to their preference.

(Based on the UK service Access Strategy document, BUPA.)

'I'm in charge of my car': the Peugeot website

Keywords: personalized customer care; online service support database

Introduced in early 2000, the interactive personal website is designed to provide a 'one-stop shop' for all the motoring needs, to take the stress out of ownership, of Peugeot owners. Using relationship marketing techniques, Peugeot aim to organize their customers' motoring and to offer competitive deals.

Registered users can access their own 'My car' profiled site to:

- receive emailed alert notices in advance of service due dates;
- be notified of renewal dates for car tax, insurance, and MOT;
- order information on the latest finance deals and product offers;
- request car brochures and current prices;
- arrange a test drive;
- buy accessories online;
- get a valuation of their car from *Glass's Guide*;
- get tailored information on a range of topics, including traffic news, hotel guide, etc.;
- receive tailored offers on insurance, accessories, etc.;
- request a call from the call centre to get answers to questions via a 'call me' option.

The success of this approach depends on customers' willingness to provide personal information to indicate their interests, and the use of this to make relevant offers in return. Although such one-to-one interaction may seem intrusive, the aim claimed by Peugeot's Manager of Direct Marketing, Bill Sullivan, is to develop rapport and thereby offer continuing added-value.

The website builds on the established customer service and dealership network, to initially promote the brand and support sales, then to facilitate after-sales care. The major benefit claimed is the personalization and proactive information.

A CD-ROM showcasing the services and providing free Internet access through Virgin Net was mailed to 350,000 readers of the loyalty magazine *Rapport*, which is mailed to Peugeot owners four times during the year. A supporting 'Peugeot Open-line' is provided on 0345 56 55 56.

(For more, see the Peugeot Owner's website @ www.peugeot.co.uk)

Getting involved with Ben & Jerry's Homemade, Inc.

Keywords: human values; quality; care and responsibility

Ben Cohen and Jerry Greenfield established their super-premium ice cream business in Vermont in 1978. Since then, they have pursued a values-led caring and socially responsible way of doing business that seeks to prosper through the finest quality products, profitable growth, and commitment to the community. In their Caring Capitalism, while relationships with customers need to be profitable to sustain the business, there is the deepest respect for each person, whether employee, customer, supplier, or other, and for the communities of which they are part.

Relational bonds are acknowledged and rewarded. Loyalty is earned through caring and responsible response to customer issues, rather than engineered in loyalty programmes and 'lock-in' arrangements.

Customers and employees participate in tours of the production plants, roadshows, charity events, and new product development contests. A number of successful ice cream flavours have been named by customers (e.g. Cherry Garcia, and New York Super Fudge Chunk). Creative ideas can be logged on the website. The 'Great British Flavour Name' competition led to the Cool Britannia flavour.

A range of websites are provided in a number of countries for interaction and involvement of customers in the business. In the UK, the Cool Club has 25,000 members who receive a monthly newsletter on events and ways to get involved. Some activities are tied to the social mission of the business. For example, as part of the National Blood Service student blood donor drive, B & J's helped to promote sessions and gave free tubs of ice cream to donors.

Since the takeover by Unilever, has anything changed, and will the core philosophy prevail?

(See www.benjerry.co.uk, http://lib.benjerry.com/index.tmpl and Cohen and Greenfield, 1997.) The assistance of Lauren Nola, Brand Manager, Ben & Jerry's Homemade Ltd, is gratefully acknowledged.

Modelling fashion and finance – the J D Williams home shopping challenge

Keywords: predictive modelling; purchase behaviour database; home shopping

As J D Williams expanded their interests beyond one-to-one home shopping in to financial services, they faced a problem of communicating about appropriate product offers with a growing and diverse customer base.

J D Williams is the UK's largest, independent home shopping company with a long-established reputation for leadership. From a focus on fashion for 45–65-year-old people, they have expanded into the youth market and into financial products. This has produced annual sales of more than £350 million, driven by a commitment to innovative application of ICT.

In 1997 several partnerships were established with established financial service providers, generating sales of £1 million in the following year. Some 15,000 customers now hold life assurance policies. The marketing database computer now holds 20 million account records and transaction data for six trading years. They have gathered lifestyle and age data through catalogue questionnaire inserts and outbound telephony. Data are also transferred from their third-party providers. The result is a rich 'customer view' database that is refreshed on a monthly cycle.

(Based on a case study at www.crm-forum.com)

Building customer relationships with old and new media at Oticon

Keywords: contact; supporting problem-solving; relational knowledge

Oticon are rather unconventional Danish manufacturers of hearing care products who emphasize relationships in their way of doing business. Dr Peter Mark sees Relationship Marketing as always being there for your clients on their terms.

Oticon are already anticipating the massive growth in wireless mobile services that will allow people to be online all of the time. In this way, their products can be used to counteract hearing deficiencies or for wireless communication purposes. Clients are acquiring masses of information through the Internet, and the role of professional care will include helping them 'digest' this in to their decisions, choices, and problem-solving.

High-cost, low-efficiency mass promotional techniques can attract new sales prospects, but the more cost-effective new technologies and new media will be used to nurture relationships over the typically 8–10 years of trying to cope with progressive hearing loss.

Dr Mark advocates using a variety of relationship marketing options: cross-selling to clients, prospecting and networking, personal letters and personal calls, referral programmes, direct mail offers, email and print newsletters, and events. The aim is to stay in touch.

An informational website is a forum for delivering information about goods and services, allowing clients to make informed choices. 24-hour user support is provided, for example, on the www.DigiLife.com site.

The key is establishing willing communication based on mutually agreed interests so that the relationship is personal, and contact is neither sporadic nor always initiated by the supplier. Dr Mark terms this kind of relationship as 'eDating'. For the supplier, the advantage is obvious – other suppliers can copy business strategy, products, marketing, and way of working. On the other hand, knowledge of customers and the relationship cannot be copied.

(Based on a company report from their *International Human Link Conference*.)

Coming on strong with the HOG

Keywords: owner group; membership; brand loyalty; charismatic brand

Once, a Harley-Davidson motorcycle was the symbol of rebellion – today it is a status symbol and so popular that new orders take more than a year to deliver. Customers are certainly loyal! Some even tattoo the company name onto their bodies.

All new owners are given a 1-year membership of the Harley Owners Group, and receive regular mailings of literature and manuals. Dealers support the relationship by sponsoring local HOG chapters. A customer retention direct mail programme was devised with help from the US Postal Service Tactical Marketing & Sales Development division. This aims to encourage HOG members to renew their $40 annual membership by mailing humorous reminder cards, member magazines, and easy-to-use renewal kits. When the HOG was launched in 1983 there were 33,000 members. With a 75% renewal rate, this has grown to more than 500,000 members.

In 1999 the HOG.com website was launched to provide on-demand membership information and administration. As the site proudly proclaims, 'some HOG benefits you hold in your hand – some you hold in your heart.'

(For more details, see www.harley-davidson.com and www.hog.com and www.harley-davidson.co.uk)

Is Air Miles ® *a Relationship Marketing programme?*

Keywords: loyalty; frequent shopper; reward; incentive

Air Miles® are points earned by spending money on purchases from a coalition of sponsoring retailers and service providers. These are 'travel miles' that can be redeemed against airline tickets as a discount on fares.

What does the programme actually achieve? If so-called loyalty is increased, is this loyalty to the participating brands or to the scheme? Is loyalty developed, or does the scheme merely stimulate purchases, regardless of the participating partner brands? We should not equate the duration of a series of interactions with loyalty. The travel miles are a reward for repeat purchases that are taken to be an incentive to encourage people to buy more.

Scheme members can look up offers on the website but cannot immediately confirm availability. During a follow-up telephone call, other offers may be presented by the service representative. Arguably, some degree of short-term emotional bond develops during the several telephone conversations needed to confirm a deal. However, the convenience of online purchase is missing.

Should Air Miles® be properly termed a frequency marketing or frequent shopper reward programme, rather than a loyalty scheme? Perhaps the scheme is behaviourally driven in producing repeat buying behaviour? What evidence can we find for an emotional bond being developed? There is an attitudinal aspect of trading that is not treated in so-called 'loyalty programmes.' So-called 'loyalty' is really repeat purchase – the reasons for this behaviour may not be fully understood by the seller.

The telephone company: how not to listen by phone

Keywords: customer satisfaction; service; listening to customers

A long-established public sector telecommunications company is facing de-regulation of the industry by developing strong marketing skills, and conducts regular customer satisfaction measurement in the face of growing competition. Staff members are, however, secure in the knowledge that their career progression and rewards are linked to seniority, not to the business activity. Products are as good as any from competitors, yet customers take every opportunity to change to another supplier. In response to this apparent paradox, more products are offered to targeted customers through customer profiling.

A customer, JD, classified as 'professional' by the company, is offered products to satisfy his special needs. He is informed by letter that *his* agency has opened, and he calls by telephone to arrange installation of a fax machine. He is told by a company representative who is obviously well trained in the 'customer welcome process' that he cannot accept an order by telephone. Surprised by the lack of confidence in the very medium of communication that they are themselves promoting, he asks how he can place an order. He is informed that orders must be sent by mail. After 10 days since mailing his letter, he receives a personalized reply from a named 'correspondent'. The letter states that the new line will be installed on that very day within a 2-hour time slot, to avoid unnecessary delay. JD is a professional and when suddenly and unexpectedly faced with the prospect of having to stay away from work to be at home for this installation, he calls the correspondent. The representative is surprised to get the call, explaining that he is simply the person who entered the order on to the computer system. The call is trans-ferred to another representative. JD explains that he cannot wait at home for the installation. The representative apologizes for the mix-up and states that the company could not have foreseen that he would not be at home. JD is surprised that (as a phone company) they could not simply have phoned to make an appointment. He is told that they have called several times to contact him, but as they had been unable to speak to him, the time had been fixed and the letter sent out. JD is, of course, in their own classification, a professional (who could reasonably be expected to be at work during usual office hours). JD suggests that a message could have been left on the answer phone that they had supplied. The representative states that the company does not conduct business in that fashion. JD suggests that they could have called in the evening, and is told that the company has not resorted to after-hours working.

The company's products are technically very good and priced very reasonably. Yet, they have not listened to their customer – the complexity of his needs are not understood. There is no concrete organization set up for him as a real person – he has been virtualized in a database. The company 'listens' as a bureaucratic function, but does not listen. This real listening is a set of actions or arrangements of co-operative efforts.

(This case is a summary interpretation of a story told by Dupuy, 1999, pp. 40–43.)

Nothing interpersonal at Amazon.com

Amazon.com customers have access to a much wider range of books, CDs, videos, and so on, than could be stocked by a physical shop, and the service never closes. Acquisition is convenient as purchase is done at home and delivery to the door is quick and reliable. Customers are allocated an account number and are offered recommended books, etc. by email and on the website, selected by the system on the basis of previous purchases, stated likes and dislikes, and links between products. Order progress updates are also sent by email.

This arrangement offers considerable benefits to the supplier since distribution and storage costs are minimized. Premium rents for high street locations are not paid, inventory is minimal, and (expensive) knowledgeable sales staff are not needed.

However, books cannot be browsed online and there is no sales clerk to advise, so buyers have to rely on titles, publisher 'blurb', cover images, and published and customer reviews. The risk of buying an inappropriate book is much higher than would be the case in visiting a book shop.

This is a clear case of replacing face-to-face customer service with systematized service that feels 'personal'. Various means are employed to try to demystify the abstract system so as to reduce feelings of risk, but still there is very limited scope for human relationships. What customers do get is a convenient way to buy, as the conditions for efficient transactions are preconfigured.

(Based on Ritzer and Stillman, 2001.)

VHI's lifestyle education programme

Keywords: tailored marketing; membership; learning relationship

October 1999 saw the launch of the 5-year *VHI Says Go For It* lifestyles education programme in Ireland. With a total budget of £1,560,000 this is a serious effort to position VHI as Ireland's champion of healthy lifestyles.

The Dublin-based Voluntary Health Insurance Board (An Bord Árachais Sláinte Shaorálaigh – united budget and planning horizon) (VHI for short!) was established in the 1950s as a not-for-profit service to encourage Irish residents to become more self-reliant in providing for their health care needs. Their market monopoly was ended by legislation in 1994. Today, VHI has 1.43 million members, including 6,500 group schemes (this is 40% of the Irish population, whereas only 11% have opted for private insurance in the UK!). A further 1,000 people are joining the VHI membership every week, with an average age of 28 years. The defection rate (to competing health care insurance schemes, such as BUPA) is only 1%. VHI strongly support community rating, in which all members pay the same premium irrespective of age, as an alternative to the UK's risk-rated premiums that increase as the member gets older. Income in 1999–2000 is around £400M.

The *VHI Says Go For It* brand is being developed through a series of lifestyle education programmes, targeting five defined life stages (based on age), and based on national and international research and sound medical advice, that promote a positive, practical, and light-hearted approach to healthy living. The brand is to be incorporated into all communication strategies, and will be an important asset in positioning VHI as an innovative provider of integrated health care products that meet all members' health care needs. *VHI Says Go For It* will be the focused vehicle for:

- direct positive contact with members;
- enhancing emotional ties to VHI;
- providing added-value, especially for those members who do not claim;
- attracting positive media attention;
- meet VHI's commitment to invest a portion of profits in promoting healthy living.

Following an extensive review of sponsorship opportunities, a VHI-initiated and wholly owned project was designed, with the following strategic communication objectives:

- to establish VHI as Ireland's champion of healthy living;
- to provide new positive communication opportunities that offer practical advice on healthy lifestyles, particularly to the 18–40 age group, families, and corporate customers;
- to present VHI as innovative, efficient, and member-oriented;
- to provide a significant national profile for VHI;
- to build emotional ties with VHI;
- to support brand, sales, marketing, advertising, and public relations strategies.

In the first year, the project has been concentrated on lifestyle education for 5–10-year-old children. In subsequent years of the 5-year project, programmes will be tailored to each life stage segment (niche group) by selecting the relevant lifestyle research findings and appropriate media for communication. For example, the Healthy Children programme has mailed 80,000 posters to those VHI members with young children, and a further 195,000 posters were circulated by the RTÉ Guide (Irish television – weekly programme guide), and to schools, GPs, and other requests via a freephone line. More than 3,500 people responded to *VHI Says Go For It* competitions in the local and national press. A Go For It page was added to the VHI website. Following a comprehensive circulation of press releases the programme was covered in almost all the national and regional press and radio, with a 20-minute feature on TV3. A promotional video was produced for use in VHI presentations.

The new brand is being used to rebrand VHI's healthy living activities and to initiate some new activities, including:

- *Go For It* magazine;
- Go For It public seminars;
- Go For It on the Web, including joint marketing ventures;
- Go For It health columns in local newspapers;
- Go For It magazine-style programmes for syndication to local radio stations and as audio content on the website;
- *Irish Times* Business 2000 case study as part of this multimedia education pack;
- supporting outdoor advertising at sports events and on 48-sheet bill-boards, and on prime-time TV;
- sponsorship of the time checks on national and local radio.

The impact of the project will be measured annually by independent omnibus research and the VHI customer satisfaction survey. Annual budgets will be reviewed when content and implementation of the life stage programmes are decided.

The marketing budget is not always deployed only for promotional purposes. At VHI, we see an investment in engaging people in issues that, if successful, will change the way the market operates.

(The assistance of Mark Cohen, Marketing Director – VHI, and Tara Buckley, General Manager for Corporate Communications – VHI, is gratefully acknowledged. More at www.vhi.ie. This case originally appeared in Varey, 2002.)

GM Saturn: ensuring legendary service

Keywords: customer enthusiasm; quality; communication network

Saturn was conceived by General Motors in 1982 and went to market in 1990 with 130 retail facilities in 33 US states. Today the family extends to more than 400 retailers in the US, 15 in Canada, and 22 in Japan.

An important part of Saturn's brand identity is its relationship with its customers. This is founded on a defining aspect of the corporate culture – the commitment to treat customers thoughtfully with respect for them as individuals and as friends. A strong connection has been established between brand personality, interpersonal relationship, and emotions. The personified Saturn might be characterized as young at heart, genuine, honest, friendly, and down to earth. This person is competent and reliable, and thus respected and trusted.

Saturn dealers speak of customer pride in a US car that has beaten Japanese firms on quality, reliability, and service, in the employees for their commitment and achievement, and in themselves for buying a home-produced car. Because the brand is not built on product attributes, the purchase and use of a Saturn expresses a customer's values and personality. Like other charismatic brands, such as Apple Computer and Harley-Davidson, as follower to a much larger competitor Saturn has developed intensely loyal relationships, resulting in a strong user group with its own identity. Users encourage others to buy.

Saturn owners, for example, have attended several 2-day, nationwide, Homecoming customer enthusiasm events. In 1999, some 60,000 owners descended on Spring Hill, Tennessee, the birthplace of the Saturn, for entertainment shows, athletic competitions, displays, and, best of all, plant tours. A further 150,000 (1 in 6 of all owners) participated in dealer events with barbecues, car washes, car care seminars, rallies, and amusement park outings. Dealers also organize caravans to the main event. These depart several days before and travel to the landscaped and still-farmed Spring Hill site, stopping at Saturn stores and attractions along the way. The Homecoming is about building a great relationship and enthusiasm among users.

People featured in Saturn TV commercials are users, not actors. The Spring Hill welcome centre is housed in a renovated barn. All employees are Union of Automobile Workers (UAW) members and termed 'team member' – they all eat in the same cafeteria and there are no punchcard time clocks in the plant. The terms 'labour' and 'manager' are not used.

Consumers can order 'Saturn Stuff' apparel and gifts through an online catalogue at www.saturnstuff.com. The website provides Saturn with a competitive advantage in giving customers another convenient no-hassle shopping experience, selling products, building customer loyalty, enhancing accessibility, and capturing information about customers.

In 1991, improperly formulated antifreeze resulted in the recall of 1,836 cars. These were all replaced as part of Saturn's commitment to providing a superior level of customer satisfaction. In May 1995, Saturn produced the millionth car. In 1997, Saturn Corporation became the only manufacturer to have every vehicle in the range selected as a 'Best Overall Value of the Year' product by IntelliChoice (the independent automotive information service for consumers).

Saturn wanted to ensure that the relationships they worked hard to cultivate would continue to flourish. The IT services corporation EDS were commissioned to integrate IT services for finance, engineering, manufacturing, HR, purchasing, material flow, corporate communications, sales, service, marketing, and customers, in a mature network infrastructure. This created an enterprise-wide view of each vehicle and Saturn-owner relationship. The corporate website (www.saturn.com) is used to inform employees, customers, and suppliers. For example, customers can configure a car with desired options from a photo gallery, calculate loan repayments, and begin the credit application process. Dealers can access a comprehensive online vehicle file that records vehicle performance, parts inventories and service trends. This enables them to keep well stocked with the parts that customers need. On-demand information provision helps engineers to notify dealers when issues arise. Customers' comments are considered to improve the design of new models. The www.gmbuypower.com website makes buying a car an easy shopping experience by providing online and telephone vehicle shopping services. Customers can check inventory, incentives, dealer's best price, and financing options, and schedule a test drive.

Mission: Market vehicles developed and manufacturer in the United States that are world leaders in quality, cost, and customer enthusiasm through the integration of people, technology, and business systems and to exchange knowledge, technology, and experience through General Motors.

Philosophy: We the Saturn Team, in concert with the UAW and General Motors, believe that meeting the needs of the Customers, Saturn Members, Suppliers, Retailers, and Neighbors is fundamental to fulfilling our mission.

Saturn Values: Commitment to Customer Enthusiasm; Commitment to Excel; Teamwork; Trust and Respect for the Individual; Continuous Improvement.

Commitment to Customer enthusiasm: We continually exceed the expectations of internal and external customers for products and services that are world leaders in cost, quality, and customer satisfaction. Our customers know that we really care about them.

Saturn's founders took a long-term, total business approach to creating customer loyalty – achieving a triumph in relationship marketing. Technology has been used to create a ring of communication with the customers at the centre. Excellent press coverage and word-of-mouth enthusiasm has helped to produce record sales (increasing 25% in one year).

(This case is based on material located at www.saturn.com)

Royal Mail's Strategic Customer Relationships

Keywords: strategic relationship management; capability; measurement

Royal Mail North East, one of nine regional divisions, was given the objective of establishing Strategic Customer Relationships with 25 key customers, with the aim of being rated by them as best in terms of service, solutions offered to business problems, and value for money. In the financial year 1996–1997, some 74% of revenue was generated by these 25 customers. Results from this development programme were to be improved satisfaction with Royal Mail service, loyalty in a competitive environment, and improved profitability.

An independent survey was commissioned to provide data from face-to-face interviews among key customer staff for a customer perception and satisfaction index (CPSI). Issues discussed were: the trading relationship – past, present, and desired (ranging from purely transactional to partnership); the character of the relationship in terms of commercial vs. operational orientation, understanding the customer's business and market, and degree of flexibility and adaptability to meet needs; satisfaction with services performed by sales, finance, operations, and marketing departments; level of commitment; and value for money.

The central issues that were found to counter moves to establish partnerships were: continuity (staff and other internal organization changes that interrupted the relationship), and matching customer needs.

The review revealed that increased commitment was needed among senior executives, managers, and front line staff in both the Royal Mail and their customers. Relationship Managers were appointed and made responsible for establishing the SCRs. Issues around long-term planning, reward structure, and resources to support the networks were identified.

(This case is based on Nuttall, T. (1997) 'Relationship Marketing', MBA dissertation, The Management School, University of Salford.)

Personalized marketing, direct from Dell

Dell Computer Corporation grew to almost $14 billion sales in just 12 years – an average annual growth rate of almost 50%. By 1996, they were the third largest PC manufacturer, yet had a mere 18,000 employees. Today, they generate 80% of their revenue by selling to business users, although in 2000 half the annual website sales ($6 million per day in 1998, and $25 million per day in 2000) came from home users. The website records 400,000 customer visits each day.

The online option allows the maintenance of relationships through self-service. Customers can help themselves. The website structure and features are designed for self-help. This extends to information, online transactions, order status checking, payments, and service access. The strategy of adding an online service was to enable customers to interact through whatever media they choose, and to enable them to design their own products.

Each of the 40,000 order status checks each week saves the business $8 (no call centre is needed).

Launched in early 1995, the Dell online e-commerce site mirrors the business model established by Michael Dell in 1984. Dell sell direct to their customers and build efficiently to order. They bypass distribution channels (inventory, work-in-progress, sales agents, etc.) that do not add value.

The website carries 80,000 pages of detailed service and support information, including more than 100 detailed trouble-shooting scenarios. Customers are provided with a rich information and interaction resource so that they can make educated decisions on what to buy. A Quote Generator provides a personal price quotation for the product configuration specified by selecting from a range of performance and accessory options. Online ordering is then available.

A natural language search engine fields 400,000 questions each month. There is a discussion forum and a Frequently Asked Questions knowledge base. At www.dellauction.com, customers can buy and sell used and refurbished equipment.

In 1997, the 'My Dell' capability was introduced. Customers were then able to create their own customized web page. This was upgraded to 'Premier Pages' that are fully customized, password-protected websites with interactive catalogue and diagnostic applications for troubleshooting and problem-solving. At least 40,000 pages, in 12 languages, are now operating, producing a direct relationship between supplier and end-user and enabling transparency in dealings. All PCs sold carry a 'service tag' number to enable information tailored to the individual machine to appear on the website.

In addition to the corporate website, some 12,000 supported personalized customer Extranet sites are hosted, each with intuitive navigation for the customer's tasks. Sales staff are able to build a site in just 20 minutes. By 1998, some 46 country-specific websites were operating – this was expanded to 80 by 2000.

Customer surveys reveal that 80% of online buyers would buy online from Dell again. The value of an online order is generally higher than that of a telephoned order (due to the openness and flexibility of the personal configuration facilities). With 10 million end-users, Dell have a phenomenal information base that provides the capacity for learning to all who use it.

The Dell business model is consistently operated with a consistent brand image and one-to-one relationship management (personalized marketing) through 'high-touch' support. A central e-commerce group ensures integration among several largely autonomous business units specializing in serving particular markets. There is a relentless pursuit of opportunities to improve the buying and support experience for corporate and educated consumer customers. They have to do this – Compaq and Gateway 2000 (and others) are following behind.

Loyalty drivers are specified as:

- order fulfilment, as specified by the customer, on time;
- product performance (i.e. absence of technical problems);
- post-sale service and support (i.e. all problems fixed first time, on time).

The online system enables Dell to characterize customer groupings by clusters of actual behaviour in using the website, rather than by demographics. Therefore, personalized offers are based on actual behaviour, including what visitors to the site look at, even if they don't purchase.

You actually get to have a relationship with the customer. And that creates valuable information

(Michael Dell, quoted by Magretta, 1998, p. 74)

Dell may be hailed as the leaders in personalized marketing. They aim to apply their PC technology to put customers 'in the driving seat'. At the time of writing, I haven't received a promised reply to my mailed pricing query. Will I still choose to buy a Dell PC? Affinity comes through personal and personalized experience in service and support.

(Based on Chandiramani, 1999; Magretta, 1998; Dell, 1999; Seybold and Marshak, 1998.)

Branson's Virgin: promise-keeping

Keywords: brand relationship; promise-keeping

The proliferating range of products and services bearing the Virgin name is surely evidence that Richard Branson's Virgin way of trading defies the conventions of marketing and brand management. In every case, the Virgin business makes and keeps promises about making trading easier and fairer for customers. This is a differentiating winner if the promises of lower prices and better value through intensified competition among suppliers, emancipation, a better retail and service experience, and so on, can be kept.

The ever-expanding Virgin group of businesses has been built into a business institution personified almost from the outset by a famous celebrity leader and creative entrepreneur. The strong values of 'the Virgin Way' have, in many markets, been applied to champion consumer interests for value for money and responsive service. This recognizes that consumers' needs are not owned by marketers for manipulation. It is their expression that is owned, and this has to be unique. Virgin's *depositioning* approach emphasizes that the right, not necessarily different, values that meet basic human needs are expressed attractively, acceptably, and originally. Marketing, this way, is no longer comparative as the basis of competing.

Maintaining mutuality in the Britannia Building Society

Keywords: CRM; integrated information systems; loyalty programme

With 2,600,000 customers served by 4,000 staff through 191 branches and a call centre, The Britannia Building Society faced a challenge in sustaining an independent position as a mutually owned building society. The decision was taken to implement a loyalty scheme and to enhance customer service.

Britannia needed to retain their strengths in providing competitive products in a friendly and approachable way. They also sought to express their distinctiveness by sharing their success with their members. What emerged was a concept of modern mutuality that gives them the opportunity to differentiate themselves in the financial services market.

With the help of FINEOS Corporation, The Britannia has taken the first steps in understanding customers through customer segmentation, propensity-to-purchase modelling, and customer profitability modelling. Data are rapidly transformed into information, opening up new possibilities for the control of the business. This has helped to draw them closer to their customers, facilitating their offering of superior customer care, and increasing their retention rates.

The Britannia also chose to start the Members Loyalty Bonus Scheme (MLBS). The scheme pays members a bonus by distributing a portion of profits based on each member's financial holdings and the length of time they have been a customer. The mutuality strategy requires the company to control the number of members they have in relation to profits carefully. When the project was initiated, the quality of their customer data was not adequate for them to be able to make accurate bonus payments based on a customer's total product holdings. It was not good enough to permit meaningful customer analysis such as customer segmentation and purchase propensity modelling.

The company needed to build a customer registration database that was integrated with their legacy systems, and to set up a telephone helpdesk to advise customers and sort out account discrepancies. The database formed the foundation of the customer database that is now accessed by staff in contact with customers (face to face in branches, and via the telephone in head office).

The development of this customer relationship management (CRM) system not only allows access to customer data but also allows delivery of data to customer-facing points – branches, postal, or telesales units – and eventually also directly to customers via interactive units and the Internet. Direct marketing, corporate communications, distribution strategy, sales targeting, corporate strategy, product design, and sales training are all now enabled and enhanced. Employees now have the ability to speak to customers in a manner which makes them feel that The Britannia understand them. This enhances the customer 's assessment of service.

(Based on a case study @ www.crm-forum.com)

Carlsberg – possibly the best music sponsor in Malaysia?

Keywords: brand relationship; Internet interaction; sponsorship

Malaysia has severe restrictions on the print and broadcast advertising of alcoholic products. To build a relationship with men aged 20–39, Carlsberg established a website music programme called HOTtrax (www.hottrax. com.my). Mandarin and Cantonese singers are sponsored for CDs, concerts, and autograph parties. Visitors to the website can download PC wallpaper images and interact with the brand by participating in skilled online games to win CDs and other prizes.

The website is promoted through traditional media advertising and inserts in CDs. Website users provide demographic information that is used to personalize e-mailed publicity about events and launches.

HOTtrax has helped to reposition the Carlsberg brand away from its 'older generation' image in Malaysia.

(Henderson, 2000.)

Building a relationship business the Streamline way

Keywords: knowing the customer; CRM; online servicing

Streamline, Inc. are a virtual store who retail groceries. Established in 1993 in Westwood, Massachusetts, Streamline have gone a step further than the growing number of online grocers who offer Internet-based ordering and home delivery. In order to improve quality of life by alleviating some of the most mundane hassles facing overworked and stressed people, customers in the Boston, Chicago, and Washington, DC areas pay a monthly fee for the use of a refrigerator, a freezer, and storage shelves. A ring barcode reader, worn on the finger and linked to a wrist-worn, computer-radio frequency data communication unit, is used to record what each customer keeps in them, in their medicine cupboard, and in their kitchen cupboards. A personal shopping list is then posted to the Streamline website. This allows editing by the customer. When the customer orders an item, Streamline people know what brand they prefer. Over a period of weeks, the list is refined, allowing ordering, via the Web or fax, of a selection from over 10,000 grocery items, video rental, dry cleaning, parcel delivery, shoe repairs, picture processing, ready-made meals, and bottle and can recycling. Typical orders are placed 47 weeks a year for 75 or so items totalling $110 and paid for by credit card or electronic funds transfer. So, the annual value of the relationship is around $5,000.

Rather than being based on leading-edge technology, the Streamline offer is a home-based learning relationship that attends to necessity, frequency, and reliability. The corporation has carefully selected who they want to trade with. 'It's easy to get customers. It's harder to get the right customers,' argues Gina Wilcox, Director of Strategic Relations. In choosing to do business with young and middle-aged couples with high incomes and at least one child, 'we collaborate with families that want to run better,' explains Vice President of Marketing & Merchandising Frank Britt. Consumers are coming to depend on the corporation to help them make their lives simpler and better, thereby freeing up time to do the things that really matter. For example, almost 50% of customers use the 'Don't Run Out' service that has Streamline staff regularly replenishing the items that the family identifies as 'must-have'. This redefines loyalty and marketing, suggests Gina Wilcox. They are pioneering new supply chain strategies with their customers and their suppliers to provide 'lifestyle simplification'. The relationship is very tangible and interactive. Apart from the weekly orders, Streamline representatives have permission to enter the customer's garage even when they are not at home. How many businesses have that level of trust? The website has 'smiley faces' that allow customers to rate the service at every interaction, and 'Streamline Screamline' provides telephone access for feedback and venting of any frustrations.

The Streamline business model follows the notion of a 'products for customers' strategy as explained by Don Peppers. There is fast learning during the installation phase, then a strong understanding of the customer's purchasing patterns arises and needs can be very effectively anticipated. Using sophisticated databases and telecommunications, the customer-response centre tracks orders and maintains a customer profile. There are immediate benefits to everyone. Only competitors, who find it hard to attract customers way from the service, are disadvantaged. A number of partnerships are being built to provide the kinds of product and service that customers want. UPS collect and deliver parcels, while Kodak process pictures in a variety of formats. Marketing and advertising partnerships are being developed with leading packaged-goods companies (FMCG) to provide revenue from fees, merchandising, and other direct marketing activities. Fresh foods, such a fish, are supplied just in time direct to the consumer

Founder Tim DeMello is clear that 'We are not in the grocery business. We are in the lifestyle-solutions business. We are not a product business. We are not a service business. We are a relationship business.' The asset is the consumer relationship. What prompted the launch of the business was the 'commoditization' of time and the introduction of technology that enables people to interact with service providers. Streamline becomes a consolidator and gatekeeper to its customers. Bills, delivery, and problem-solving are easily accessed together, while the corporation recognizes each customer's needs, learns from them, and responds accordingly.

Streamline, Inc. plan to roll out their service to 20 US metropolitan areas by 2004. The business publicly issued shares in June 1999. More than 75% of orders are received over the Web. By August 1998, the company was ringing its office bell to welcome another new family every hour or so. The annual customer retention rate is about 90%. DeMello claims that in the categories of consumer spending served, his corporation gets around 85% of the money that their customers spend each year. The referral rate is also very high.

Automatic replenishment is perhaps the ultimate loyalty programme for packaged goods suppliers and will have a profound impact on consumer marketing. Retailers will increasingly orient away from 'push' selling to 'pull' customer relationship management.

(An earlier version of this case study appeared in Varey, 2002.)

Club membership @ Tesco.com

Keywords: online shopping; CRM; brand loyalty; shopping experience

Tesco has built the world's largest and most profitable online grocery business in the UK with over 70,000 orders each week. Tesco.com is the most widely used online shopping website in the UK. Some 30% of their customers shop nowhere else online.

In 1995, Tesco plc launched the Tesco Club Card as a highly personalized loyalty programme. Members now account for 80% of in-store shopping, increasing product turnover by 51% with only a 15% expansion in store floor space. By capturing and analysing massive data sets, Tesco can mail personalized letters and coupons to members with an average redemption rate of 90%. Over 5,000 needs-based segments are differentiated, based on eight primary 'life stage' definitions of needs. Quarterly magazines are 'mass customized'. Profits from this customer-centric strategy have grown from £600M in 1995 to £880M in 2000. Today, some 7 million households shop with Tesco each week – 75% have signed up to the loyalty programme.

The customer call centre established in 1996 has expanded from the initial 180 staff to over 650 to become a productive, profit-driven part of the Tesco network by implementing appropriate technologies, in the process setting call centre benchmarks for others to emulate. Through Interactive Voice Response (IVR), service representatives can determine the nature of a call, contact history, Club Card membership status, and purchasing history. Computer Telephony Integration (CTI) is allowing call centre staff to retrieve data prior to call allocation.

Tesco.com, originating in the Tesco Direct service, was launched in 1998 and became a subsidiary company of Tesco plc in Spring 2000. In early 1999 some 250,000 customers had registered, generating £125M in revenues and a startling 12% profit margin. By February 2000 annual sales had reached £200M with 48,000 orders per week. The millionth order was processed in August 2000. By September of that year, the number of registered customers had risen to 750,000, with the online service available to 90% of UK grocery shoppers. In 2002, UK sales may hit £300M and Tesco.com is expanding into the USA (in partnership with Safeway USA), Japan, Thailand, and parts of Western and Eastern Europe.

By carefully integrating local store inventory and pricing to the customer's view of the website, data on all purchases – in-store and online – are captured to create a Club Card purchase history and a seamless shopping experience. Some 40,000 products are offered on the website, including clothes, home furnishings, books, and videos. The virtual store has everything the physical store has and much more.

As the leading operator, Tesco.com is almost certainly attracting customers who have been shopping at other stores. Exceptional service is necessary if the other operators are to win back their own customers. The mountains of data generated make it easier for them to target direct mail campaigns. Tesco's recently launched insurance service was offered directly to those who had recently bought cat litter and dog food in-store.

Stuart Anderton, head of the Tesco marketing team, believes that they have created a strong brand relationship that ensures that customers get the same feel at all stores visited. Barnes (2001) explains that meaning is created for their customers by offering a consistent quality experience. Does the online service engender customer loyalty in a strong brand relationship (i.e. continued repeat purchase and a broadening of the range of products purchased)? Is there a 'genuine', meaningful, lasting relationship between supplier and buyer, as seen from the customer's perspective? Is Tesco.com an example of managing customers, or managing relationships, or managing relationship resources?

There are more than 14 million active Tesco Club Card holders. In January 2002, ASDA announced that they were cutting back their Internet shopping service (Asda@tHome.com) because of customer apathy and technical hitches that led to unsold groceries languishing in two distribution warehouses (Fisher, 2002). Asda@tHome.com is the third largest Internet grocery retailer, after Tesco.com and Sainsbury'stoyou.co.uk, in a UK market worth £800M in 2002 and forecast to increase to £6b by 2005. Tesco.com are, at the time of writing, expected to make special offers to Asda@tHome.com customers to induce them to defect.

Tesco.com seems to be working for many people because they bring the corner shop to the doorstep, including the convenience of an electronic shopping list that never forgets, and a delivery driver with a personality. What does it take to identify with 'my home delivery grocery supplier', then 'my Tesco.com man'. What of the person who does the picking? Can the customer be sure that they are as 'picky', 'fussy', 'hard to please' when he or she is doing the shopping for them? (as promoted in a recent Sainsbury's brochure). How will the customer be assured that they pick the same things that the customer would have and are the groceries fresh? Tesco.com encourage their pickers to contact the customer by telephone if they have any doubt about the suitability of substitute products when the request item is out of stock. They have also commissioned the development of 'personal shopping assistants' (from the Autonomy Corporation) who will suggest products and services that are appropriate to customers' needs and interests in a stock-out situation and for cross-selling. This will enhance personalization during website use.

Tesco.com have used CRM to move a long way ahead of Sainsbury's to become the number-one online grocery store.

Online shopping does provide an alternative to store visits that is appealing to those with lifestyles in which traditional browsing shopping is not convenient. For the retailer, a differentiated shopping experience can be constructed. The addition of the online service has increased general awareness of the Tesco brand, and store use. Patterns of shopping can alter according to tastes and lifestyles. Some are expecting online/home delivery shopping to become the norm.

But what of a trading relationship? Perhaps this is really with the deliverer, rather than with the store. This is an interpersonally mediated brand relationship. The deliverer is the representative of the brand. Are those who are Tesco.com customers forming a relationship with their own 'my grocery man'?

Is the apparent success of this online shopping service sustainable? Are Tesco.com over-delivering now, like many dotcom businesses, relative to the price charged, in order to gain market share and a leading dominant position? Is ASDA's decision to drop CRM a prompt for a further reflection? Do we really need a CRM system? Is there an alternative business model that is at least as profitable?

This case was developed from material contained in Seybold and Marshak (1998), Newell (2000), Seybold (2001), Barnes (2001), and the other sources cited in the text above. The co-operation of Pete Hampson and Ian Danton, Blackburn store, is gratefully acknowledged.

The Altro/IAS Brand Progression ® *contact management system*

In business-to-business trading, most commercial relationships are with buyers who are prospective customers, and with people who don't buy goods and services themselves – specifiers, influencers, and users. Much of the activity is preparation for selling–buying. This could be understood as commercial courtship. From the marketer's point of view, their work is to break buying habits and create new preferences. Therefore, brand relationship development with a key potential customer might take continuous activity along a considerable timeline.

This case study outlines the work done by branding/marketing consultants IAS to produce a comprehensive brand development system specification for their clients Altro. Brand development is managed by controlling contact using a systemic contact management strategy and integrated supporting information and communication system.

The system allows co-ordination of regular maintenance and development interactions as well as event-driven tasks (such as quoting on a project tender). The managerial framework is based on understanding, systematizing, automating, and delegating regular and task contact with selected potential, latent, and active customers, specifiers, contractors, and users.

Increasingly, commercial interaction is customer-driven. Contrary to popular assertion, IAS believe that commercial relationships prosper through the establishment of preference rather than through loyalty. A business-to-business brand is constructed in the totality of all contact. A commercial relationship starts when a buyer, specifier, influencer, or user gains confidence in the competence of the seller with whom they are interacting, to provide relevant valued benefits, and they decide that they like them. Since, in a business-to-business market, trading is premised on a recognized need for goods and services that are not necessarily wanted, brand relationships and professional relationships are central elements of commerce. This is different from business-to-consumer trading, where products are wanted, but not necessarily needed.

Altro is a leading supplier of high-performance flooring products for commercial and public buildings. Research among customers and potential customers, specifiers, users, and influencers, has shown that the Altro brand was seen as helpful, reliable, friendly, knowledgeable, professional, efficient, innovative, and confident. This seemed very encouraging. However, Altro was also seen as conservative, snotty, boring, distant, middle-aged, and too serious. Some significant change for the better was necessary if valuable business was to be attracted. IAS have been working with Altro to develop a contact strategy and management system. This was to be capable of strategic functional integration of all interactions with customers and potential customers. The aim was to be able to consistently express brand values and benefits at all 'touchpoints', and to support marketing efforts with coherent ICT systems. Likeability and benefit messages were not consistently expressed in Altro's work. It was realized that the importance of relationships had to be recognized.

This all would require cultural and electronic integration in the deployment of people, strategy, processes, and technology. Therefore, the system would have to be capable of capturing, storing, and providing use of relationship data captured in and used in a variety of points of contact and interaction: sales meetings, advertising, brochures, telephone conversations, training, hospitality events, recruitment, and so on.

> CRM should be strategically driven Relationship Marketing that incorporates IT, rather than vice versa.
>
> (Tim Hazlehurst, IAS)

A relationship marketing strategy was adopted to manage the progression of selected commercial relationships with distributors, contractors, architects, building users, and influencers, from prospect to advocate over time. Using professionally prepared databases, the total market membership for each product group was classified on the basis of behaviour. For example:

- unaware – there had been no inward contact (about 15,000 people);
- interested – up to two inward contacts (about 10,000 people);
- customer – two or more purchases (about 5,000 people);
- advocate – some enthusiastic endorsement (about 200 people).

In addition, each commercial relationship was valued in terms of realistic future business. This allowed a segmentation of the total contact database so that a differentiated contact management programme could be operated. Altro strategically decided to move away from contacts driven by building and refurbishment projects, to relationship-based contact that could anticipate future buying requirements.

Altro and IAS are anticipating a number of major business benefits from the establishment of the system:

- enhanced market knowledge to identify sales and product development opportunities;
- increased customer satisfaction as people are able to choose their means of contact and services are more personalized, productive, and efficient through the differentiation of services in the management of the relationships;
- improved customer information for targeted promotion and product offerings;
- better co-ordinated internal working arrangements with a common goal of brand clarity.

IAS believe that the traditional definition of CRM implies no need for relationships with people other than as customers, and a confusion with software systems. Their approach is to encompass the entire supply chain, and they have called this Contact Relationship Management. This is a brand management approach that centres customers, prospects, and specifiers, and focuses on making it easy for people to access the business at all 'touchpoints'. In this way, the IAS version of 'CRM' achieves the integration of all contact with the market with the brand performing in a consistent, unified manner across all 'touchpoints'. The starting point is to map and define how the brand must interact with the market in all 'touchpoints' for mutual benefit. But, as far as the 'traditional' customer relationship management goes:

> CRM is like high-school sex – nobody is really doing it, but everyone thinks that everyone else is.
>
> (heard at a conference)

The co-operation of Tim Hazlehurst, Chairman, and Claire Buchanan, Consultant, IAS Marketing & Communications, in discussing this case is gratefully acknowledged. Brand Progression® is a commercial consulting process of IAS. IAS are specialists in business-to-business brand management.

Commentary

The cases gathered in this chapter were selected to illustrate some of the key points raised in the journey from revisiting the concept of relationship marketing in a changing context, to examining the capability required for ICT support in the era of expanding social networks mediated by the Internet. Perhaps you will read them and use them as stories for discussion. In each case I have identified the key concepts and maybe prompted some discussion questions. Please take them as starting points for your consideration, rather than as definitive answers to any questions I have posed or catalysed in your thinking about eCRM.

The reward for adopting CRM is supposed to be commercially beneficial 'trust' and 'loyalty'. Exchange-based market interaction emphasizes the taking to market of goods and services that meet the needs and wants of consumers, rather than what they can produce and sell. On the other hand, Relationship Marketing requires that managers take a long-term perspective to look beyond single transactions to recognize their work duty and purpose is supporting mutually beneficial (trading) relationships with customers.

Much of what is termed Relationship Marketing and Customer Relationship Marketing is, on the one hand, 'persistent provocation to purchase' and, on the other hand, 'systematized sales and service'. Could we aspire to a more productive Relationship Marketing? This, as we will see in the final chapter, will require a much more reflective practice.

References

Barnes, J. G. (2001) *Secrets of Customer Relationship Management*, New York: McGraw-Hill.

Brown, S. A. (2000) *Customer Relationship Management: A Strategic Imperative in the World of e-Business*, Toronto: John Wiley & Sons.

Chandiramani, R. (1999) 'Dell – life support for the machine', *Revolution: Business and Marketing in the Digital Economy*, available online at www.revolutionasia.com, June 2001.

Cohen, B. and Greenfield, J. (1997) *Double Dip*, New York: Simon & Schuster.

Cooren, F. (2000) *The Organizing Property of Communication*, Amsterdam, Holland/ Philadelphia, PA: John Benjamin.

Dell, M. (1999) *Direct from Dell: Strategies that Revolutionized an Industry*, London: Harper-Collins Business.

Dupuy, F. (1999) *The Customer's Victory: From Corporation to Co-operation*, London: Macmillan Business.

Fisher, D. (2002) 'Asda cuts Internet shopping', *Manchester Metro Business News*, 7 January.

Fitchett, J. and McDonagh, P. (2001) 'Relationship Marketing, e-commerce and the emancipation of the consumer', in A. Sturdy, I. Grugulis, and H. Willmott (eds) *Customer Service: Empowerment and Entrapment*, Basingstoke, UK: Palgrave, pp. 191–199.

Gilmore, A. (2001) 'Call centre management: Is service quality a priority?', *Managing Service Quality*, Vol. 11, No. 3, 153–159.

Henderson, C. (2000) 'Relationship Marketing: I want to be your friend', *Revolution Asia*, 31 December [www.revolutionmagazine.com]

Johnson, D. T. (2001) 'Is this a real person?', *Management Communication Quarterly*, Vol. 14, No 4, 659–665.

Leibs, S. (1997) 'Shop, don't drop', *Information Week*, 18 August, 69.

Magretta, J. (1998) 'The power of vertical integration: An interview with Dell Computer's Michael Dell', *Harvard Business Review*, March–April, 74–84.

Newell, F. (2000) *Loyalty.com: Customer Relationship Management in the New Era of Internet Marketing*, London: McGraw-Hill.

Ransdell, E. (1998) 'Streamline delivers the goods', *Fast Company*, No. 16, 154–156.

Ritzer, G. and Stillman, T. (2001) 'From person- to system-oriented service', in A. Sturdy, I. Grugulis, and H. Willmott (eds) *Customer Service: Empowerment and Entrapment*, London: Palgrave, pp. 102–116.

Seybold, P. B. and Marshak, R. T. (1998) *Customers.com: How to Create a Profitable Business Strategy for the Internet and Beyond*, London: Century Business Books.

Seybold, P. B., Marshak, R. T., and Lewis, J. M. (2001) *The Customer Revolution: How to Thrive When Your Customers Are in Control*, London: Random House.

Streamline, Inc. online at www.streamline.com

Thomas, K. (2001) 'E-grocers fight for custom', *IT Week*, 12 November.

Varey, R. J. (2002) *Marketing Communication: Principles and Practice*, London: Routledge.

Where to Find More on CRM Applications

Association for the Advancement of Relationship Marketing:	www.aarm.org
The CRM Forum:	www.crm-forum.com
CRM Benchmarking Association:	www.crmba.com
CRM Community:	www.crmcommunity.com
The Gartner Group:	www3.gartner.com
The Conspectus Report:	www.conspectus.com

Chapter 7

WHAT NEXT?

Getting beyond telling and listening, to creating and sharing value

Every complex problem has a simple solution, and it's usually wrong
H. L. Mencken

Marshall McLuhan observed that most people live in the rear-view mirror – using the lenses of yesterday to assess what is experienced today

Getting from 'the supplier' and 'a supplier' to 'my supplier'*

Introduction

Relationship Marketing is a trading process that focuses attention on people-relating through buying–selling interactions. Customer Relationship Management supports this through the deployment of information and communication technologies to create a dynamic knowledge system. CRM can be the enabler of RM, but often isn't. In my view, CRM has to be a logical development of enterprise-wide Relationship Marketing, not merely from Enterprise Resource Planning (ERP) to integrated 'front office' and 'back office' hardware and software systems.

Many people are increasingly demanding and increasingly sophisticated in their expectations of, and response to, marketing. New technologies are enabling marketers to become more sophisticated in constructing information, and more sophisticated in using information.

The promise of greater value for all is in the air. What more could be done to bring CRM nearer to promise-keeping? This requires Relational Marketing, not relationship marketing that is operated on pseudo-relationships. This is fundamentally responsive and responsible marketing.

---

*With thanks to Professor Jim Barnes (2001, p. 4) for this insight into what this discussion is all about.

Summary of Relational Marketing Principles

Is Relationship Marketing another term for the same shifted management attention as Integrated Marketing Communication? Is this Brand Management? Clearly, communication is the common integrative process. Yet, I think not, since for me IMC aims to ensure that all corporate voices are strategically consistent and compatible. Brand management widens managerial concern to all corporate actions that can be meaningful to observers.

The essence of Relationship Marketing, and the Customer Relationship Management that enables it, is that the respective co-marketers seek mutually desirable interactions as their way of finding satisfiers for their respective needs/wants/desires.

Forget H. B. Barnum's way of doing business. Marketing is a dismal craft if nothing more than a way of separating buyers from their money and of shifting 'product'. Better we realize the huge potential for bringing people together to connect with investment opportunities to originate, produce, create, resolve, reconcile, and so on. So, marketing can be inherently dialogical.

Diary of an Internet-age consumer

Monday: Web pages don't provide easy routes to find staff.

Tuesday: No response to an emailed request is received.

Wednesday: Mailshots are irrelevant.

Thursday: There is no proactive personal contact, even from long-term suppliers (subscriptions, etc.).

Friday: Multilevel automated telephone systems require information input every time a selection is made.

Saturday: Web links don't work, and pages provide information that is no longer valid or correct.

Sunday: Mailshots that contain two different offers on the same products, and the related website has another offer, confusing the customer and making it hard to do business with the supplier.

It is no good simply telling people that you care about them and about satisfying their needs. You have to do it. Then you don't need to express these values – they are demonstrated in your promise-keeping, value-creating, value-delivering performance (including the critical treatment of people in the trading interaction). As part of the marketing decision process, managers should ask themselves: 'how will what we propose make our customers feel?' and 'how would I feel if a loyal supplier did that to me?'

A Relationship Marketing way of trading requires the strategic application of ICT to move back from mass communication to interpersonal communication. The focus of management decision-making is ongoing relationships of exchange rather than on single transactions in isolation or aggregated markets. This 'outside-in' marketing competitively customizes rather than institutionally standardizes. The process is participative rather than informative and persuasive. This may require suppliers to change their behaviours.

Conventional theory described and explained a 'marketer' who attempted, through product development and promotion, either to meet existing customer attitudes, or to change their priorities of needs and/or brand attitudes. Relationship Marketing is a hybrid of adapting and changing strategies. The relationship is a series of connected 'projects' of mutual learning through interaction. Relationship Marketing is a formal management system that is inherently communicative and that measures satisfaction of both parties in relational terms.

Kalle Lasn's Adbusters Media Foundation advocate a powerful metameme, which they have called the 'Media Carta':

> Every human being has the right to communicate – to receive and impart information through any media.
>
> (Lasn, 1999, p. 124)

Managers have to rethink the concept of a relationship as a necessary basis for organizing – relating is a mode of trading, rather than a means. How is it that we have a widely accepted common sense notion of a relationship as a resource for competing, and that relating as the primary manifestation of connectedness seems to be generally reserved for friendship and family? I urge managers to choose collaboration as an imperative for managing, in place of confrontation, competition, and manipulation.

Three Levels of Management Rationality

I have drawn from a critical reflection on management, organization, communication, information systems, learning, and knowledge. The impetus was twofold. The reading of a text on 'interaction strategies' (for health professionals) revealed, unnervingly, a 'theory' of human communication as a technology for objective informing that seems incapable of producing the higher order 'connection' outcomes required (in situations of illness and trauma). This is not an isolated example, with a transmissive conception of communication prevailing in management literature.

With the advent of customer relationship management (CRM) systems, much of the discussion has been exhibiting an impoverished notion of relationships. This has produced, for me at least, a sense of the impotence of managerialistic rhetorics that promise that things are and will be better than they are. The deployment of relationships understood with an objective and rational understanding of reality – as an essentially selfish instrument – is far from taking a relational stance to treating collective problems of creating and sharing valued actions (services) and objects (goods).

That practical reason (acceptability to all parties concerned) and instrumental reason (utility or success) are complementary, is the basis for reflective practice.

Applied sciences tend to reduce practical rationality to no more than instrumental rationality – thus capturing only the expediency of actions for attaining the chosen ends of those in control of actions. Practical reason is seen as merely utilitarian. Yet, as Habermas (1984, p. 8) observed, 'rationality has less to do with the possession of knowledge than with how speaking and acting subjects acquire and use knowledge.'

Three ways of managing can be discerned: Instrumental, Strategic, and Communicative.

The *management of cost* is enacted in pursuit of productivity in the efficient allocation of scarce resources – this is an instrumental rationality that is found in the hard systems tradition. The justifying logic is optimization. This is *instrumental action*.

The *management of complexity* is enacted in pursuit of strategic advantage and competitive success in the effective direction of complex systems – this is a strategic rationality that is found in the hard systems tradition. The justifying logic is leadership (steering) in the face of uncertainty and change. This is *strategic action*.

The *management of conflict* is enacted in pursuit of mutual understanding in the social integration of conflicting interests – this is a communicative rationality that is found in the critical systems tradition. The justifying logic is capability for interaction and opportunities for discourse. This is *communicative action*.

Implications for Managing

Most so-called relationship marketing and customer relationship management is instrumental management, or, at best, strategic management, in nature.

In principle, relationship marketing initiates contact and provokes purchase by promise-making – but is it authentic? In principle, CRM integrates marketing and service production (that may include goods): facilitating customer service interaction in which goods and services are presented as carriers of value in exchange for money or co-operation. This is inherently a process of communicating, as promises are realized, renegotiated, or reneged.

The attempt to use the notion of a relationship as an instrument of manipulated exchange must be recognized as inherently cynical (unethical) and the manifestation of an arrogant delusion. Marketing is not a tool kit but rather a way of thinking (a 'state of mind') about how to treat buyers who can be attractive customers.

Relationship Marketing does not have to be a managerialistic weapon deployed solely for shareholder profit maximization. Trading relationships can be socially productive if they are more than asymmetric information-driven control systems.

People participating in, and contributing to, healthy relationships can mutually benefit from interdependence when they are committed to working to overcome dependence and dominance. In this way, a relational perspective transcends 'contact' between individuals and focuses attention of the possibility of emergent characteristics of interactions of co-producers of identities, meaning, and knowledge. Of course, dialogue raises awareness of differing understandings, rather than automatic acceptance.

Active communication is necessary for the engagement that produces value beyond the redistribution of fixed imposed outcomes in trading events. Managers become stewards charged with co-ordinating value-creating resource configurations. Interaction is productively contrived as interaction. Communication is capable of more than the distribution (circulation) of information as a means to an end. Interactive communication is better taken to be communicative interaction.

Commentator and consultant Drayton Bird has described the meeting of CRM and e-commerce as 'the ultimate marketing nightmare' – 'a conjunction of the deluded and the arrogant' (Bird, 2001). He sees much CRM effort as ignoring the fundamental need to serve customers and to forge what Godin (1999) would call trading 'friendships'. In e-commerce, it is worse still – many customers are treated as though they are wrong and stupid – the antithesis of customer service!

In 1996, Francis Buttle urged us to reflect on where we might go, intellectually and practically, with 'relationship marketing'. Six years later, as we revisit this question, is eCRM the encapsulation of a perfected 'RM' (technology) and thus a building block of the panacea (i.e. universal remedy) for all the woes of the market-based society? Has this enfolding (trapping?) of RM into CRM killed the prodigy? Can we, as citizens, afford to let this happen? The future of RM *is* in eCRM, but RM must be the foundation. The information and communication technologies (ICT) (of automation) should be servant and not master.

The Emerging Tradition of Customer Relationship Management

The creation of customer satisfaction with the product and their treatment is a sure way to earn repeat business. This is not, of course, solely the responsibility of the marketing team. Generative, productive, and representative work is necessary (Wikström and Normann, 1994). The managerial problem is one of integrating this specialized work. The starting point of a relationship marketing strategy is a deep understanding of why customers would want a relationship with a seller (as provider of value?). The answer, stated simply, is that a sustained relationship between buyer and seller must itself provide additional value to the customer. Such a developing committed relationship will come from:

Knowledge, privilege, co-operation

Organization around products and technologies is already giving way in many corporations to organization around trading relationships and capabilities.

Information that is interpreted and transformed into satisfying products is essential. Increasingly, it is this transformation of knowledge from one form to another that is the basis if the business (i.e. the customer–product relationship). Then, customers have to be treated differently from prospects. Commitment must be reciprocated, if the provider is to be rewarded for their relationship management efforts with profitable sales and favourable word-of-mouth publicity and promotion.

The growing adoption of a Customer Relationship Management (CRM) system is, it could be argued, evidence that more and more providers are trying to put the customer's interest at the heart of their business by integrating marketing, customer support, and other functions to maximize added value in a dialogical relationship. Instead of finding customers for products, providers are managing relationships in which they find products for customers (Peppers and Rogers, 1993, 1997). Marketing communication no longer simply tries to create and refresh product awareness and identification. Instead of saying 'we are here, look at what we have got', providers are saying 'we are here with you continually providing value'.

CRM is a holistic approach to the generation, production, and representation of a value-creation system (i.e. marketing, customer service, and logistics). The aim is to move the supply chain nearer to the customer to link customer needs more directly into the management of supplies, design, manufacturing, packaging, transport, and the ultimate purpose of all of this – profitable exchange. This enterprise view is a shift away from a departmental view. The technology captures and provides information about preferences and interaction history, enabling a consistency of experience for valuable customers in all inter-actions – inquiry, order, delivery, maintenance, upgrade, and so on.

CRM systems can send customers reminders about essential servicing and tailored offerings based on past trading history and personal information profiles. Customers can self-select the level of assistance through the provider's website, and gather information about products, billing, order progress, and so on.

In business-to-business situations, Relationship Marketing requires and/or leads to a process of gradual 'cementing' of formal structures and integration of procedures and systems and informal mechanisms. The supplier and customer systems come to 'mirror' each other, at least at the interface between the two. This requires special internal co-ordination structures and collaborative auditing and design and improvement of subsystems of communication between and within the respective systems, to ensure that the partnership is effective and efficient in pursuit of shared (or at least compatible) goals. Managers then have to design their own adaptations and influence their counterpart's adaptations to make the exchange process easier. Spillard (1991) has termed this 'organizational mating'.

This development should challenge the marketing communication manager because it includes knowledge management, marketing automation, customer care, call centres, and salesforce automation. This is obviously much more than promotional advertising design. Is this really all there is to CRM? I seek a more sophisticated and coherent, reflective perspective.

Managing Relationships for Marketing

I have pondered the apparent reinvention of relationship as a component of trading markets for some time. How could it be that until the final decade of the 20th century, marketing was not concerned with interaction, but merely with exchanges? This seems to be a matter of scale – mass production requires mass consumption. So people can't get close – they are too busy! Bigness is a burden! (Sale, 1980). Small is beautiful (Schumacher, 1973). We need a human scale, not an industrial scale, in which people actually do matter as humans and not mere trading resources. Surely, a relationship was the context or environment within which such trading had meaning? By backgrounding relationship, marketing ideology placed communicating in the role of informing instrument – advertising flourished. Latterly, branding has surfaced in recognition of the active role played by people in constructing meaning. Now, it is difficult to pursue a logic that does not recognize the centrality of the concept of relating. But much of the burgeoning literature has simply married an unreflective instrumental notion of information systems with an unreflective instrumental notion of marketing (Varey and Wood, 2001). Gordon (1998) and Brown (2000) are examples of well-written rhetoric on CRM. The resulting eCRM is unhealthy. Through our reflection, we see the present manifestations, in eCRM, of a convergence of re-lationship marketing and ICT as fundamentally flawed due to what we might term the 'intellectual BSE effect'. When a major new capability is heralded, yet constructed in the unreflective feeding of one distorted/flawed discourse upon another, a recipe for disappointment (at least) and potential for a fall might reasonably be anticipated. Is the mutant that is being created from the damaged marketing and ICT (both spawned of a limiting managerialistic rationalism) really what we want?

Barnes (1995) has drawn on knowledge in the social psychology field to raise the question of what is a trading relationship? Managerially, the purpose of this orientation is to engender continuing trading in place of fleeting encounters. For some, this means no more than 'locking in' customers by raising switching costs through various means. Others have spent vast amounts of resource on database-driven promotion and product development. Barnes was motivated to investigate what was missing – genuine relating.

Stephen Brown has been particularly vociferous in countering the erupting crowd frenzy that has raised relationship marketing (and therefore CRM) to the status of mantra and (yet another) 'strategic imperative'. He and his colleagues, in considering the death of marketing, saw relationship marketing as 'a false con-ceptual idol' (Brown et al., 1995, p. 14) and just one of a number of enthusiastic attempts to recycle 'long-dead' elements of the 'marketing' intellectual tool kit – part of 'the vast bulk of contemporary marketing scholarship [that] comprises [sic] little more than intellectual necrophilia' (Brown et al., 1995, p. 11).

Brown is clearly concerned that relationship marketing, with the 'ostensibly communal, co-operative, egalitarian ethos of all-pervasive harmony' (Brown and Maclaran, 1995, p. 269), is no more than an enthusiastic (at least by some manage-ment gurus and their disciples) pursuit of a capitalist consumer society utopia. He describes relationship marketing as having a 'co-operative rhetoric', and, as one of several philosophically unrobust catholicons of marketing, seems concerned that this is basically mendacious and false (Brown, 1994). Of course, even if relation-ship marketing is authentically dialogical, we should realize that dialogue raises awareness of differing understandings, rather than automatic acceptance.

Cultural theorist, Raymond Williams (1961) was dismayed at the economic cynicism of casting people as consumers, and thereby instrumentalizing relationships as means to supply consumption demand. Citizens are treated as commoditized consumers to be 'understood' as a target for product sales. On the other hand, it can be believed (hoped) that the social mind is yet greater than the consumption mind.

Relationship Marketing is not only concerned with marketing actions, but also with who are co-operators in trading. Paul Wang, of Northwestern University, has described the 'relationship buyer'. These people, as consumers, are different from 'transaction buyers' (who emphasize purchase price), in that they look for a friendly supplier who they can trust, who remembers them and recognizes them, who does favours for them, and who builds a relationship with them. These people will pay to save time and emotional energy by trading relationally. But what of those citizens who can't be customers in a relationship marketing regime? To 'play the game', we have to become a consuming customer and give up (at least some of) our citizenship in order to be included and to avoid exclusion. When some citizens are not included, we could term the actions as *repulsive marketing*.

Some marketers can choose to act as facilitators in community bonds (e.g. Harley-Davidson HOGs and GM-Saturn 'Homecomings'). Staff can be treated as brand owners, rather than as intermediaries. Managers as marketers have relationships with employees (as 'internal customers') as well as 'external' customers. Service-motivated employees motivate buyers. Trading relationship management (TRM) is supported by employee relationship management (ERM). These are essential aspects of the much bigger stakeholder relationship management (SRM) (this is addressed elsewhere in my Corporate Communication Managing System – CCMS – see Varey and White, 2000).

Elsewhere, I am studying the impact of forms of interaction in institutional settings – specifically in team-based working – as joint action – that is (at least potentially), inherently and fundamentally organizing in nature. This stems from a semiotic analysis of language in use (Cooren, 2000). Perhaps such contributions to the pursuit of a utopian 'marketing practice' might just help to avoid further risk of the undesirable consequences of ignoring Albert Einstein's advice – that we should simplify things, but not too much.

The Politics of CRM

The meeting of two personalities is like the contact of two chemical substances: if there is any reaction, both are transformed.

(Carl Jung, 1961)

Paravatiyar (1996) defined Relationship Marketing, from the seller's point of view, as 'the process of co-operating with customers to improve marketing productivity through efficiency and effectiveness.' We also need to ask: 'What is Relationship Marketing from the buyer's point of view?'

The argument for e-commerce-enabled Relationship Marketing is simple and compelling. Employees, suppliers, and stock/shareholders get the possibility of a greater say in the strategic decision-making of the producer/provider. For customers, the managers and front line service workers are more knowledgeable about consumer intentions and motivation: constructive and productive aspects of consumption (as the driver for production?) are identified. In summary, the providers will prosper only if the consumer's long-term desires are central influences on their managerial and productive activities.

What is wrong with this portrayal? Of course, we realize that corporate strategy and marketing activity are determined by managers as agents of their employer, not as representatives of customers.

According to Fitchett and McDonagh (2001), the rhetoric of RM mediated by cyberspace only socializes and naturalizes the power differentials inherent in a market system. The 'consumer commitment' agenda clashes with the notion of citizen as 'collaborator/partner' rather than self-motivated need satisfier.

Who started the move toward 'relationship' as the basis for trading in contemporary society? Of course, corporate interests provided the impetus as managers come to explain market interactions as partnership. Intriguingly, the very notion of an 'open market in cyberspace' offers consumers greater scope for promiscuity, deceit, and subterfuge (as identities can be disguised and multiple contacts sustained without commitment or mutuality).

It is not yet clear that e-commerce provides the ideal for realizing all that is good and desirable in Relationship Marketing.

Relationship Marketing is, fundamentally, a hegemonic practice, according to Fitchett and McDonagh (2001), for the following reasons. Corporate actions are determined by managers as corporate agents, not as representatives of customer interests. It is they who have chosen to describe market interactions as partnership. All but the wealthiest and most influential consumers are much less able to exercise control over the form of a relationship, yet managers can include and exclude people. Relationship terms and conditions are not negotiated mutually, but imposed by the corporate managers (see also Gabriel and Lang, 1995). Once accepted, there is little scope for renegotiation, and judicial responsibilities (relevant in the case of conflict in the relationship) in trading relationships are attributed unequally. Corporate legislative authority and economic power allow the resolution of disagreements in favour of the stronger party (the corporation).

Fitchett and McDonagh (2001) do not see e-commerce as a new business paradigm, but as a new additional marketplace. Further, the logic of Relationship Marketing 'denies the role of citizenry and regulation and, in the process, reinforces existing imbalances of power which favour the corporation over the customer in any relational episode' (p. 197).

> *The relational terms of e-commerce transactions have some unique and contradictory features which do not necessarily favour or enhance consumer representation and expression.*
>
> (p. 197)

While corporate agents have greatest access to technologies and greatest influence over how they are developed and applied, power imbalances in the consumer–producer relationship cannot be equalized. Is CRM (to be) no more than a lie? As it is currently understood and applied, the CRM logic is incapable of delivering on the promise of authentic and credible trading relationships. Many CRM systems are little more than a customer information storage facility. Can a relationship reside in, and be conjured up from the contents of, a database? If so, how exactly?

IT hardware and software cannot replace authentic human interaction, and connected databases, online purchasing information systems, and email management software does not constitute a holistic customer care capability – even if these components don't technically conflict with existing systems.

Access to the Internet as a means to transact in the market may allow consumers to be more promiscuous rather than causing them to be more loyal. This seems to be in contradiction to the basic notion of Relationship Marketing held by some, that RM fosters customer retention.

Studies have shown that while there has been, and still is, broad support among managers for relationship marketing principles, the actual behaviour of many do not facilitate implementation. Relationships are not dealt with systematically, the necessary investments are not made, and the major changes to organization are not accomplished (Morris et al., 1998). Very few managers really care about customers, business processes are not geared to customer expectations, and software is incompatible (and even within) CRM systems that are too often being treated as add-on, rather than integral to, the corporate business system.

The main issue is the full recognition by management teams of the co-dependency among functional groups in the corporation. It is the team effort of all the contributing functions that produces a sense of relationship among all parties involved in making and keeping promises and the creation and delivery of value for customer and their stakeholders. Yet, I discern an undermining conflict. How can servicers be expected to work relationally when they are treated transactionally? Read the marketing literature and you find a shift from transactional to relational. Read the human resource management literature, and the picture is rather different. Thinking is shifting away from relational toward transactional.

Despite the burgeoning developments in the integration of electronic information and communication technologies into business operations, many adopters are still failing to produce real interaction between buyers, producers, and sellers. Buyers respond to Internet stimuli, for example, but their requests are not treated as a priority for action in the seller's system. An abundance of information is now captured and processed, but much of it is still not used in building relationships (despite the very high cost, in many cases).

Without the deployment of information and communication technologies, the full benefits of Relationship Marketing would be almost impossible to realize. Yet, vendors and systems integrators are, as yet, over-promising, and managers are overoptimistic about the ease with which an RM strategy can be adopted, accepting the claims of vendors and consultants all too readily.

Compared to database-driven 'relationship marketing', members of Internet-based consumption communities are more active and discerning and thus less accessible to one-to-one (i.e. addressable) marketing communication (Kozinets, 1999).

Expectations and intentions, in some cases, have shifted from marketers performing to an 'audience-of-one', to 'one-to-one' and 'many-to-one' co-production and sharing of meaningful value. Trading conversations have to be dialogues about respective needs, rather than tactical discussions of putative problems and promises of hypothetical solutions. All *points of engagement* between buyer and seller must be informed by previous contact and focused on the buyer's need. The problem is not one of interactive communication, but one of managing (i.e. creating and directing) communicative interaction to the mutual benefit of buyer and seller.

The traditional notion of salesperson will have to be replaced with a new role of *relationship promoter* or *relationship manager*. This person identifies appropriate partners, brings them together, and facilitates the dialogue and the exchange process between them. This is a development from the Customer Liaison Manager, requiring a strategic perspective that is more proactive and concerned with more than mere pacification.

The investment has to be in deploying a customer service strategy and a relationship development strategy. This has to be underpinned by a reorientation and a restructuring of the way the business operates. Otherwise, counterproductive conflicts between internally focused operations and production and externally focused relationship developers will be rife. True Relationship Marketing is an all-or-nothing mind-shift.

So what next? Mattsson (1997) for one argues that proponents of Relationship Marketing, as a normative pursuit, must conceive of markets as networks, so as to properly recognize that other actors can be similarly involved in a relationship strategy. A limited view of Relationship Marketing deploys a Marketing Mix Management mentality, whereas an extended Relationship Marketing view is rather more like a Market-as-Network approach. The distinctions are summarized in Table 7.1 (note that the limited view of Relationship Marketing is identified in italics and the extended view in bold).

Mattsson's analysis tells us that Relationship Marketing has attributes of both marketing mix management and market-as-network management. The limited view of RM is largely a marketing mix approach used to increase customer loyalty, satisfaction, and retention, and this dominates the eCRM provision currently. ICT aids individualized advocacy communication with customers in a mass market. The extended view of RM is rather more like the network perspective, in pursuit of true interaction and mutual dependency within a network of relationships, but retains some characteristics of marketing mix management in the manner in which relationships at the macro (society) and meso (market) governance levels are handled. This must be addressed in further refinement of conceptualizations and resulting managerial (not managerialistic) practices. It seems that RM could benefit from a greater attention to buying and not just selling. Is this a clear case for marketing and consumer behaviour scholars to co-operate? Gummesson (1999) suggests that the advent of Relationship Marketing is a paradigm shift – an alternative set of values, assumptions, and methods that offer us a more general theory of marketing in a more fluid and less compartmentalized management system. This requires systemic thinking (beyond cybernetic) about the management system.

Beyond the walls of the 'ivory tower' of the academy, arguably, we can discern networks of trading relationships that naturally do not follow a managerial desire to control contrived relationships. CRM is capable of lifting marketing from dismal craft to social benefactor if it enables citizens to fairly purchase spontaneous excellent service in the form of promises that make sense to both

TABLE 7.1 Identifying the scope of Relationship Marketing
(based on Mattsson, 1997, p. 454).

Marketing mix approach	*Network approach*
Theoretical foundations Monopolistic competition and *psychology*. Microeconomic analyses	Dynamic industrial economics, sociology, and *organization theory*
Character of exchange **Stimulus-response model** (with feedback). Economic exchange, at the *seller's initiative*, satifies the needs and wants of buyers and sellers in a specified time period *through the seller's creative act*. **Aggregate response (from market or segment)**. Transactions and delayed responses – **buyer learning**. *Buyers and sellers are not very dependent* (seller has many customers and buyer can choose substitutes)	*Exchange through interaction in exchange relationships*. Exchange co-ordinates production systems and *creates valuable relationships within ongoing individualized exchange relationships*. *Transactions are episodes in long-term relationships that focus on economic and social exchange*. Exchange is conditioned by prior exchange, adaptation, and institutionalization. Initiative may be taken by seller, buyer, or a third party – there is *strong mutual dependency between each buyer and seller*
Exchange system **The market has clear, objective boundaries, and is defined as a group of buyers and sellers exchanging highly substitutable products (i.e. the market is competitive), and divided into segments**	The market is *defined by complementarity and substitutability* of products in subdivided networks formed by relationships at *several levels* – boundaries are unclear and subjective – the market is emergent
Implications for marketing managers Emphasis on short-term **optimization of the marketing mix** and resource allocation through **market analysis and marketing planning and control. Information from sales and discrete market research. The focus is planning and the marketing function**	*Emphasis on establishing, developing, and breaking relationships over the long term* to create access to external resources and to improve the position in various networks, requiring *inter-functional co-ordination*. *Information from day-to-day interaction. A whole-firm problem of strategic action – marketing is an investment*

parties, and are valued and fulfilled. For me, this implies inherent ethicality, and thus the need for systemic management thinking.

Marketing development is occurring in the context of shifts from modernism to post-modernism, and from an industrial society to a value society. Having written this book, I am now much happier with the notion of *Relational Marketing*, as part of relational management, than I am with the rather imprecise (even muddled) idea of relationship marketing or relationship-based marketing. A trading relationship is certainly an asset for the participants, but does it really have to be treated as a tool or weapon? I think not. Managers really have to address the question of who defines and interprets what constitutes a trading relationship? Problems are created when managers do so, but do not

TABLE 7.2 Nine obstacles to real CRM (based on Millard, 2001).

- Requires thinking outside traditional silos of expert knowledge
- Strategy is required for meeting specific customer needs with capabilities that cannot flourish in an inflexible command-and-control management regime that is long on specialist turf wars and short on good information
- Short-term 'hard' financial 'cost' targets will always mitigate against the long-term investment case
- Technology is too attractive and will rarely enable real dialogue with customers unless the system is carefully designed for this
- Requires systemic redesign of the way the business operates from the customer's perspective
- Human beings don't fit very well into a rigid 'machine'-type organization, so significant hard work is needed to ensure that people are able to build relationships
- Customers are in control – they are longer 'lawful prey', but want to be recognized as trusting persons
- Traditional market segmentation no longer works because customers are human beings
- Customers choose whether or not to consent to a relationship

take into account the points of view of customers, their experiences, and their responses. Table 7.2 summarizes some critical obstacles to the realization of a responsive, responsible eCRM management system.

The End of the Beginning (with apologies to Sir Winston Churchill)

This book was started with the view that CRM was a solution in search of a problem. A review of the theory of relationship marketing should, it was thought, be conducted in the light of an alternative business model (e-commerce). Accordingly, the discourses of marketing and knowledge management have been explored to continue the debate about CRM by re-presenting and re-viewing the idea of relationship marketing to ask 'what is the use of it at the nexus of producer and consumer?'

Much that is wrong with marketing is due to the governance of commerce (a trading culture) with political pressures (from a taking culture). Relationship Marketing, in basic principle, promises reciprocally fair treatment, and this requires that such a management system be deployed fairly. For Relationship Marketing to be anything more than a cynical obscuring of manipulative taking, it must operate in a realm of harmony and conversation to produce consensus and co-operation. Marketing communication (i.e. communication for marketing purposes) must be both talking and listening to ensure an authentic expression of consumers' needs and an honest adaptation of marketers' actions to these. A genuine relationship is the basic condition for this if we are to escape from damaging reciprocal manipulation. Sellers who continue to adopt a dominatory stance toward buyers, premised on assumptions of resource manipulation, winning customers as trophies from competing suppliers, and teaching consumers about what is important and best will find that they eventually have no valuable customers.

Relationship Marketing facilitated by ICT must help sellers to attract people in order to create customers in committed trading relationships. Installing technology to answer calls quicker, route calls more effectively, and to handle customer requests more efficiently are necessary but not sufficient. Where is the service? Technology alone is not enough to please people in trading. A crucial question for all CRM projects, is (how) does eCRM make sellers more attractive to buyers? How do eCRM technologies add any real substance to trading relationships?

From here, my work is to be further developed. At this point, my feeling is that what relationship marketing practice (often crudely) recognizes is not a recently invented phenomenon – there has always been relating implied and inherent in trading. Relationship marketing is not merely a means for trading, it is the mode of responsive and responsible trading.

But, through the justification of exchange, reciprocal manipulation takes an instrumental notion of the nature and purpose of a trading relationship. Yet, unreflective CRM/eCRM may be self-defeating in inauthentically presenting relationship as more than an instrument. Practices and underlying theories in use may be capable of no more than supporting unethical (manipulation) and dishonest promise-making because the contacts/interactions that are 'managed' are not 'strategic talk' and are not co-operative interactions. How can CRM really enable the keeping of the seller's promises? That seemed to be a good question for a book project.

So, does society really need eCRM to realize the benefits of trust-based, committed trading relationships? Or does it get in the way? Is there an alternative model for organizing trading that can produce the desirable benefits sought for all stakeholders in the contemporary consumer society? Time, money, and energy are spent on things we like another person to do for us. These, however, may not be the things that the other person appreciates. Dialogue is required to create the match.

Is the next book to be about open network marketing in the open society? It will probably be titled 'Dialogical Marketing: Network Marketing in the Open Society'. Watch this space! We have to get beyond behavioural data-driven contact control. When value is created and shared by customer and supplier, a truly relational way of trading will have been accomplished. This will require communication however and whenever either needs the co-operation of the other. Technologies and processes will be integrated in a relational marketing system that is user-friendly. Then, who is to say that it will not be customers who will be the managers of trading relationships? Real-time processes will have to be integrated to produce customer value – so that sellers are ready to sell when buyers are ready to buy – by providing customers with a seamless way to manage their relationship with the production system, in a way that suppliers can learn *with* their customers (and not merely about them).

References

Barnes, J. G. (1995) 'Close to the customer: But is it really a relationship?', *Journal of Marketing Management*, Vol. 10, No. 7, 561–570.

Barnes, J. G. (2001) *Secrets of Customer Relationship Management: It's All About How You Make Them Feel*, New York: McGraw-Hill.

Bird, D. (2001) 'CRM and e-commerce are sure to send shivers down any spine', *Marketing*, 19 April, 20.

Brown, S. (1994) 'Marketing as multiplex: Screening postmodernism', *European Journal of Marketing*, Vol. 28, No. 8/9, 27–51.

Brown, S. A. (2000) *Customer Relationship Management*, Toronto: John Wiley & Sons.

Brown, S. and Maclaran, P. (1995) 'The future is past: Marketing, apocalypse and the retreat from utopia', in S. Brown, J. Bell, and D. Carson (eds) *Marketing Apocalypse: Eschatology, Escapology and the Illusion of the End*, London: Routledge, pp. 260–277.

Buttle, F. (ed.) (1996) *Relationship Marketing: Theory and Practice*, London: Paul Chapman Publishing.

Cooren, F. (2000) *The Organizing Property of Communication*, Amsterdam: John Benjamins Publishing.

Fitchett, J. and McDonagh, P. (2001) 'Relationship marketing, e-commerce and the emancipation of the consumer', in A. Sturdy, I. Grugulis, and H. Willmott (eds) *Customer Service: Empowerment and Entrapment*, Basingstoke, UK: Palgrave, pp. 191–199.

Gabriel, Y. and Lang, T. (1995) *The Unmanageable Consumer*, London: Sage.

Godin, S. (1999) *Permission Marketing: Turning Strangers into Friends, and Friends into Customers*, New York: Simon & Schuster.

Gordon, I. (1998) *Relationship Marketing*, Toronto: John Wiley & Sons.

Gummesson, E. (1999) *Total Relationship Marketing: Rethinking Marketing Management – From 4Ps to 30Rs*, Oxford: Butterworth-Heinemann.

Habermas, J. (1984) *The Theory of Communicative Action*, Volume 1: *Reason and the Rationalization of Society*, Boston: Beacon Press.

Knowledge Lab @ www.knowledgelab.com

Kozinets, R. V. (1999) 'E-tribalized marketing? The strategic implications of virtual communities of consumption', *European Journal of Marketing*, Vol. 17, No. 3, 252–264.

Lasn, K. (1999) *Culture Jam: The Uncooling of America*, New York: Eagle Brook/William Morrow & Co.

Mattsson, L-G. (1997) '"Relationship Marketing" and the "Markets-as-Networks Approach" – A comparative analysis of two evolving streams of research', *Journal of Marketing Management*, Vol. 13, 447–461.

Millard, N. (2001) 'The future of Customer Relationship Management', *Journal of the Institution of British Telecommunications Engineers*, Vol. 2, No. 2, 92.

Morris, M. H., Brunyee, J., and Page, M. (1998) 'Relationship marketing in practice: Myths and realities', *Industrial Marketing Management*, Vol. 27, No. 4, 359–371.

Paravatiyar, A. (1996) Statement made during the *12th International Conference on Industrial Marketing and Purchasing (IMP), Karlsruhe, Germany, September*, reported by Mattson (1997).

Peppers, D. and Rogers, M. (1993) *The One-to-One Future: Building Business Relationships One Customer at a Time*, London: Piatkus Books.

Peppers, D. and Rogers, M. (1997) *Enterprise One-to-One: Tools for Building Unbreakable Customer Relationships in the Interactive Age*, London: Piatkus Books.

Sale, K. (1980) *Human Scale*, London: Secker & Warburg.

Schumacher, E. F. (1973) *Small is Beautiful: A Study of Economics as if People Mattered*, London: Blond & Briggs.

Spillard, P. (1991) 'Organisation for marketing', in M. J. Baker (ed.) *The Marketing Book*, 2nd edn, Oxford: Butterworth-Heinemann, pp. 49–72.

Varey, R. J. and White, J. (2000) 'The corporate communication system of managing', *Corporate Communications: An International Journal*, Vol. 5, No. 1, 5–11.

Varey, R. J. and Wood, J. R. G. (2001) 'When marketing met ICT: The mutant CRM child',

Proceedings of the International Workshop on (Re-)defining Critical Research in Information Systems, Salford, UK: Information Systems Institute, University of Salford, July.

Wang, P. *Integrated Marketing Communications*, Evanston, IL: Media Management Center, Northwestern University.

Wikström, S. and Normann, R. (eds) (1994) *Knowledge and Value: A New Perspective on Corporate Transformation*, London: Routledge.

Williams, R. (1961) *The Long Revolution*, New York: Columbia University Press.

INDEX

Customer Relationship Management

A Strategic Imperative in the World of e-Business

Stanley A. Brown

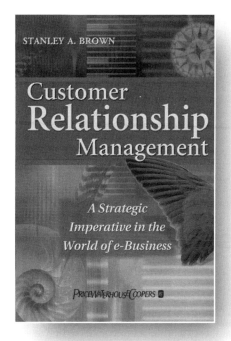

Over the last decade, too many organizations have assumed that their products or services were so superior that customers would automatically keep coming back for more. But in order to compete effectively in today's marketplace, organizations must change their strategy needs to become more customer focused, not product focused. Customer Relationship Management (CRM) is the best way to integrate this customer-facing approach throughout an organization. Aimed at understanding and anticipating the needs of an organization's current and potential customers, this innovative book shows how CRM links people, process, and technology to optimize an enterprise's revenue and profits by first providing maximum customer satisfaction.

Covers developing a market-oriented strategy, innovation in products and services, sales and channels transformation, customer relationship marketing, and customer care.

0471 64409 9
376pp
Hardback
£22.50 / €37.20

The Lifebelt
The Definitive Guide to Managing Customer Retention

John A. Murphy

Customer Relationship Management, or CRM, is a concept that senior managers in any kind of business ignore at their peril. At its heart is the successful management of customer retention by being customer focused as an organization. The concept is not rocket science, but its implementation is more of a challenge. It involves a fundamental change within the organization. In this book, John Murphy introduces "The Lifebelt" – quite literally an aid to keeping afloat in this pressured environment.

The Lifebelt is a framework that offers a practical way forward to integrating and mobilizing the entire oragnization toward a holistic CRM programme. The framework is based on research and proven in practice, that will, if effectively implemented, dramatically improve loyalty and retention. The book is a step-by-step route to completing the framework. Each chapter follows the individual components of the Lifebelt.

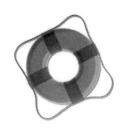

THE LIFEBELT
The Definitive Guide to
Managing Customer Retention

John A Murphy

WILEY

0471 49818 1	
304pp	
Hardback	
£19.99 / €33.00	

3737

Performance Driven CRM

How to Make Your Customer Relationship Management Vision a Reality

Stanley A. Brown and Moosha Gulycz

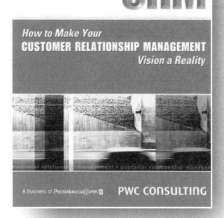

Customer Relationship Management is now facing its toughest challenge yet – the company evaluation. Measuring what gains CRM has made for your company, if any, is sound business. *Performance-Driven CRM* lets you determine how sound your investment has been with practical tools for measuring and monitoring CRM initiatives and its impact on operations and the bottom line.

- Includes questionnaires, assessment tools, exercises, and action plans.

- Measurement tools are applicable to the firm's internal culture as well as external customer care.

- Features e-business applications-using Web tools in research and assessment; what to measure in an Internet environment.

- Brown is a partner in PwC's Global Customer Relationship Management Practice, an international authority on the subject of customer care and the author of several books.

0470 83161 8
320pp
Hardback
£22.50 €37.20
May 2002

3738

Relationship Marketing

New Strategies, Techniques and Technologies to Win the Customers You Want and Keep Them Forever

Ian H. Gordon

A practical guide to best practices in the revolutionary new marketing strategy that's sweeping the business world. Relationship marketing is all about forging strong, enduring and unique relationships with a core of most valuable customers. This book explains how to implement a relationship marketing program in your organization, supplies tools for measuring results, and explores the practical role of technology as a key enabler in successful relationship marketing. It also discusses relationship management, or the forging of relationships with investors, suppliers, and employees, as well as customers.

Most of the literature on relationship marketing to date focuses on the marketing relationship between a company and its customers; this book will expand the discussion of "relationship marketing" into "relationship management," to include relationships with investors, suppliers, and employees, as well as customers.

0471 64173 1	
336pp	
Hardback	
£22.50 / €37.20	

3739